D1713349

*Capitalist Control and Workers' Struggle
in the Brazilian Auto Industry*

Capitalist Control and Workers' Struggle in the Brazilian Auto Industry

John Humphrey

Princeton University Press
Princeton, New Jersey

Publication of this book has been aided by the Whitney Darrow
Publication Reserve Fund of Princeton University Press

This book has been composed in Linotron Times Roman
Clothbound editions of Princeton University Press books
are printed on acid-free paper, and binding materials are
chosen for strength and durability

Printed in the United States of America by Princeton
University Press, Princeton, New Jersey

To my parents

Table of Contents

List of Illustrations

(pages 90-97)

The plants and products shown in these photographs are not related to any particular plant discussed anonymously in the text. The illustrations were compiled four years after the initial research in two São Paulo auto plants, and the author did not take any photographs when researching them.

Credits: 8, 9, and 11 courtesy of Chrysler do Brasil. All others, the author.

List of Tables

List of Tables

Preface

THE AUTO INDUSTRY is never far from the headlines. In Brazil, where over one million vehicles were produced in 1978, the growth of the auto industry was the centerpiece of the "economic miracle." Its phenomenal expansion and rapid rise into the world's top ten auto producers in the nineteen-seventies made the news often enough, but after 1978 the headlines were of a different sort. Instead of miracles, strikes began to make the news—so much so that by April 1980 even the British press carried regular reports on a strike of auto and metalworkers in São Paulo. For forty days a strike of tens of thousands of workers continued in spite of fierce opposition from the State and the employers. The union was taken over by the Ministry of Labor, the strike declared illegal, and union leaders put into prison. This strike was just one major clash in a prolonged period of tension and opposition between the auto workers and the Brazilian State. At issue were not merely wages and working conditions but also the nature of trade unionism and the course of democratization in the country.

Clearly, the workers supporting the 1980 strike must have been motivated by serious grievances and sustained by determined organization. At the same time, the State must have been extremely perturbed by their activities if it was willing to take such stern measures against the union. In view of the importance of the strike and the general context of relations between workers, unions, employers, and the State which led to it, one might have expected social scientists in Brazil and abroad to have devoted considerable attention to the matter. However, had an interested lay person gone to the library in search of enlightenment, he or she would have been disappointed. Up until late 1979 only one book had been published in Brazil on workers in the auto industry (Rodrigues, 1970). Based on research carried out in 1963, this had found that the workers in the industry were generally satisfied with their situation and did not look to the union for assistance in resolving their problems. This is hardly the kind of situation that provokes a forty-day strike. A more generic approach to the problem would have been equally unilluminating. The standard analysis of the working class in Latin America holds that workers employed by large, multinational firms in the most modern sectors of industry tend to form a privileged group within the working class as a whole. Once again, the privileges of high wages and good working conditions would not appear to provide the basis for protracted and bitter confrontations with the employers and the State, particularly when the "privileged workers" are sustained by support from other unions and the Catholic Church. Finally, an examination of the available work on the Brazilian working class would have found an almost exclusive concentration on the period before 1964, and the literature uniformly refers to the absence of plant organization and the dependence of unions on State support. Once again, this hardly seems to be in line with the capacity of workers to sustain a forty-day strike in open and defiant opposition to the State, even after the union has been taken over and its leaders imprisoned.

I experienced a similar problem of the lack of fit between what was apparently happening and what the written word had led me to expect when I first arrived in Brazil in 1974. I had been led to believe that the working class had been silenced by the military regime's fierce repression after 1968, that the labor movement in Brazil had no tradition of organization in the workplace, and that the press would not carry reports of strikes anyway because of censorship. I was rather taken aback, then, to pick up a magazine one day and read an article about stoppages in some of the metal-working plants in Greater São Paulo. I was just as surprised to find reports about one union in particular, the Metalworkers of São Bernardo do Campo, which was quite openly demanding radical changes in the structure of the trade unions and the rights of workers. Not only were such demands quite out of line with the State's policy, but they also ran contrary to the dominant traits of trade unionism in the period before the military coup in 1964. The Metalworkers of São Bernardo was a union whose workers were concentrated in the auto industry, and the auto industry had figured quite prominently in the stoppages in 1973-1974. I decided to investigate matters further.

The auto industry in Brazil was, by 1974, a major employer and a key sector of the economy. In that year it produced over 900,000 vehicles with almost 100 percent local content. The five largest assembly firms (all multinational companies) employed over 90,000 people, and in the industrial suburb of São Bernardo do Campo on the south side of the city of São Paulo there were over 50,000 people working in three large plants. The largest, the Volkswagen plant, produced 400,000 vehicles in 1974, and it employed more than 30,000 people. Ford and Mercedes, too, had factories which employed over 10,000 workers. But in spite of the size of these plants and the importance of the auto industry, I could find little information about such matters as wages, working conditions, and occupational structures. Behind the public face of auto consumption was a private and somewhat inaccessible productive sphere. Everyone seemed to know that auto workers earned high wages, and on the basis of this it was often asserted that they formed a privileged elite within the working class, but even this information and opinion sat uneasily alongside the evidence provided by the stoppages in 1973 and the union's complaints about high turnover, excessive overtime, and accidents.

At that time, it seemed that the best way to find out more about auto workers would be to go to the plants and examine the situation there. Good fortune enabled me to gain access to two assembly plants owned by one of the major auto companies, and I spent some months interviewing production workers and management in them. The information obtained at this time provides the basis for the analysis of working conditions and management strategies presented in chapters three and four. At the time of the interviews, it was possible to see that auto workers did not correspond to the stereotype of "privileged workers" that was widely held in Brazil, but the State's firm control over both the unions and political opposition meant that the full implications of this fact did not emerge until later. It was only in 1978 and 1979 that strikes and stoppages in the auto industry brought to public attention the extent and nature of conflict between labor and management. Although it was not possible to go back into the two plants in 1979, I did return to Brazil and discuss the new developments with managements in three auto firms, union leaders, and rank-and-file activists in the auto industry. The development of industrial relations in the auto industry and the significance of the strikes in 1978 and 1979 are discussed in chapters five, six, and seven. A further visit to Brazil in 1980 enabled me to discuss the impact of the 1980 strike with management and unionists, and this has been incorporated into chapter seven.

The purpose of this book, then, is to explain the system of labor use and labor control in the Brazilian auto industry in the seventies and to show how this derived from the specific social and political conditions existing at that time. On the basis of this analysis it then becomes possible to explain the development of the labor movement in Brazil in the latter part of the seventies. In particular, two questions can be answered. Why did auto workers play such an important part in the mobilization of the working class at the end of the seventies? Why did auto workers and their union raise demands that were different in character from those put forward by the labor movement in Brazil before 1964? The answers to these questions are important not only because of the re-emergence of the Brazilian labor movement in the political arena but also because they can shed light on certain aspects of class formation in other underdeveloped countries which are at present experiencing rapid industrialization.

Acknowledgments

THIS BOOK has developed from an initial interest in Brazil acquired in 1973, and in the intervening period many people and institutions have given support and encouragement. Only a few of them can be mentioned here.

In Britain, my supervisor, Emanuel de Kadt, gave me the patient encouragement that enabled me to finish my thesis without undue difficulty, and it is only now that I am supervising research students that I am beginning to appreciate the amount of effort and time that he gave so ungrudgingly. The Social Science Research Council financed my stay in Brazil in 1974-1975 and also a further visit in 1979. John Peel, the head of the Sociology Department at the University of Liverpool, allowed me time to get on with my research.

My debts to people in Brazil are enormous. Above all, the Centro Brasileiro de Análise e Planejamento, CEBRAP, in São Paulo gave me a place to work, along with all the friendliness, advice, and understanding that went with it. In particular, Juarez Brandão Lopes acted as an informal supervisor and contributed a lot to my work. Needless to say, my research would have been impossible without the cooperation of management and unions in the auto industry. Without the openness of the auto company whose identity must remain undisclosed and the friendliness of the Metalworkers of São Bernardo nothing could have been achieved. Of the many others who helped me in Brazil I will only mention the Trade Union Research Department, DIEESE, whose researchers were unfailingly helpful. They, and many others in Brazil, patiently guided me into the subject when I knew nothing and then gave me the encouragement and interest to go on when I began to develop my own ideas. They made me feel it was worthwhile.

Other influences are less obvious and direct, but no less important. At various stages in my work, certain people gave val-

Acknowledgments

uable advice and criticism. I will mention only Regis Andrade, Ron Dore, Ken Mericle, and Juan Carlos Torre. I have not always followed their advice, but sometimes they set me thinking about things that had never occurred to me, enriching my outlook and forcing me to try and do better. Two groups have been valuable sources of intellectual development. The Brighton Labour Process Group was the most stimulating group in which I have ever participated, and the working group on the Latin American Auto Industry, sponsored by the Social Science Research Council in New York, provided the stimulus to continue working on the Brazilian auto industry after I had completed my doctoral dissertation.

Finally, I would like to thank the people whose support at times of despair, frustration, and doubt helped me keep moving. In particular, Alan and Mary Tomlinson, fellow graduate students at the University of Sussex, lived through and shared the same anxieties as I did, and Susan and David Storr kept me aware of the fact that there was more to life than Brazilian auto workers.

List of Abbreviations

ANFAVEA	Associação Nacional dos Fabricantes de Veículos Automotores (National Motor Vehicle Constructors Association)
CLT	Consolidação das Leis do Trabalho (Consolidated Labor Laws)
DIEESE	Departamento Intersindical de Estatística e Estudos Sócio-Econômicos (Inter-Trade Union Statistical and Socioeconomic Studies Department)
FGTS	Fundo de Garantia do Tempo de Serviço (the law relating to stability of employment and dismissal compensation)
FIESP	Federação das Indústrias do Estado de São Paulo (São Paulo Federation of Industry)
FSP	*Folha de São Paulo* (a São Paulo morning newspaper)
FT	*Financial Times* (a London morning newspaper)
GDN	*The Guardian* (a London morning newspaper)
GEIA	Grupo Executivo da Indústria Automobilística (the presidential steering group set up by the Kubitschek administration to supervise the implantation of the auto industry)
IBGE	Instituto Brasileiro de Geografia e Estatística (a para-statal organization which produces many official statistics, including the censuses and the annual statistical abstracts)
JB	*Jornal do Brasil* (a Rio de Janeiro morning newspaper)
JT	*Jornal da Tarde* (a São Paulo afternoon newspaper)
OESP	*O Estado de S. Paulo* (a São Paulo morning newspaper)
SINFAVEA	Sindicato Nacional da Indústria de Tratores, Caminhões, Automóveis e Veículos Similares (The National Union of the Tractor, Truck, Automobile and Like Vehicles Industry—the legally constituted vehicle producers' "union" and constituent member of FIESP)

Capitalist Control and Workers' Struggle
in the Brazilian Auto Industry

Introduction

A NOTABLE FEATURE of the development of the Brazilian working class in the seventies was the central role played by the workers in the auto industry in the southern industrial belt of Greater São Paulo. Although workers in the auto assembly industry constituted only a small fraction of the working class, the fact remains that auto workers more than any others defined the shape of the labor movement in Brazil and led the struggle for change. In the early seventies, the auto workers' union, the Metalworkers of São Bernardo do Campo,[1] established a pattern of union activity and union strategy often called the "new unionism," and this became an important current with the labor movement in the course of the decade. In 1978 workers in the auto industry started the strike wave that gave rise to a prolonged period of industrial conflict, and in 1979 and 1980 strikes led by the Metalworkers of São Bernardo shaped the pattern of conflict between workers and the State. In 1980 and 1981 the struggles over industrial-relations practices and workers' representation in the auto industry signaled both to employers and the State that a commitment to liberalization in the political sphere would have to be accompanied by changes in the workplace. The growth of working-class resistance and the particular forms it took in the seventies were fundamentally molded by auto workers and their union.

[1] Auto workers do not have their own union. By law, they are represented by the Metalworkers Union in the local district. However, in the seventies over half of the metalworkers in the district of São Bernardo do Campo in Greater São Paulo worked in the large auto assembly plants. At the same time, most of the country's auto workers were concentrated in this one district. Although the industry gradually decentralized in the seventies, in January 1978 57 percent of all workers in the auto assembly industry—as registered by the auto assemblers association, ANFAVEA—still worked in São Bernardo. All but 900 of the 69,000 auto workers in São Bernardo at this time worked in just five plants.

3

Introduction

It follows, then, that an examination of the auto assembly industry[2] and its workers is a prerequisite for an understanding of the development of the Brazilian working class in the period. This book attempts to provide that examination and understanding. It is addressed to a series of specific problems concerning the reasons why auto workers displayed the combativeness they did, why it was channeled in certain directions, and how it influenced other sections of the working class. The book is, therefore, concerned with a series of specific questions about one particular section of the working class in Brazil at a particular time. It is not about Brazilian workers in general, nor labor under authoritarian regimes in general, nor auto workers in general. Rather, it tries to explain why and with what effects auto workers rather than any other group played a leading role, and the implications of their struggles and strategy for the rest of the working class.

It follows from this that a significant part of the analysis should be devoted to an examination of the situation of auto workers and patterns of labor-management relations and trade unionism in the auto industry. The specific characteristics of auto workers cannot be explained by an analysis of the working class in general. At the same time, the analysis starts from the premise that a crucial determinant of the behavior of auto workers and the role they have played within the working class was their work and employment situation. In other words, it is not sufficient to examine their union activity and strike behavior alone. Merely to state this involves breaking with the dominant patterns of analysis of the working class in Brazil.[3] Studies of trade unionism and specific strikes are much more common than studies of workplaces and the work situations of particular groups of workers. Unionism is studied because of the importance of the labor system and the trade union structure imposed by the State on the working class. Strikes are studied because they are considered to reveal more

[2] In this book, the assembly firms will be called the "auto industry." Components firms will be called the "auto components industry." Collectively they will be referred to as the "motor industry" or "automotive industry."

[3] See Vianna (1978a) for an exposition and critique of various tendencies in the study of the Brazilian working class.

Introduction

about workers' consciousness than the daily routine of factory life.

To some extent, the decision to concentrate on the workplace was forced by circumstances. In 1974-1975 there was little material available on strikes because the stoppages in the previous year had been incipient and short-lived. Not only this, but it also seemed prudent at the time not to delve in a politically sensitive area. Similarly, there seemed little point in studying the "new unionism" directly because it was still embryonic. As important, the "new unionism" had a strategy of direct negotiations between labor and management and the development of union organization in the workplace, and this suggested that an evaluation of its practical functioning and chances of success would be done best by a concentration on the workplace. However, there is a more fundamental reason for not beginning an analysis of auto workers and their union with a discussion of strikes and unionism. These two manifestations of the state of the working class cannot be explained satisfactorily by analysis only of the manifestations themselves. Therefore, works on these topics in Brazil have tended either to describe strikes and patterns of unionism solely in terms of their internal dynamics or to explain them by appeal to untheorized external causes. For example, analyses of unionism have tended to explain the existence of the State labor system by reference to modernization and rural-to-urban migration. Explanations of strikes, too, have tended to oscillate between the determinism of social-structural variables and the voluntarism of the activities of political agents.[4] This is inevitable unless the determinants of the social structure are themselves theorized.

In this book an attempt is made to avoid the pitfalls of both reductionism and voluntarism by, firstly, locating auto workers immediately in a relation with capital—at the point of production—while at the same time examining the general social and political conditions within which that relation is constituted. Secondly, the examination of the development of workers' resistance

[4] There is, of course, a further variant which attempts solely to describe events in a particular strike. The theoretical eclecticism involved in the selection of significant events to describe is left untheorized.

5

and union activity is put in a specific historical context. The starting point, then, is the point of production, but merely starting in the factory does not, by itself, define a satisfactory approach. The few factory studies carried out in Brazil before the nineteen-seventies tended to produce reductionist analyses in much the same way as the trade union studies. The factory was seen as a site at which the effects of modernization produce certain behavioral patterns among workers. In the work of Lopes (1964) and Rodrigues (1970) the main explanatory factor for workers' attitudes and industrial relations was the urban or rural origin of the workers themselves. The factory had no life of its own. Diametrically opposed to this kind of analysis are those studies which view the factory as a largely self-contained system. The operation of the system determines the opportunities open to workers and the forms of struggle they adopt. The variations in this approach are enormous, ranging from, for example, Chinoy's (1955) classic study of the adaptation of auto workers to the reality of the job (a reality that Chinoy took as given) to Braverman's (1975) analysis of the determination of the capitalist labor process. In both cases, the "system" has a life of its own, unaffected by the historically given and specific conditions of capitalist reproduction and class struggle.

Neither of these two types of study is satisfactory. The former reduces the factory to a passive site at which broader social processes take effect, while the latter largely abstracts the factory from society. The former leaves no basis on which to distinguish the auto workers from any others in Brazil, while the latter gives no reason why auto plants in São Bernardo should produce workers' struggles and organizations any different from those in Detroit, Barcelona, or Birmingham. And yet it is precisely the fact that auto workers in São Bernardo are different from other workers in Brazil, and also different from auto workers in other countries, which is of greatest interest. The analysis of the factory, therefore, must locate it within a definite social context.

The factory in capitalist society is the site of capitalist production. Capitalist production is the production at one and the same time of use-values (specific material products or services) and exchange-values (commodities which can be sold). In the factory, work is organized under the control of capital in order for commodities to be produced at a profit. Management organizes production to this end, selecting equipment and organizing work around it. This involves not only the specification and integration of different tasks and the monitoring of performance but also the creation, control, and motivation of workers through what can be termed employment policies: wage rates and structures, recruitment, training, promotion, stability of employment, grievance procedures.

Employment policies are both important and problematic for management. They are important because production is not merely a technical process in which a ready-formed factor of production, labor, is combined with capital to produce commodities. Labor has to be formed and controlled. Employment policies are also important because control cannot be maintained by the specification of tasks and the vigilance of management alone. Capital's inability to specify tasks completely and its difficulties in obtaining suitable labor (not only because of training problems but also because of competition between firms for labor) nearly always give the workers some opportunity for resistance. Hence a management needs employment policies to control its work force. However, these policies are problematic, because both use-values and exchange-values are being produced. Given that the object of production is the creation of specific use-values, there are constraints on the ways in which control can be achieved. It may be easier to control unskilled workers, for example, but in some kinds of production skilled workers are indispensable.[5] Since at the same time the object of production is the creation of exchange-values and profit, management cannot maximize control in a way that is either costly in terms of supervision or directly inefficient (for example, specifying exact work tasks even though efficiency requires flexibility). Management has to control and train labor

---

[5] This position is contrary to that taken by Edwards, who suggests that technologies are abundant and can be selected in accordance with the control system in force (1979: 179).

while at the same time producing efficiently. These aims can be contradictory.

The precise strategy adopted by management will, of course, vary from industry to industry and from factory to factory. The kinds of products made, the technologies used, and the size of plants will all present specific problems for the formation and control of labor. In some industries, such as textiles, technical change has been a major feature affecting employment policies in the seventies in Brazil,[6] but in the auto industry events in the same period have highlighted the way in which conditions outside the workplace crucially influence management control strategies.

Three types of influence should be mentioned. The first type is that derived from factors affecting the supply of labor. Patterns of capital accumulation and industrial concentration influence local labor markets, and management operates within the constraints of these markets. The kinds of workers available, their previous experience, and competition from other firms influence the options and strategies open to both management and labor.[7] Secondly, management strategies are affected by labor legislation. In Brazil the State plays a large role in determining wage increases (but not wage rates), protection against dismissal, and grievance procedures, and these provide the initial framework from which labor-management relations in the plants develop. Thirdly, the ability of management to impose strategies is influenced by the form and

---

[6] On the question of technological change in the Brazilian textile industry and its implications for labor-management relations, see Acero, 1981.

[7] The issues raised by this consideration go far beyond labor-market theory. At the time of the study in 1974-1975 the combination of the difficulties in carrying out studies of workers outside plants and a desire to concentrate on labor-management relations in production led me to ignore such issues as the development of religious and political organizations in working-class districts. In the 1980 metalworkers' strike, for instance, the Catholic Church's base organizations played an important role in organizing and sustaining workers' resistance, and this is an area which merits more attention. More generally, workers arrive at the factory gates with definite characteristics which are important for a study of labor processes and management strategies. Relevant characteristics include union experience, family and community situation, and political affiliation. These vary not only from country to country and from area to area but also within these areas according to such factors as race, sex, and skill.

8

extent of union organization and activity. The freedom of unions to organize and mobilize, along with the liberties allowed rank-and-file activists in the plants, are major factors in workers' ability to resist management pressure.

When these influences are taken into account, the factory is no longer seen as a subsystem largely independent of the wider society. Rather, it becomes a site at which the relations between labor and capital as a whole are brought to bear on the particular terrain of concrete labor processes and concrete management practices. The workplace is integrally related to the general conditions of capitalist production, and it is a vantage point for studying the effects of class formation, labor legislation, labor markets, and patterns of union activity.

The first half of this book examines the auto industry in the light of the above discussion about employment policies and management strategy. Following the opening chapter, which examines the development of the Brazilian labor system, chapter two situates the auto industry in the context of, firstly, the expansion of Brazilian industry before and during the period of the "economic miracle," and secondly, the transformation of the labor system in Brazil following the military coup in 1964. This then allows an examination of the auto industry itself, which is carried out in two stages. It begins in chapter three with a rebuttal of dual-labor-market analyses of the auto industry in Brazil and an empirical examination of wages and working conditions. It is shown that the patterns of wages, stability of labor, and training found in the industry are incoherent when analyzed from a dual-labor-market perspective. In chapter four, these patterns are shown instead to be the result of a coherent management strategy of labor use and labor control in operation in the mid-seventies. The combination of this strategy at plant level with general bargaining procedures and the State's control over unions is illustrated, and its points of weakness are specified.

It is shown in chapter four that the imposition of this system of labor control depended on the ability of employers and the security forces to contain struggles within the plants, together with State restrictions on union activity. An account of the system,

Introduction

therefore, cannot be confined to the workplace. As a result, chapter five examines not only the growth of union organization in the plants and the potential organizational strengths of auto workers, but also the development of the policies and strategies of the "new unionism" and the impact on the union of the liberalization policy introduced in the latter part of the Geisel administration's term of office.

On the basis of this examination, it becomes possible to explain why the 1973-1974 stoppages were confined to a few plants, whereas in 1978 the initial stoppage at the Scania plant rapidly developed into a large-scale strike movement. But this is only the beginning of the story: three tumultuous years followed the May stoppages. In chapter six, attention is focused on the reasons why new patterns of industrial relations were not developed following the first conflicts. Once again, it is shown that a major factor influencing the course of the struggles, important to both employers and unions, was the general conditions in which labor-management relations were situated. To challenge the employers, the Metalworkers of São Bernardo had to challenge the State and the labor system itself. The conflict between the union and the State is analyzed in chapter seven. The effects of the 1979 strike on management, on the unions in the southern industrial belt of Greater São Paulo, and on the rest of the working class are discussed, with particular attention being paid to the politicization of the "new unionism." In the latter part of chapter seven the dismissal of the union's leaders and the takeover of the union by the Ministry of Labor in 1980 is described, but it is shown that this line of action by the State does not resolve industrial-relations problems in the plants. The need for a new system of labor control more compatible with the democratic reforms begun in the mid-seventies is shown by the problems encountered by Volkswagen and Ford and by the continuing influence of the deposed union leadership.

Chapters five, six and seven show how the "new unionism" and management control strategies in the plans developed and changed in three years of conflict following the first stoppages in May 1978. The prior analysis in chapters three and four provides an important insight into this development, but the specificity of the struggles in the period is not denied. It follows from this that specific predictions cannot be drawn from the analysis. Therefore, chapters eight and nine consider only certain factors of importance for the future course of trade unionism and industrial relations in Brazil. Chapter eight considers the reasons why employers were so resistant to the development of workers' organizations in the workplace and goes on to consider the implications of democratization for industrial relations, placing emphasis on the variety of options open to management. Chapter nine concludes by discussing the implications of the "new unionism," and its demands for reform, for the future unity or division of the working class. A detailed and specific analysis of labor-management relations in the eighties cannot yet be carried out, but the evidence of 1980 and 1981 suggests that what happens in the auto industry will have crucial and widespread repercussions on both trade unionism and political development in Brazil during the rest of the decade.

1

The Development of the Brazilian Labor System

FOR MANY YEARS relations between employers and workers in Brazil have been regulated by a sophisticated and extensive machinery of legislation, judicial procedures, and outright State control. When the auto workers of São Bernardo do Campo went on strike in 1978, 1979, and 1980 they were not only defying the overall control of the State but also setting themselves against a labor system which had functioned even before the military coup in 1964. The system had been created in the nineteen-thirties and forties, and it survived both the democratization of 1945-1946 and the military coup in 1964. In the democratic period from 1945 to 1964 the trade unions had operated within the confines of the labor system, using it increasingly to their own advantage. They regarded it as a weapon that could be turned against the employers. The ''new trade unionism'' rejected this approach and sought to develop a pattern of industrial relations less constrained by the intervention of the State. To understand the context in which the auto workers and their union were forced to operate in the seventies, and to appreciate the significance of their rejection of the established labor system, it is necessary first to outline the system's development.

The Establishment of the Labor System

The Great Depression beginning in 1929 was a turning point for Brazilian society. It was by no means a complete rupture in its historical development, but the economic and political crisis brought on by the collapse of the international coffee market led to a lasting shift in political alignments and economic development.

The sharing of power among regional oligarchies that had dominated the country's political life from the declaration of the First Republic in 1889 was swept away by the 1930 revolt. The crisis of the agrarian-export economy and the measures taken to support coffee growers led indirectly to an expansion of industrial output and a shift in economic policy toward what was later to be theorized as import-substitution industrialization. A national economic framework replaced the regionalism that had dominated previously, and the goal of national development began to take precedence over free trade and support for coffee. Although the working class did not play an important role in 1930, it was able to grow in strength in the climate of political turmoil that followed. Initially, the new government headed by Getúlio Vargas was content to use an unsystematic mixture of repression and legislation to contain urban labor, but after the rapid growth of the radical Aliança Nacional Libertadora in 1935, a much more severe policy was adopted. The ANL was outlawed, and when an abortive Communist uprising took place later in the year, the government repressed political parties and trade unions. State control over the labor movement was extended further when the political crisis resulting from the uprising and the continuing uncertainties over economic policy and political institutions led, in 1937, to Vargas's definitive break with liberalism. Following the foundation of the corporatist Estado Novo, independent unions were banned and strikes made illegal. Previously, trade unions had been more or less independent organizations protecting the wages and working conditions of their members, but under the Estado Novo regime they became adjuncts of the State.

In Brazil, as in Italy, corporatism required a system of control over the working class and mechanisms for representing the interests of different sections of society through the State. In the six years following the establishment of the Estado Novo a comprehensive system of labor legislation was created, perfected, and consolidated into the Consolidação das Leis do Trabalho (CLT). This codification of labor legislation into a unified body remained more or less intact for the whole of the period to be considered. Inspired by the Mussolinian model, the CLT was designed to ensure social harmony by guaranteeing the interests of both labor and capital under the tutelage of the State. By regulating the activities of the different productive elements in society, the State was to guarantee social progress and harmony between the classes. Getúlio Vargas's own description of the aims of the State at this time provides a good sense of the purposes of the new labor system:

> The government does not want under any circumstances strife between classes, nor the predominance of some over others.
> . . . The proper organization of work at a time of disturbance and profound economic and social transformations as we have at present cannot be established to the profit of the employing classes and with benefits to workers except through intelligent, thoughtful, and systematic coordination to conciliate and guarantee their mutual interests. . . . The Estado Novo does not recognize the rights of individuals in opposition to the collectivity. Individuals have duties, not rights: rights pertain to the collectivity! The State rises above the struggle between interests, guarantees the rights of the collectivity, and ensures the fulfillment of duties. The State does not want and does not recognize class struggle. The labor laws are laws of social harmony. (Getúlio Vargas, cited in Souza Martins, 1979: 36, 47, 61.)

The trade unions lay at the center of the State's system of control over labor. Unions had to be recognized by the Ministry of Labor, and there was one for each category of workers, defined by industry and geographical area. So, for example, the Ministry recognized metalworking unions in different geographical areas to represent all the workers in the metal-mechanical and electrical industries, and in each area the recognized union had the sole right to act on behalf of workers employed in that category. The Ministry regulated the greater part of the unions' finances through a levy on all workers known as the Trade Union Tax (in 1966 this was renamed the "Trade Union Contribution"). The Ministry could, at its own discretion, suspend and replace union officers and veto candidates wishing to run in union elections, and it maintained statutory powers to regulate union statutes and oversee expenditures. This mass of legislation guaranteed the unions a role, however circumscribed, in the regulation of relations between labor and capital, but only at the expense of a complete subordination to the State. In the Estado Novo period the unions functioned mainly as adjuncts to the Ministry of Labor, representing workers in the State apparatus and distributing welfare services. Trade unions were transformed from active, if precarious, defenders of workers' interests and rights to financially secure, bureaucratic welfare agencies, as Troyano illustrates in her account of the Chemical Workers Union in São Paulo (1978:60-65).

Responsibility for resolving conflicts between capital and labor rested with a system of Labor Courts, which judged individual and collective disputes. From 1930 onward new laws had been introduced that gave employees new rights or extended old conquests to new groups. The CLT combined these laws into a comprehensive series of regulations covering such matters as pensions, female and child labor, holidays, the working day, hygiene, accident prevention, and many others (see Almeida, 1975:53-54, for a comprehensive list). If a worker was dissatisfied with his or her employer's treatment and felt that the law had been broken, a case could be taken to the Labor Court. The Courts also had the power to regulate collective relations between employers and unions. Although the CLT allowed for direct negotiations between employers and unions without the intervention of the State (CLT, Articles 611-616), in the event of a refusal to negotiate by either side the dispute would go to the Regional Labor Office for conciliation and, if that failed, to the Labor Court, where an agreement would be imposed by compulsory arbitration. In practice, this compulsory arbitration, known as the *dissídio coletivo*, became the standard form of collective bargaining in Brazil.

Within the logic of this system, the unions were not in an antagonistic relation to capital, and any conflicts could be resolved by the mediating guidance of the State. Therefore, no provision was made for strikes (or lockouts) or a union presence in the workplace. It was argued that strikes were supplanted by the Labor

Courts and that problems within the workplace could be resolved by recourse to the same organ. Similarly, trade unions were allowed to group together only in vertically structured federations and confederations because direct links between unions were superfluous: there would be no cause for a general mobilization of workers. Thus, while the new system granted some protection to labor, this was at the expense of any freedom of action. The working class was dependent on the State for its rights, and where the law was silent, incomplete, or inadequately enforced, there was little recourse. The protection given by the law was limited by the need to protect the interests of capital as well as those of labor, and within the terms established by the CLT for individual contracts and general working conditions employers had a free hand to organize production and pursue profits as they pleased. In practice, the enforcement of the law was often so minimal that they were able to ignore many restrictions laid down in the CLT. There were gains for capital as well as for labor in the new system.

However, it is important to realize that in some areas there were mutual interests, and a gain for one party was not necessarily a loss for the other. An objective basis for the ideology of harmony between the classes lay in the need for the ordering of labor markets at a time of rapid industrial expansion and migration from the countryside to the towns. The CLT regulated training and instituted a system of employment cards for all workers, and it also confirmed two items of legislation that are of particular importance: the minimum wage and the Lei da Estabilidade, which regulated the terms and compensation for dismissal from employment. In addition, the standardization of labor legislation and its extension to most categories of urban, non-State workers meant that many more groups were brought under the umbrella of the labor system. If this system was later presented as Getúlio Vargas's gift to the working class, then the basis for the claim lies here. Estabilidade and the minimum wage were regarded as major gains. However, it has been argued more recently that the minimum wage and the Lei da Estabilidade benefited capital as much as, or more than, labor. Vianna, for example, has argued that the minimum-wage legislation allowed industrial employers to reduce their wages toward the nonindustrial level and, at the same time, contained wage dispersal above the minimum rate (1978b:235-240). Similarly, Ferrante analyzes the Lei da Estabilidade as an attempt to reduce labor turnover by giving job security to long-term workers and increasing compensation for dismissal according to length of employment (1978:43-44). This would then consolidate an urban labor force and make training at the workplace more profitable to the firms.

The ambiguity of the CLT, its combination of protection and control—minimum safeguards combined with constraints on the working class's ability to improve them—allowed it to be the subject of much debate in the years following its introduction. Was it a shield or a manacle for the working class, and should it be retained in part or scrapped completely? During the Estado Novo's lifetime, the working class had little choice, but with the end of the war in 1945 and democratization in Brazil, the issue opened up.

The Labor System in a Democratic Period

Toward the end of the Second World War, Getúlio Vargas began to dismantle the more repressive aspects of the Estado Novo and prepare for democratization. His strategy for maintaining power included gaining the support of the working class, and to this end he made concessions to labor. In 1945 strikes were allowed, de facto, and in April of that year the Communist Party secured the right to organize freely. Although many of the Estado Novo union leaders maintained their positions, new groupings emerged which sought to mobilize workers and build up the kinds of links between unions that the official union structure had forbidden. The unions and the working class had more freedom than they had enjoyed in the previous decade, and it might have been expected that the downfall of Getúlio Vargas in October 1945 would have strengthened this freedom: the corporate system falling with the State that created it. Plans were made for a Constituent Assembly which would draw up a new Constitution, and presidential elections were held early in 1946. The working class appeared to be taking advantage of the situation when a rash of strikes broke out in the first few months of the same year.[1] However, this proved to be the high point of the working class's mobilization, not its beginning.

Even before the Constitution had been drafted and promulgated, the newly elected President, General Dutra, introduced decree-law 9070, which drastically curtailed the right to strike. The Ministry of Labor, too, exercised its powers to intervene in the affairs of the unions (see Vianna, 1978b:268). When the new Constitution was promulgated it failed to reverse the situation. Although its wording on the question of the right to strike was ambiguous enough to place the legality of decree-law 9070 in doubt, the corporate labor system as a whole was left intact. The Dutra government was sufficiently anxious to reimpose controls on the working class that it used its prerogatives to the full. It banned the Community Party in May 1947 and imposed strict control over the unions. In June 1950, during the final year of the Dutra government's term of office, there were 234 unions still under the direct control of the Ministry of Labor, union elections had been postponed from 1947, and candidates for them required a clean bill of ideological health (Weffort, 1973:105). The working class seemed to have gained little.

A number of different explanations have been put forward to account for the continuation of the labor system after the demise of the Estado Novo. One school of thought emphasizes the backwardness of the Brazilian working class and its inability to develop and sustain an autonomous union structure. This view focuses on the effects of rural migration into the cities and the uneven and limited nature of industrialization.[2] An opposite view has been put forward by Francisco Weffort, who places great emphasis on the role of the Communist Party in 1945-1946, seeing it as the key political agent that failed to take advantage of the political conjuncture (Weffort, 1973). A third line of argument emphasizes

---

[1] For accounts of events at this time, see in particular Weffort, 1973; Maranhão, 1975; Vianna, 1978b:243-272.

[2] This and other theories of working-class development in Brazil are discussed fully in Vianna, 1978a.

the continuation of bourgeois power, and, as a result, the continuation of the repression and control of the working class that had been seen in the thirties (Andrade, 1979:9-12). Vianna, too, places emphasis on the continuity in economic policy and class alliances before and after 1945 (1978c:20). While these three lines of argument yield greatly differing views as to why the corporate labor system remained in force, had any of them been put forward in 1950 the resulting prediction would have been either a continuation of the Dutra government's policy of strict control or an end to the system entirely. When Getúlio Vargas resumed the presidency after a victory in the elections the latter prediction looked to be more secure. However, Vargas's second period of office witnessed the consolidation of a new coalition of forces, constructed around labor support for a policy of national capitalist development. The political regime based on this alliance is usually called Populism. To attract working-class support, the control of the Ministry of Labor over the unions was relaxed, and the law applied sparingly. Strikes took place, including the famous "strike of 300,000" in São Paulo in 1953, and interunion coordination bodies were set up.[3] The working class achieved greater freedom of activity and the corporate labor system was modified in practice, but the CLT remained unchanged. The Communist Party began to regain influence, but it remained illegal.

The support of the working class was only obtained at the cost of significant rises in wages, and the combination of wage rises and nationalist policies led to a climate of tension in 1954. A military coup was only averted by Vargas's suicide in August of that year. In 1955 the same forces that had supported Vargas managed to elect the new President, Kubitschek, and from 1956 to 1960 the developmentalist coalition held control. As in 1953, the influence of the left in the unions grew, but the corporate system remained intact. Instead of dismantling the system, the left used it as their power base to influence government policy. Although Kubitschek and the Communist Party were agreed about

---

[3] These are often called "parallel organizations" because they run alongside the official structure.

the need for industrial development, the economic policies pursued by the government involved rapid expansion through the implantation of new industries by foreign investment. Industrial development was secured in this way, but only through an increasing penetration of foreign firms into the industrial sector. The Community Party and other left-nationalist forces became increasingly unhappy about this, and they sought to give a more anti-imperialist content to nationalism (see Telles, 1962). The major questions for the working class were seen as national development and anti-imperialism, which meant opposition to right-wing forces, nationalization of foreign-held assets, and the introduction of an agrarian reform to lay the foundations for balanced, internally sustainable development. Far from being a hindrance to the working class in this situation, the corporate labor system was seen as a valuable source of patronage and political influence that could be used to put pressure on the government.

The influence of radical nationalist forces within the labor movement was not total, but it was dominant, and for these forces the general political questions of the time remained the most important issues for the labor movement right up to the military coup in 1964. The weaknesses of the union movement, such as the failure to develop significant rank-and-file organizations in the workplaces and the bureaucratization of the unions, were given scant attention compared with the battle for agrarian reform, nationalization of oil refineries, and the general strikes in the early sixties. This orientation toward the general questions of national development influenced the nature of the labor movement itself, and the results can be seen in two ways. Firstly, as Weffort has argued, the emphasis on the State and on political issues gradually caused the movement to become dominated by its activities in the State sector (1974:74). This can be seen as either an attempt to avoid a confrontation with the national bourgeoisie or a concentration of effort in those sectors where the movement's influence on the State apparatus would have most effect. In either case, an increasing distance between public- and private-sector support for labor mobilizations became evident in the late fifties and early sixties. The main parallel organizations for coordinated action shifted toward the public sector, and the strike calls in the early sixties were much less effective in private industry than among public-sector workers. They were less effective in São Paulo, the center of private industry, than in Rio de Janeiro, close to government power (see Erickson, 1977:102-122).

Secondly, the orientation of the labor movement to the State led it to play down issues not resolvable at that level. This can be seen clearly in an agitational pamphlet published in 1963 in the series *Cadernos do Povo* (People's Notebooks). This pamphlet, about strikes in Brazil, included an evaluation of different types of strikes. The author, J. Miglioli, argued that strikes over working conditions were a thing of the past, whereas the strike by workers at the State oil-exploration and production monopoly, Petrobrás, in support of the appointment of a nationalist chairman to head the company was an important new development for the working class:

> If strikes resulting from administrative issues are an example of a new type of stoppage in Brazil—which will tend to grow in number and importance as the number of State enterprises grows, and as the strength of the working class and its consciousness that it, too, is an owner of these firms increases— strikes over conditions of work are an old type which is diminishing in numbers and importance. (Miglioli, 1963:101).

He went on to argue that the Labor Courts were equipped to deal with any problem that arose in the workplaces and that, in general, strikes over working conditions were no longer necessary because "nowadays working conditions are much better" (1963:102). In this argument, the State sector was given an overriding importance, and the State was seen as inherently progressive. Far from challenging the corporate structures, Miglioli accepted them wholeheartedly. In doing this, he ignored questions of fundamental importance for the working class because he included in his definition of working conditions such matters as hygiene, intensity and forms of work, hours of work and rest, and personal relations at work. In spite of his assertion that such matters were resolvable through the Labor Courts, they were not being ignored by the working class at the time. In the motor industry there were strikes and protests in the early sixties over such matters as food and shift systems, while in the case of the chemical workers in Campinas, a union meeting in 1963 instructed the executive to "negotiate agreements with Rhôdia about dangerous and unhealthy conditions, a wage increase, and a new shift system, and to prepare forms of struggle against the firm's intransigence, including strike action" (Minutes of a union meeting held 20/9/1963). Miglioli's assertions are more a reflection of the dominant currents within the Populist labor movement than an accurate assessment of working-class concerns in Brazil. The leaders of this movement were gaining political influence at the expense of their ability to mobilize workers in the private sector.

In the early sixties the weakness of the State's control over the unions allowed the union leaders considerable flexibility in their approach. They could negotiate at a broad level and concentrate on such matters as the minimum wage and State policy, or they could negotiate directly with the employers, even at a plant-by-plant level (see Mericle, 1974:244). In principle there is no contradiction in the unions' making demands on both the State and their employers. Chemical workers, for example, demanded the nationalization of the private refineries in São Paulo while at the same time pursuing their own wage agreement with Rhôdia, as mentioned above. However, there were signs of a disjuncture between traditional- and modern-sector workers, even during joint negotiations and strikes in the early sixties. In the case of the negotiations in 1963 between the São Paulo Federation of Industries and the National Confederation of Industrial Workers (representing unions in the food, textile, chemical, and metalworking industries, among others), the different unions approached the common negotiating platform in different ways. While the textile unions concentrated attention in their meetings on questions relating to the minimum wage, metalworkers hardly discussed this issue at all in their meetings, preferring to spend time on the question of union delegates in the plants.[4]

The difference between union strategies in the traditional and

[4] Information on union treatment of the issues arising in these negotiations is taken from handbills announcing union meetings and from minutes of meetings.

modern sectors lay not in their overall political attitudes but rather in their degree of reliance on the State for the determination of wages and working conditions. Workers in the newer, dynamic industries were not necessarily antinationalist or antileft, but issues such as the minimum wage and nationalization (takeovers by the State) were of limited relevance to them. The large firms in the new industrial sectors implanted by the Kubitschek industrialization strategy attempted to widen this divide within the working class by instituting direct negotiations and offering fringe benefits such as social clubs and medical schemes. As a result, modern-sector workers were largely marginal to the mobilizations of the labor movement.

In the fast-developing political situation of the early sixties, the operation of the corporate labor system was transformed, even though its formal structure remained intact. The left-nationalist forces in the union movement managed to gain control of much of the corporate structure and use it to change the political balance of power in Brazil. As Erickson aptly puts it, it was a case of "patronage, traditional means for a radical end" (1977:83). The drawback in this strategy was that although the left-nationalist forces controlled the labor machinery, this control did not mean that organized labor as a whole was in support, because the system had been designed to inhibit the mobilization of workers. In spite of this limitation, a serious challenge was mounted to the political arrangement that had served the dominant classes since the thirties: oligarchic control in the countryside and containment of the workers in the cities. Demands for agrarian reform and a much tougher stance on the role of foreign capital threatened the bases of dominant-class control in both rural and urban areas. At the same time, the resistance of the working class to wage cuts and reductions in public expenditure complicated economic policy-making. The Brazilian economy had gone into a recession in 1962, but there was no agreement as to how this should be countered. The government's plans for cuts in spending to control the money supply, reduce inflation, and increase profitability were not accepted by the labor movement, and the 1963 Three-Year Plan did

23

not go into operation.[5] The restructuring of capital and a renewed industrial expansion would require drastic measures that could only be carried out in a new political climate.

The labor movement had achieved some measure of influence over the government, but it had achieved this within the corporate structure, reproducing the top-heavy bureaucratic model that had been developed by Vargas in the Estado Novo period. The failure of the left-nationalist labor movement to develop either a solid rank-and-file base or a political strategy that went beyond a reliance on the State and on the supposedly similar interests of the Brazilian bourgeoisie in national development left it vulnerable to a right-wing offensive, and its weaknesses were cruelly exposed by the military coup in 1964.

The Working Class Under Military Rule

The immediate effects of the military coup were the elimination of the labor movement's influence within the State apparatus and the reimposition of strict controls on the unions. Almost all strikes were made illegal, many unions placed under the control of the Ministry of Labor, and leading unionists arrested. New policies to restructure industry and raise productivity led to cuts in wages and increasing unemployment. The disarticulation of the labor movement gave it little chance of mounting serious opposition to the new military rulers, and it was not until 1967 that a relaxation of State control allowed some discussion and criticism of government policies and the beginnings of renewed union activity. This took the form of an interunion coordination grouping, the Inter-Union Anti-Wage-Squeeze Movement (Movimento Inter-Sindical Anti-Arrocho, MIA), organized on the same lines as the Populist parallel organizations of the fifties. It constituted no threat to the State because its constituent elements, the unions themselves, were still firmly under control (Almeida and Lowy, 1976:110), and it foundered in 1968.

When serious opposition to the military government did finally

[5] For the background to the economic crisis, see Oliveira, 1977:76-98.

come from the working class, it emerged from a rather unexpected source. In April 1968 a mass strike developed in Contagem, an industrial suburb on the fringe of Belo Horizonte, and in July of the same year there was a further mass strike in Osasco, one of São Paulo's peripheral industrial zones.[6] Both strikes displayed two features that broke with the past practice of the labor movement and foreshadowed its development in the seventies. Firstly, they took place in the new industrial suburbs and large metal-mechanical plants that had developed in the fifties and sixties. In Contagem and Osasco large and foreign-owned firms were much in evidence. Although the new industrial suburbs had been expanding in the fifties, they had not played a significant role in the working-class mobilizations of the Populist period for the reasons outlined in the previous section. Secondly, the strikes were based on organization at the rank-and-file level, and they opposed the State instead of relying on it. In Osasco, in particular, the movement was based on the prior development of workers' committees in the major plants, and the leadership of the Metalworkers Union was closely linked to them. As Weffort has argued: "In their orientation and in their organization, these strikes showed an attitude of *independence* to the State and the employers. Whatever qualifications might be made, this is very different from the traits of trade unions in the Populist period. As it appears to me, it is precisely this position of independence that makes them interesting for an examination of the current possibilities of trade unionism in the country" (1972:11). In the Populist period the mass strikes in 1953 and 1957 had been organized and channeled by the official trade union movement, and the unions had looked to the State for a resolution of their grievances. After 1964 the unions faced a hostile State, and this forced them increasingly to try and negotiate with their employers and openly oppose the State.

The strike movements in Contagem and Osasco were contained by the regime, and from December 1968 a further shift to the right within military circles led to tougher repressive measures.

[6] For a long time, Francisco Weffort's account of the two strikes was the only one readily available. However, a collection of short accounts and analyses of the Osasco strike was published in 1978 (Cadernos do Presente, 1978).

The following few years were very difficult for the working class, but in the course of the seventies a new current developed within the trade unions. Centered on the dynamic industries, and above all on the auto workers in the industrial suburb of São Bernardo do Campo, the new current gave considerable importance to plant organization and the resolution of workers' problems by the actions of workers themselves. There were, without doubt, differences between the Metalworkers of Osasco in 1968 and the Metalworkers of São Bernardo in the nineteen-seventies. Whereas in Osasco the aim of the leadership was to provoke a political crisis by outright opposition to the regime, in São Bernardo the strategy was to build up strength slowly by pushing to the limits allowed by the regime without going so far as to provoke an all-out confrontation. In Osasco, the official union structure was merely something to be captured by militants in the plants and used in pursuit of their political and organizational aims, whereas in São Bernardo the bases in the plant were developed under the guidance of the leadership. However, in both cases there was a decisive break with the Populist style of mobilization and activity.

Two questions have to be asked about this new orientation of trade unionism in Brazil. Firstly, why was there such a decisive break with the dominant strategy of the Populist period and a switch to an emphasis on plant struggles and rank-and-file organizing? The new orientation pursued political objectives, but only from strong bases in the workplaces. Secondly, given that the workers in the dynamic industries appeared to be marginal to the trade-union movement in the early sixties, what can explain their rise to dominance in the following decade? In trying to answer these questions, different aspects of the transformation of the working class in the period have been emphasized by different writers. Two basic approaches to the problem can be discerned: those which emphasize the change in the internal structure and composition of the working class, and those which stress the change in the political and trade union situation faced by the class. Each of these approaches has two main variations in the literature. This gives four different positions, each of which is not only an analysis of why the labor movement developed as it did after 1964 but also an evaluation of Populist practice and an implied prediction of what might happen in a future democratic period in Brazil:

1. The development of industry creates new groups of workers linked to the dynamic sectors. These groups are strong enough to adopt forms of relationship to the employers and the State that do not depend on the latter's tutelage. Taken on its own, this position implies that most sections of the working class were unable to break with State control in the Populist period, but that the workers in the modern sectors are strong enough now and will continue to be so in a future democratic period. It can be implied that the sectors favoring independence from the State will be forceful enough to set a new pattern of behavior that will benefit the working class as a whole.

2. The development of industry produces a structural heterogeneity within the working class between the workers in the modern and traditional industries. The uniformity of treatment established by the labor legislation becomes increasingly inadequate to cope with the diversity of work situations. In particular, it cannot resolve the specific problems of workers in modern industry. This position implies that not only was the majority of the working class favored by the labor system established in the Populist period—the system "corresponded" to the nature of industry—but that the majority of workers are likely to continue to derive benefit from it.

3. The military coup in 1964 leads to a blocking of the systems of power-bargaining and influence in the State apparatus from which the Populist unions derived their strength. In the light of the failure of the Populist strategy in the new period, new strategies are developed. This position does not judge, necessarily, the usefulness of the Populist system, but it implies that the old system could be re-established if a political regime more open to the working class were established.

4. The military coup forces the working class to break with its

ideology of reformism and its collaboration with the ruling class. This involves a rejection of the strategies dominant in the Populist period and such a fundamental change in orientation that the Populist system cannot be resurrected.

These different explanations contain different assessments of the benefit of various patterns of trade union orientation. The fourth position, put forward by Quartim (1971:105), implies that the orientation of the Populist period was not inevitable, but rather a harmful imposition on the working class by the bourgeois State. In contrast, the second position, advanced by Almeida among others (1975 and 1978), is less critical of the Populist unions and more critical of the new lines of trade union activity developing in the late sixties and seventies. This line of argument is diametrically opposed to that of Weffort (1972 and 1973), who sees Populism as a fetter on working-class development, compared with the potentially liberating practice of the workers in Contagem and Osasco.

These four positions, and their combinations, differ not only in their emphasis on, on the one hand, the composition of the working class, and, on the other hand, the working class within a set of class relations mediated through the State, but also in their assessments of both the content of old and new forms of organization and the potentiality for changes in these forms. Unfortunately, none of the positions as they stand are satisfactory. Quartim fails to take into account the real differentiation that has taken place in the working class and cannot, therefore, explain why resistance to the military regime should be located in the modern industries; Almeida misinterprets the nature of working-class differentiation and abstracts modern-sector workers from their situation of class domination. In the work of a perceptive writer such as Francisco Weffort, elements of positions one and three are merged (1972:90-92), but their different implications and the relation between them are left unspecified.

An explanation and evaluation of the emergence of new forms of trade union action can only proceed by means of a close examination of their roots in the development of modern industry in a period of authoritarian rule. In this book, industrial relations in the auto industry are taken as the point at which the development of modern industry and the repressive nature of the State combine to create a new basis for trade union activity. However, before the argument can be sharply focused on the auto industry it is essential to map out the broad lines of industrial development and authoritarian control in the period under consideration.

2

Industrial Development and the Working Class

THE WORKING CLASS in Brazil has been transformed since the Second World War by a considerable expansion and modernization of industry. Whilst the manufacturing sector still employs only a minority of the economically active population—16 percent of males and 12½ percent of females in 1976—the manufacturing and construction sectors together increased their share of employment more rapidly than any others. Between 1950 and 1976 employment in manufacturing and construction rose from 13 to 22 percent of the economically active population (all figures from IBGE, 1978). Although agriculture still employed one-and-a-half times as many people as manufacturing and construction in 1976, the difference had narrowed greatly from a ratio of about five to one in 1950. Manufacture is by far the largest nonagricultural sector. The greater size of the labor force in agriculture is more than offset by the political and economic importance of the urban areas and the urban working class. Brazilian industry is a vital and booming part of national development, and in the political arena the cities and the working class have been crucial elements in the postwar period.

The nature of industry has been significantly altered by the industrialization strategy adopted in the fifties. New industries producing heavy electrical and mechanical goods, domestic appliances, and automobiles were developed, and their impact on the working class will be examined in the first section of this chapter. However, as Oliveira has demonstrated so well (1977:76–113), the expansion of the Brazilian economy in the period involved much more than merely creating new factories and jobs. It required a restructuring of capital and labor. The development of the consumer-durables industries required the provision of internal resources, large inflows of foreign capital and technology, and a change in the role of the State. The transfers of wealth and changes in economic policy required to sustain the new model of accumulation provoked the political conflicts and social unrest that led to the military coup in 1964. Therefore, as part of the examination of the transformation of the working class, it is essential to see how the policies adopted after the coup to restructure capital and labor affected such things as wages, working conditions, and union organization.

Industrial Development and Working-Class Differentiation

As a result of the developmentalist strategy pursued by the Kubitschek government, first the consumer-durables sector and later the capital-goods industries grew rapidly. The State took responsibility to provide the stimulus and basic conditions for the implantation of whole new industries as part of a crash program of industrialization summed up by the slogan of "fifty years in five." The extent of the change can be seen if manufacturing industry is split up into three groups: the "traditional," the dynamic-A (intermediate goods), and the dynamic-B (consumer durables and capital goods):

> *Traditional*: timber, furniture, leather and hides, textiles, clothing and shoes, food products, beverages, tobacco, and printing and publishing.
> *Dynamic-A*: nonmetallic minerals, metallurgical, paper and cardboard, rubber (including tires), and chemicals.
> *Dynamic-B*: mechanical, electrical and communications equipment, and transport materials.[1] (Taken from Mata and Bacha, 1973:303.)

Between 1949 and 1969, output in the traditional sectors in Brazil grew by 4.1 percent per annum, in the dynamic-A sectors by 8.7 percent per annum, and in the dynamic-B sectors by 13.5 percent

---

[1] These industrial sectors are the ones used in the census classification. The list does not contain the plastics, pharmaceuticals, and perfume sectors, which will be included in the dynamic-A group.

per annum. The traditional sectors' share of total manufacturing output fell from 70.4 percent in 1949 to 46.8 percent in 1969, with the sharpest falls being registered in the fifties (Mata and Bacha, 1973:305).

The transformation of industry was even more marked in the State of São Paulo, the industrial center of the country, as can be seen in table 2-1. The dynamic-B sectors tripled their share of industrial value-added between 1949 and 1970, while the traditional sectors' share fell from over one half to less than a third. In all the traditional sectors the share of value-added declined, while the dynamic-A shares remained roughly constant and the dynamic-B sectors' shares of value-added rose sharply. The process was not uniform in the two decades. The traditional sectors declined in both, but it can be seen that in the fifties the most rapidly expanding sectors were chemicals, rubber, transport materials (vehicles and components), and electrical equipment. In the sixties, the metallurgical, pharmaceutical, mechanical, and electrical-goods sectors showed the largest gains in share of value-added. This indicates the increasing importance of the capital-goods industry in the latter period.

The employment impact of the growth of the new industries was equally profound, and in table 2-2 the changes in employment in São Paulo are presented. Between 1949 and 1974, the three dynamic-B sectors increased their share of manufacturing employment from 6.7 to 29.6 percent, even though the total labor force tripled in size. In 1949 the number of workers employed in the three sectors was insignificant, but by 1974 it totaled 418,000 workers. This had a pronounced impact on the trade unions. In 1949 nearly one third of all workers in the State of São Paulo were employed in the textile industry, but by 1974 this figure had dropped to just under 12 percent. For the metalworking unions, the opposite happened. In 1949 the four sectors represented by the metalworking unions—mechanical, transport materials, electrical materials, and metallurgy—employed 16.3 percent of the total manufacturing labor force, compared with 43.3 percent in 1974. In view of their rapid expansion and their grouping together in the metalworking unions, these four sectors will be referred to as the "dynamic sectors" or "dynamic industries" from here on.

TABLE 2-1

Value-added by sector as a percentage of total value-added in manufacturing
industry: São Paulo, 1949, 1959, 1970

Sector	1949	1959	1970
Traditional	*(55.0)*	*(37.9)*	*(31.2)*
Textiles	22.1	12.3	9.9
Clothing and shoes	4.2	3.5	3.3
Food	14.7	12.0	10.2
Beverages	3.7	2.4	1.7
Printing and publishing	3.4	2.7	3.3
Others[a]	6.9	5.0	2.8
Dynamic-A	*(34.2)*	*(37.3)*	*(38.4)*
Non-metallic minerals	7.4	6.0	5.0
Metallurgical	9.4	9.2	10.5
Paper and cardboard	2.6	3.2	2.9
Rubber	3.2	4.6	2.8
Chemicals	7.3	10.0	9.3
Pharmaceuticals	2.7	2.3	3.9
Others[a]	1.6	2.0	4.0
Dynamic-B	*(8.9)*	*(22.5)*	*(26.7)*
Mechanical	3.1	4.9	8.3
Electrical materials	2.6	5.8	7.3
Transport materials	3.2	11.8	11.1
Others[b]	*2.3*	*2.3*	*2.5*
TOTAL[c]	100	100	100

SOURCES: 1949 and 1959: IBGE, n.d. 1970: IBGE, 1974b.

[a] Those sectors which produced less than 3 percent of total value-added in all
three years for which figures are presented are grouped into the category "Other."

[b] This is an unspecified category in the census classification.

[c] The columns do not add up to 100 percent exactly because of rounding. In
addition, the census in 1970 did not provide figures for two small traditional
sectors, leather and tobacco.

Where necessary, the dynamic-A sectors will be termed the "intermediate sectors."

The dynamic industries have certain characteristic features, and
their growth has changed the face of Brazilian manufacturing.
Firms in these industries are more likely to be located in the São
Paulo region, produce for the national market (as opposed to
regional markets), be owned by or associated with foreign capital,
use a relatively sophisticated technology, and control a significant

Development and the Working Class

TABLE 2-2

Average number of workers employed per month by sector: São Paulo, 1949 and 1974[a]

Sector[b]	1949	Per-centages	1974	Per-centages	1974/1949
Traditional	*(274,526)*	*(60.1)*	*(469,756)*	*(33.3)*	*(1.71)*
Textiles	145,696	31.9	164,861	11.7	1.13
Clothing and shoes	23,659	5.2	92,719	6.6	3.92
Food	49,758	10.9	98,522	7.0	1.98
Beverages	9,861	2.1	11,728	0.8	1.21
Printing and publishing	12,884	2.8	33,366	2.4	2.59
Others	32,848	7.2	68,560	4.8	2.09
Dynamic-A	*(141,689)*	*(30.9)*	*(461,612)*	*(32.8)*	*(3.26)*
Nonmetallic minerals	44,508	9.7	83,160	5.9	1.92
Metallurgical	44,063	9.6	193,066	13.6	4.38
Paper and cardboard	11,703	2.6	39,958	2.8	3.41
Rubber	6,414	1.4	30,619	2.2	4.77
Chemicals	25,304	5.5	50,686	3.6	2.00
Pharmaceuticals	5,111	1.1	15,613	1.1	3.02
Others	4,586	1.0	48,510	3.4	10.58
Dynamic-B	*(30,740)*	*(6.7)*	*(418,156)*	*(29.6)*	*(13.60)*
Mechanical	13,613	3.0	183,383	13.0	13.47
Electrical materials	9,806	2.1	114,527	8.1	11.68
Transport materials	7,321	1.6	120,246	8.5	16.42
Others	*9,716*	*2.1*	*61,872*	*4.4*	—
TOTAL[c]	456,671	100.0	1,411,396	100.0	3.09

Workers employed spans the 1949, Percentages, 1974, Percentages columns.

SOURCES: 1949: IBGE, n.d. 1974: IBGE, 1976.

[a] In 1949 the census definition of workers excluded foremen. In 1974 the equivalent census category was "persons linked to production," which included workers, foremen, and also technical staff. This category has been selected because it excludes white-collar staff and top management.

[b] The same sectors as in table 2-1 have been included in this table.

[c] The columns do not add up to 100 percent exactly because of rounding.

share of the market (Fajnzylber, 1971:56). The average size of establishment is also larger in the dynamic industries, and they are disproportionately located in the industrial suburbs. Above all, the firms in the dynamic sectors pay higher than average wages. The differences between the dynamic sectors and the longer-established industries can be summed up in the stereotypes of, on the one hand, the large, modern, high-wage, foreign-owned establishment in the industrial suburbs and, on the other hand, the small, traditional, low-wage, nationally owned firm in the old industrial center of São Paulo. In many ways this contrast encapsulates the transformations that have taken place in Brazilian industry since the Second World War: all of the features attributed to the large, modern firm became more prevalent in Brazilian industry in the course of the postwar period. However, it would be wrong for two reasons to take these stereotypes as an adequate illustration of the changes that have taken place. Firstly, within the dynamic sectors there is a considerable differentiation with respect to wage levels, foreign control, and location. The mechanical sector, for example, has relatively high wage-levels but small firms owned by Brazilian capital and located in the city of São Paulo. The electrical-materials industry, on the other hand, has wage levels much closer to the industrial average. The dichotomy between "traditional" and "modern" often hides more than it reveals. Secondly, the longer-established sectors were *not* traditional in the sense of remaining unchanged and fixed to past practices: the development of the new industries was accompanied by a considerable transformation of other sectors. Mata and Bacha provide figures on output per worker for the period from 1949 to 1969 which show that increases in the dynamic-A and dynamic-B groupings were almost matched by those in the traditional industries (1973:307). In the textile and food industries there was a lot of modernization in the larger firms as synthetic textiles, advanced spinning and weaving machinery, and modern forms of food processing and packaging were introduced. In 1968, six of the ten largest firms in both sectors were foreign-owned (Fajnzylber, 1971:44). Similarly, it is worth noting that in 1970 the textile industry was the second-largest importer of foreign machinery and equipment (IBGE, 1974a). The stagnation of employment in the traditional industries was due to rapidly rising productivity, and this led to low overall rates of job creation in manufacturing in the fifties.[2]

---

[2] Gerchunoff and Llach make the same point for Argentina (1975:14).

The transformation of Brazilian industry resulting from the Kubitschek industrialization strategy went far deeper than merely the implantation of some new industries. The conditions for the successful introduction and development of these industries also had to be secured, and this required major changes in the role of the State and the use of resources. According to the structuralist model of economic development, employment growth in the post-war period was to be achieved by the controlled inflow of foreign capital into the manufacturing sector and State support for private national capital.[3] Foreign capital would merely provide the know-how to develop industry and some limited capital to ease the burden of raising the necessary funds and resources. However, in Brazil as elsewhere in Latin America the role of foreign capital and the effects of the new development strategy turned out to be rather different.

Rapid industrial growth placed great strains on the economy. On the one hand, the vast amount of resources needed to develop completely new industries could only be provided by reductions in disposable income, either directly or through inflation. On the other hand, the State needed to finance spending on basic industries and on the infrastructure of energy and transportation essential for rapid industrialization. To do this it was forced to resort to the printing of money because the tax base could not be expanded sufficiently. While the economy was booming, this problem was not serious, but when the economy moved into recession in 1962, the Populist government was placed in the impossible position of trying to control inflation and restore growth without penalizing the labor movement whose support was so vital.[4] At the same time, its labor support was voicing increasing concern about the buildup of foreign capital in manufacturing industry and demanding tough policies to curb the activities of multinational firms. The economic crisis and the political crisis over the measures to deal with it—I.M.F.-style stabilization versus agrarian reform and control of foreign capital—were significant factors

[3] For a straightforward exposition of the structuralist view on the role of foreign capital, see Prebisch, 1969:40–43.

[4] See Oliveira, 1977:90–91. Much of this account is taken from this source.

leading to the military coup in 1964. Following the coup, new economic policies and new political arrangements were introduced to cope with the crisis. The economic and political implications of the new pattern of development introduced in the fifties were profound, and for this reason the transformation of industry before and after 1964 cannot be accounted for by a concept such as the ''structural heterogeneity of industry'' (Pinto, 1965). The new pattern of development could only be introduced and sustained by a change in the general conditions of capital accumulation in the economy as a whole. This change was seen in its fullest extent after the military coup in 1964.

The Working Class under Military Rule

The military government came to power in 1964 with a commitment to restore political and economic order. From the point of view of relations between different units of capital, this involved fiscal and financial reforms and a policy of controlled crisis in order to restructure the role of domestic and foreign capital in the economy (see Oliveira, 1977:92–97). In relation to the working class, the first priority was to cut short the increasing radicalization of the labor movement and restore State control so that new and unpopular policies could be implemented. Once this had been done, it became possible to substitute for the policy of ''tutelage'' (protection and control) a policy that subordinated labor to the new needs of capital, as expressed in the centralized and rational planning of the State. In practice this meant the subjection of the class to policies designed to reduce or contain wages and increase productivity.

In an analysis of the decade 1964–1974, Roberto Campos, Minister of Planning in the period of restructuring (1964–1967), outlined four stages of economic policy.[5] The second of these stages he termed the ''discovery of hard reality,'' which included

---

[5] Made in a speech to the Brazilian Chamber of Commerce in March 1975, when Ambassador in London. Reported in fully in JT, 31/5/1975.

the ending or reduction of subsidies on food and transport, an option in favor of the "Productive State" instead of the "Distributive State," and the acceptance of an "Executive power sufficiently strong to implant budgetary discipline, define national priorities, and control wage indiscipline." This period of adjustment was difficult for capital as well as labor, particularly for the smaller national firms, but the government regarded it as necessary, even if undesirable. But whereas the "hard reality" was a temporary phase for capital, and a prelude to the economic miracle, for the working class it lasted much longer. Of the three temporary measures introduced to "clean out" the economy when Campos was Minister of Planning—fiscal policy, monetary policy, and wage control—only the third was either rigorously applied or kept in force for long (Fischlow, 1974:8–36). Together with direct repression of the working class and trade unions, and changes in the law on stability of employment, the wages policy was a permanent feature of a new situation for the working class after the coup.

REPRESSION

The measures taken after the coup put labor firmly back under the control of the State. Labor leaders were imprisoned or forced to go into hiding, the Populist political system which had been the source of their power was dismantled, and political organizations of the working class were persecuted. The unions also suffered direct measures. In 1964, 409 unions and forty-three federations were put under the direct control of the Ministry of Labor, with the larger and politically active unions being disproportionately affected (Erickson, 1977:45 and 158). A new law regulating the right to strike was passed in July 1964, and this made legal strikes almost impossible. As well as forbidding strikes in certain essential services and productive activities, no strike could take place if the issue in dispute had been the object of a judgment in the Labor Court, which could, of course, be requested by just one of the parties to the dispute.

The repression of the working class was designed to eliminate the political elements within the labor movement, and one of the themes of Ministers of Labor after the coup was the need to develop an authentic, nonpolitical trade union movement.[6] However, the unpopularity of the government's policies meant that any liberalization of the control over the unions led to working-class resistance, as happened in 1967–1968. An "authentic" union would oppose the State and defend the interests of its members, and declarations by Ministers of Labor about rising real wages were not sufficient to contain working-class discontent. Therefore, the State was forced to keep a permanent grip on the unions. After the initial period of direct Ministry control, unions were slowly allowed to elect new executives and return to "normal" functioning, but this normality had narrowly circumscribed limits. Particularly after the closure of Congress and the passing of Institutional Act Five in December 1968, the Ministry of Labor's vigilance over the unions was intense. Any kind of radical action or mobilization was sufficient to provoke a further period of direct control, and the selective use of this instrument, as well as the arrest and imprisonment of trade union leaders, intimidated other unions not directly affected. In this way, even a small number of interventions by the Ministry of Labor was sufficient to immobilize union leaders. For example, an opposition group won the union elections for the Metalworkers of Guanabara in 1972, and the Ministry immediately intervened. This not only neutralized opposition in this particular union but led to the cancellation of a meeting of São Paulo unionists about the wages policy (Mericle, 1974:99–100). Ten years after the coup, in 1974, the threat posed by the Ministry of Labor was clearly expressed when the Minister commented on the end of the intervention in the Confederation of Workers in Credit Establishments: "This does not mean that we will cease to be attentive to the evolution of events and ready to act whenever necessary to safeguard legality, national security, and respect for authority" (OESP, 9/11/1974).

For rank-and-file militants in the plants, the situation was much

[6] This type of declaration about nonpolitical trade unionism can be found in Arnaldo Sussekind's proposals for reform of labor legislation in 1965 and Jarbas Passarinho's declarations about a new policy in 1967 (see, for example, OESP, 27/5/1967 and 11/8/1967).

worse. Strikes and protests could be accompanied by mass dismissals, arrests, and imprisonments, and it was not until 1976–1977 that either the unions or the rank-and-file militants could feel at all confident about their chances of actively opposing the policies of the State without suffering its retribution.

THE WAGES POLICY

One of the major reasons for the State's continuing need to resolve labor issues by the use or threat of force was the wages policy adopted in 1965. The general principle of the wages legislation was that wage settlements should be adjusted to keep the share of wages in the national income roughly constant.[7] In the first nine months of implementation, wage increases were determined by judges in the Labor Courts, who could select which inflation indices they chose and also order special increases in wages to compensate for such factors as "distortions" in relative wages, losses in real income dating from before the start of the new policy, and levels of wages insufficient to purchase the necessities of life (Law 4,903 of December 1965). However, these special provisions and the discretion allowed to Labor Court judges were not the best way to bring down the rate of inflation and transfer income from labor to capital. In 1966 new laws were decreed which reduced the role of the Labor Courts in the determination of wage settlements by eliminating the special provisions and by providing an official inflation index. From this point on the wages policy was strictly subordinated to overall economic policy. Wage settlements, and the figures on which they were based, became subordinate to the needs of the ministries of Finance and Planning, and this led to a systematic misapplication of a wages formula that in theory should have maintained the share of the national income going to wages.

The wages policy, as it was defined in 1966, determined the level of wage settlements according to a formula which contained three basic variables: (1) an allowance for the effect of inflation

---

[7] For a discussion of the debates surrounding the introduction of the wages policy, see Souza Martins, 1979:139–154. A good analysis of the effects of the policy on wage settlements can be found in DIEESE, 1975.

sufficient to restore wages to the average level of the previous twenty-four months; (2) a percentage increase equivalent to half the estimated rate of inflation in the year following the settlement; (3) a percentage increase equivalent to the increase in national productivity. While the use of such a formula gave the wages policy a certain technocratic and neutral appearance, in practice it was subject to considerable manipulation. Firstly, the estimates of past inflation were not always accurate. The trade union statistics-and-research unit, DIEESE, calculated that the indices used in wage determination were below the rate of inflation from 1965 to 1968, and again unrealistically low between 1972 and 1974 (DIEESE, 1975:28). Secondly, the estimated rate of future inflation used in the wages policy was lower than the actual rate for every year from 1966 to 1974. This statement is true irrespective of whether the DIEESE inflation index is taken or the State's own figures are compared with the estimates used in the wages policy. Between 1965 and 1968, compensation for such underestimations was not made in the following wage settlement, and yet it was in this period that the gap between estimation and actual outcome was greatest. Very often the estimation bore little resemblance to the government's own predictions, and it has to be concluded that the figures used in the wages policy were deliberately manipulated in order to reduce settlement rates below the rate of inflation. For example, the estimate of inflation used in the wages policy was 10 percent between July 1966 and July 1967, and 15 percent in the following year. In March 1967, however, the Minister of Finance, Delfim Neto, predicted a rate of inflation for the year of at least 20 percent, with 25–30 percent being a more likely final figure (OESP, 3/3/1967). Thirdly, the allowance for productivity was always underestimated. In spite of rapid rises in gross domestic product, the highest figure ever reached by the productivity allowance was 4 percent (Hoffman, 1976:93–94). The net impact of these devices was to fix wage settlements well below the rate of inflation in the period of restructuring from 1965 to 1967, and to keep them at or slightly below the rate of inflation between 1967 and 1972, when the economy was expanding rapidly and productivity was rising.

Wage settlements are not the only factor determining movements in wage rates and earnings, but it is possible to show that the control of wage settlements was accompanied by a contention of wages. Some of the figures presented by Bacha on the earnings of workers in a group of large firms in south-central Brazil are shown in table 2-3. Given the area, the type of firm, and the fact that the period covered does not include the years when wage-settlement levels were most out of line with the rate of inflation, these figures for earnings can be considered to be better than would be found for the mass of workers in the decade after the military coup. Bacha's conclusion is that earnings for unskilled and semi-skilled workers fell in the period covered by his data:

> Wage control not only permitted a substantial reduction in inflation rates: coupled with a complete ban on strikes and police intervention in the strongest labor unions, it weakened wage earners' bargaining position both to contest real income losses and to compete for a share of productivity gains. Even with constant profit margins, corrective inflation of non-wage cost elements meant that prices would increase by more than wages did from 1964 to 1967: the beneficiaries were the financial sector, rentiers, real estate owners, public utilities and the government itself. After 1967 increasing productivity gains were

TABLE 2-3

Movements in real earnings of workers in selected occupations in a group of large industrial firms: 1966 to 1972

Occupation	Average number of observations	Earnings, Cr$ April 1972	Annual rate of growth of real earnings, April 1966 to April 1972 (%)
Sweeper/janitor	1,615	385	−1.4
Laborer	1,815	512	−1.2
Internal driver	152	714	−0.7
Welder	110	826	+3.4
Painter	112	766	+4.8
Mechanic	306	1,167	+3.8
Machine-tool operator	469	1,171	+2.5

SOURCE: Bacha, 1975:140.

appropriated by firms, government and upper income salary earners. Skill differentials clearly broadened during this period, given the stronger bargaining position of skilled workers; the latter, however, did not manage to maintain their income shares constant either. The clear winners were the top hierarchical positions both in government and in private firms. . . . The real wages of the unskilled positions clearly went down; the story for skilled positions is a mixed one; on average these workers managed to get some moderate increases in real wages; those on top, however, reaped most of the gains with an 8.1% real salary growth per year in the period. (This is the text accompanying the table in an English résumé of part of the Brazilian article, 1976, 15–16.)

The conclusion, that among blue-collar workers only the skilled experienced rises in real earnings, is supported by an analysis of wage movements made by DIEESE. In table 2-4 the evolution of wages in a large sample of firms in São Paulo is presented. It is based on calculations of the median wages in metalworking firms taken from their returns for the Trade Union Contribution, which is paid in March of each year.[8] The first thing to note is that the metalworkers did not do so badly as the textile workers, but even for the former wages fell very sharply in the first quinquennium, from 1961 to 1966, presumably because of the tight wage squeeze in the first two years after the military coup. In 1976, the real median wage was still below the 1961 level. Secondly, the data in the metalworking sector for wage evolution according to skill confirm Bacha's findings. The unskilled and semiskilled workers suffered big losses in the sixties which were only slightly compensated in the 1971 to 1976 period. Only in the case of skilled workers was any net rise noted in the period as a whole. Thirdly, the sample of twenty large metalworking firms shows a different trend from the sector as a whole. There are gains in the second quinquennium, but losses in the third. This is also seen in the case of five large firms (two auto assembly and three auto com-

[8] The Trade Union Contribution is defined as a day's wages, but the exact meaning of this term does not appear to be specified in the CLT.

43

ponents) in the transport-materials sector, although in this case the gain from 1966 to 1971 was much less. This point will be taken up in chapter three. While Bacha's figures and those supplied by DIEESE differ in their assessment of the degree of the fall in workers' incomes—due to the use of different inflation indices mainly—they agree about the direction of the movement. For much of the working class, the reality of capitalist restructuring and expansion was hard indeed.

STABILITY OF LABOR

The second major piece of legislation that deserves attention is the new law on stability of labor and compensation for dismissal, which was introduced in 1966. The Fundo de Garantia do Tempo de Servico (FGTS) replaced the Lei da Estabilidade that had been introduced in the Estado Novo period. It was noted in chapter one that the latter law had been designed to structure urban labor markets and stabilize a new and growing labor force. By the mid-

TABLE 2-4

Changes in the real median-wage for selected groups of workers: São Paulo, five-year intervals from 1961 to 1976[a] (percentages)

Group	1961–1966	1966–1971	1971–1976
All textile workers	− 13.5	− 15.2	− 2.7
All metalworkers	− 22.0	+ 0.5	+ 9.9
Metalworkers, unskilled	− 30.9	− 18.4	+ 4.1
Metalworkers, semiskilled	− 26.9	− 2.7	+ 6.3
Metalworkers, skilled	− 8.3	+ 4.5	+ 14.8
20 large metalworking firms[b]	− 6.1	+ 14.5	− 10.4
5 large transport-materials firms[c]	− 8.9	+ 6.6	− 6.8

SOURCE: DIEESE, 1977.

[a] The figures are calculated from a 10 percent sample of all firms returning the forms for the Trade Union Contribution. They refer to firms represented by the São Paulo textile and metalworkers' unions. The median wage has been used in order to avoid the distortions of higher-wage groups on the average (mean) wage. Nominal wages have been deflated by the DIEESE cost-of-living index.

[b] This group is made up of five large firms selected from each of the four major metalworking sectors—mechanical, metallurgical, electrical, and automotive.

[c] This group consists of two large auto assembly firms and three large auto components firms.

sixties the needs of capital were very different. Firstly, the priority
of the new regime was not the establishment of a stable, growing
labor force but rather the resolution of an economic crisis by a
restructuring of capital, which in the short term at least necessarily
involved redundancies and unemployment. In the crisis period
employers found it difficult to bear the costs of dismissal compensation, and they sought a change in the law. Secondly, the
urban labor markets in the major industrial areas had developed
significantly after the Second World War, and as a result there
was an assured supply of labor for all but the skilled trades. No
special measures were needed to structure an urban labor force.
Thirdly, industrial production had undergone a transformation in
the intervening period. Increased mechanization and the development of management control over the labor process in large-
scale production meant that productivity in industry was guaranteed less by the knowledge and accumulated experience of workers
(leading to an emphasis on training and stability) than by the
control and discipline imposed by capital. This could be achieved
by reducing job security. These long-term changes might have
led to pressure for a change in the law at an earlier stage, but
until the military coup the political conditions for removing one
of the prized gains of the working class did not exist. In the
Populist period, working-class support for the regime was essential, and this made such a radical shift in the labor system impossible. Once the coup had removed such restraints, the military
government could introduce the new law and justify it on the
grounds of capitalist efficiency.

The FGTS differed from the Law on Stability in two major
respects. Firstly, it removed the special protection afforded to
workers with more than ten years' employment with the same
firm. The old law gave such long-service workers the right to
remain in employment unless dismissed for committing a grave
error. Such a grave breach of discipline or responsibility had to
be proved in the Labor Courts before the dismissal was confirmed.
If the employer could not establish his case, the worker would
either be reinstated or receive twice the normal rate of compensation (Cesarino, 1970:219–220). The new law abolished this

protection.[9] Secondly, and possibly even more important, the financing of dismissal compensation was changed. Under the Law on Stability, workers dismissed "without due cause" (in other words, without having committed some breach of discipline or responsibility that would allow them to be sacked for a good reason) were entitled to receive a lump-sum payment equal to one month's wages for each year employed, paid at the level of the highest normal monthly wage received by them in the course of their employment. Under the new system, workers dismissed "without due cause" receive approximately the same amount of money upon dismissal,[10] but the financing is different. For each worker, the firm pays 8 percent of the basic wages into an account each month. The money in the account is used by the National Housing Bank, which pays interest and Monetary Correction[11] on it. When a worker is dismissed "without due cause" the firm adds 10 percent to the amount in his or her account and the total sum is paid in compensation.

The practical effects of the new legislation have been important for the working class. The withdrawal of protection against dismissal for employees with more than ten years' service affected few workers because under the old system firms often dismissed their employees in the eighth or ninth year, but those few workers who lost protection could be important for organization in the workplace. Protection against dismissal is now guaranteed only to workers elected as union executives. A deeper impact has resulted from the shift in the form of financing compensation. The employers' financial burden was reduced considerably by the new system because when the 8 percent levy was introduced, other taxes totaling 6¼ percent of wages were canceled by the government (Magana, 1966). This has allowed employers to cut back on employment more easily in times of recession. At the same time, the new system reduced the linkage between the cost

[9] In theory the FGTS was introduced as a second option to the Lei da Estabilidade, but in practice workers were obliged to switch to the new system.

[10] Whether the new system really provides an equal lump sum in compensation has been the subject of some dispute.

[11] Monetary Correction is a scheme to increase the values of financial assets in line with inflation.

of the compensation scheme and the number of workers dismissed "without due cause." Under the old system, firms paid compensation only to the workers they dismissed, whereas under the new they pay into the accounts of all their workers, and dismissal only costs another 10 percent over what has been deposited. This has made deliberate hire-and-fire policies much cheaper to operate than under the old scheme.

Government supporters justified the new system by reference to the needs of capital. Magana (1966), for example, pointed to the difficulties employers faced in dismissing workers during the 1965 recession, and Professor Arnaldo Sussekind, Minister of Labor in 1964-1965, argued that "Estabilidade represents . . . a severe restriction on the administrative autonomy of employers" (cited by Maragliano, 1966:49). Maragliano himself saw the old system as restricting the drive for productivity, which contradicted the need for "the rational administration of all our [Brazil's] human and material possibilities" (1966:55). The principle of tutelage, protection as well as control, was replaced by the need for productivity and the logic of capital. This was not welcomed by the more traditional labor lawyers. Cesarino, for example, wrote that the FGTS: "means that employers are entirely free to dismiss whomsoever they see fit at their complete will and caprice. . . . Dictatorship has been restored in companies" (1970:276). His judgment perhaps overemphasizes the degree of protection afforded to workers by the Law on Stability and by the old labor system as a whole, but its sense of outrage amply illustrates the ideological shift that took place. As Souta Maior put it, the new system "emphasizes the problem of labor productivity above the traditional principle of tutelage" (quoted in Cesarino, 1970:278). It was indicative of the "hard reality" that accompanied the shift in emphasis from the "Distributive State" to the "Productive State."

The Auto Industry

The development and characteristics of the auto industry typify many of the changes noted in the first two sections of this chapter. The industry's size, importance, and visibility to the public eye have made it a model on which many generalizations about industry and economic development in Brazil have been based.

The auto assembly industry first arrived in Brazil at the beginning of the century, when Fiat started truck assembly. After the First World War, General Motors, Ford, and International Harvester also began to assemble vehicles made up from kits sent from the U.S.A. Until the fifties the industry was confined to the assembly of imported kits, and the few Brazilian component firms produced only replacement parts. In the course of the nineteen-fifties all this changed very rapidly. Balance-of-payment problems led to a restriction on the import of both built-up vehicles and knocked-down kits for assembly, and this, combined with pressure from the local producers of parts, led to plans being made for the implantation of an auto industry (Martins, 1976:413). Initially, the two main assemblers, Ford and General Motors, were against the idea, and by 1956 even the local assembly of imported kits had ground to a virtual standstill. However, as a result of the developmentalist strategy pursued by the Kubitschek government, new incentives were given for auto firms to begin production in Brazil and the overall planning for the implantation of an auto industry was given to the specially created Automobile Industry Executive Group (GEIA). GEIA produced targets for a rapid shift to the use of locally produced parts in vehicles and created special incentives for foreign firms to produce and assemble in Brazil. Firms failing to meet the targets were to suffer the penalty of extremely high tariffs on imports, while firms that continued or initiated production would have concessions on profit remittances and the import of machinery and parts, and long-term loans at low rates of interest (Confederação Nacional da Indústria, n.d.:23-24).

GEIA was responsible for planning the output of different types of vehicles, approving the projects put forward by companies, and assuring that adequate supplies of labor would be available. However, the models to be produced, the techniques to be used, and commercialization were left to the companies themselves (Martins, 1976:421). The planners met with considerable success. By 1960 there were eleven firms producing vehicles, and the government's overall prioritization of trucks, jeeps, and pickups had been put into effect. Between 1957 and 1959 some 90,000 trucks, 70,000 pickups, and 15,000 automobiles had been produced (Confederação Nacional de Indústria, n.d.:31-35). But in the sixties the industry developed rather differently. From 1960 the production of trucks declined, while the production of autos continued to increase. Following the pattern of demand, rather than the priorities laid down in the Plano de Metas of the Kubitschek government, the auto industry increased its production of passenger vehicles, while truck demand stagnated and there was a lot of spare production capacity. Truck production only began to expand after 1972, in contrast to auto production, which rose steadily from 1962 to 1967 and then accelerated during the period of the economic miracle. By 1976, six passenger vehicles were produced for each truck and bus.

As the industry grew, the number of firms declined, just as it had in the U.S.A. and Western Europe. International Harvester, Kharmann Ghia, Vemag, and Willys were all taken over in the sixties, while the parent companies of Simca and the FNM were taken over by Chrysler and Fiat respectively. By 1976, therefore, the industry consisted of seven important multinational firms, whose production and employment figures are shown in table 2-5. The industry continued to undergo significant changes in the latter part of the seventies as a result of the entry of Fiat into the small-auto market, the rapid decline of Chrysler, which led to a takeover by Volkswagen, and the shift from large to small autos resulting from the oil crisis, which caused problems for the North American producers. Overall, growth in the latter part of the seventies remained at 4.5 percent per annum for all vehicles (1974-1979), which in view of the oil crisis was miraculous by world standards. However, it was a very sharp decline from 20.7 percent, the average rate of increase of vehicle output in the previous quinquennium (1969-1974). By 1974 Brazil was among the world's top ten vehicle producers (in volume terms) and it easily had the largest auto industry in Latin America, far outstripping Argentina and Mexico. Although it had not reached the level of mass production found in North America, Japan, and Europe, it was (and

Development and the Working Class

TABLE 2.5

Number of vehicles produced by firm and type: Brazil, 1976

Firm	Autos[a]	Vans/ pickups	Light and medium trucks	Heavy trucks[b]	Total production	Number of workers employed
Chrysler	17,380	1,725	8,726	—	27,831	3,777
FNM[c]	4,792	—	1,061	3,744	9,597	5,332
Fiat[d]	8,350	—	—	—	8,350	5,000
Ford	129,017	27,295	15,619	—	171,931	22,459
General Motors	144,513	23,401	13,215	15	181,144	22,933
Mercedes Benz	—	—	35,250	13,567	48,817	16,460
Saab-Scania	—	—	—	4,571	4,571	2,822
Volkswagen	463,356	66,280	—	—	529,636	39,057
ALL FIRMS[e]	767,408	118,701	73,871	21,897	981,877	117,840

SOURCES: Production: *Notícias da ANFAVEA*, February 1977. Employment: *Quem é Quem na Economia Brasileira*, 1977.

[a] Included under autos are all hatchbacks and car-derived vans of mixed use. In government figures hatchbacks are usually classified as mixed-use or utility vehicles.

[b] Includes super-heavy trucks and buses.

[c] The FNM is owned by Fiat.

[d] Fiat only initiated production in 1976. By 1979 it was producing approximately 10,000 vehicles per month.

[e] Excluded from this list are Cummins, Toyota, and Puma, which produced a total of 3,592 vehicles in 1976.

still remains) the largest producer in the capitalist world outside of the OECD countries, and it is at the stage of mass producing complete vehicles, with 100 percent locally produced parts.

The largest part of this industry is located in the Greater São Paulo area, above all in the district of São Bernardo do Campo. The concentration of the auto industry in the industrial suburbs is part of a general concentration of the dynamic industries in these areas. The four main industrial suburbs of São Paulo have a disproportionate number of workers in the transport-materials and metallurgical industries, and this is particularly true of São Bernardo, where 64.0 percent of all workers in manufacturing worked in these two sectors in 1970 (IBGE, 1974b). These industrial suburbs also show a concentration of workers in large

TABLE 2-6

Distribution of workers by size of establishment in metal-mechanical industries in selected areas of Greater São Paulo[a]

Area	Year[b]	All metalworkers		Establishments of more than 1,000 workers		Establishments of more than 500 workers	
		Number of workers	Number of plants	Percentage of all metalworkers	Number of plants	Percentage of all metalworkers	Number of plants
Osasco	1979	37,529	329	37.5	5	53.0	13
Santo André	1977	46,081	322	48.6	1C	60.7	19
São Bernardo[c]	1978	125,557	575	67.2	15	74.0	26
São Caetano[d]	1979	20,154	47	80.4	3	86.0	5
São Paulo (city)	1976	421,277	10,076	20.8	41	32.9	113

SOURCE: Unpublished figures from DIEESE.

[a] The areas are the jurisdictions of unions, not the local government districts.

[b] The year taken is the latest for which information is available.

[c] Included in this area is an estimate for one large auto firm not included in the DIEESE figures.

[d] The figures for São Caetano do not include workers in plants which did not provide detailed information on wage structures. In the other areas such firms amounted to between 10 percent and 20 percent of total employment. In all cases except that noted in (c) above, it has been assumed that firms not providing detailed information have fewer than 500 workers.

firms, compared with the city of São Paulo, as can be seen in table 2-6. In São Bernardo, above all, the dominance of five large auto firms employing 66,000 workers, along with ten other firms employing 18,000 workers in the other metal-mechanical sectors, has led to a concentration of workers in large establishments. Two thirds of all the metalworkers in the area work in establishments of over 1,000 workers, and three quarters work in establishments of more than 500 workers. In São Caetano over half the metalworkers are employed in one large auto plant. In Osasco and Santo André the degree of concentration is lower, but still well above the rate for the city of São Paulo. Information on other industries is not generally available, but in the city of São Paulo, only 13 percent of the workers in the plastic industry and 15 percent of the workers in the chemical industry were employed in establishments of more than 1,000 workers. The auto industry, therefore, more than any other in the metal-mechanical grouping, exemplifies the trends of industrial development in Brazil. It is characterized by large establishments in the industrial suburbs, and concentration of production among a small number of foreign-owned firms.

With respect to wages, too, the auto industry exemplifies the general trends found in the dynamic industries. The data available in the censuses show clearly that the average level of wages in the dynamic-B sectors is well above that found in the traditional sectors (with the exception of printing and publishing). If the textile industry is taken as the reference level for the traditional sector, the average wage for workers linked to production in São Paulo in 1974 was 44 percent higher in the metallurgical sector, 36 percent higher in the electrical-materials sector, 70 percent higher in transport materials, and 93 percent higher in the mechanical industry (IBGE, 1976). However, these general figures hide the real extent of wage differentiation because the auto assembly industry is combined with the auto components sector and other smaller nonauto sectors in the general grouping "transport materials." When the auto assembly sector is separated out, as in table 2-7, its wage levels can be seen to be exceptional. In São Paulo, the median wage in the auto assembly sector is about twice as great as in any of the other metalworking sectors, and the average wage is about 75 percent higher. In São Bernardo, the difference is less because of the larger size of firms and higher wages (relative to São Paulo) in the other metalworking sectors, but even here the median wage is between 40 and 60 percent higher in the auto industry. The only sectors which pay comparable wages are steel, machine tools (part of the mechanical industry), and the electrical-supply industry. In other sectors, such as auto components, chemicals, and heavy electrical equipment, only a few firms pay the rates offered by the auto industry.[12]

TABLE 2-7
Average and median wage-levels for metalworkers: São Bernardo and São Paulo, March 1976

Group[a]	Average wage (Cr$ per month)	Median wage (Cr$ per month)	Number of workers
São Bernardo			
Auto assembly[b]	2,870	2,307	66,304
Auto components	1,952	1,352	20,067
Metallurgical	2,113	1,444	6,207
Electrical materials	1,881	1,333	6,128
Mechanical	2,344	1,617	15,237
São Paulo			
Auto assembly[b]	3,484	2,613	12,440
Auto components	1,843	1,288	48,927
Metallurgical	1,891	1,379	36,390
Electrical materials	1,927	1,221	91,909
Mechanical	2,024	1,376	201,388

SOURCE: DIEESE.

[a] These calculations are made from firm's payments of the Trade Union Contribution in March of each year. Because the annual wage settlement for São Paulo metalworkers takes place in November, whereas in São Bernardo it comes in April, the comparison of wage levels between the two areas has to be carried out with care. When an allowance is made for this factor by computing wage levels in terms of the minimum wage during the lifetime of the contract period which includes March 1976, wage levels in the auto assembly industry in the two areas are found to be roughly equal.

[b] The "auto assembly" group also includes workers in factories making tractors.

[12] The pay rates on which these comparisons are based are taken from DIEESE's computations of the returns for the Trade Union Contribution. In the textile in-

Development and the Working Class

Because of these characteristics—large firms, high wages, concentration in the industrial suburbs—workers in the motor industry have been identified as an actual or potential labor aristocracy. The median wage in the auto industry in 1978 was four times the minimum wage and double the level in such industries as chemicals, plastics, and construction. However, it would be a mistake to believe that the workers in the auto industry escaped the difficulties facing the working class after the coup in 1964. Immediately after the coup the freedom to negotiate directly with the employers disappeared, and discipline and control were tightened up, as this description of events in a small auto plant illustrates:

> In 1964, just after the suspension of the right to strike, there was a big stoppage. It last four hours. The firm called DOPS [the political police] and they and the soldiers arrived and threatened everyone. It was a down-tools—people standing in front of the machines. They had machine guns and electric-shock machines, and they talked to the workers one by one. "Do you want to start your machine or come outside and talk with us?" Everyone was very scared, and they started working again. (Account by one of the participants, made in 1974.)

In 1969 DOPS were called in during a strike at Mercedes Benz, as Souza Martins recounts (1979:132), and in 1974-1975, 200 workers from the Volkswagen plant were imprisoned at one time (Frederico, 1978:132). These few incidents give an indication of the pressure on auto workers after the coup. The effects on wages and working conditions will be discussed in the next chapters.

---

dustry, by comparison, the median wage-rate in 1976 in the city of São Paulo was Cr$1,035, which is only 40 percent of the auto assembly figure and 15 percent below the median wage-rate in electrical materials.

3

Wages and Working Conditions in the Auto Industry

IN THE PREVIOUS CHAPTER, two different developments were outlined: the expansion of the dynamic industries and the situation of the working class after the military coup in 1964. To examine the effects of these tendencies on the workers in the auto industry, it is necessary to examine their situation. However, no examination is innocent, and so this chapter begins with a discussion of theories of dual and segmented labor markets, which have been influential and widespread in the analysis of the Latin American working classes. The assumptions and implications of these theories for job requirements, employment policies, wages, and working conditions are then compared with the situation in the Brazilian auto industry.

The empirical material analyzed in this chapter was only obtained through the cooperation of both management and unions in the auto industry. Material was provided by the managements in four auto companies, by trade union leaders, and by rank-and-file militants in the industry. However, the main empirical basis for the discussion in this chapter is a study of two auto plants in the Greater São Paulo area owned by one of the multinational firms. The management of the company provided a lot of information on wages, employment practices, and industrial relations, and allowed access to the plants and interviews with workers during working hours. In the two plants, 212 production workers were interviewed.[1] These two plants will be called AF1 and AF2.

Auto production involves a number of different processes. The

---

[1] All the production workers were male, so the sample was not sex stratified. Only one firm in the auto industry appeared to employ women in direct production work, and even in this firm women workers accounted for less than 5 percent of all employees in 1979.

main production areas are (i) the machine shops that produce the power train (engines, gearboxes, and axles), (ii) the press shops that fabricate the metal panels for the body, (iii) the body and paint shops that turn the panels into bodies, (iv) the trim and assembly areas, and (v) the ancillary services such as quality control, provision of parts and materials, maintenance, and tool and die.[2] In order to be assured of obtaining samples of workers that would reflect the effects of both skill and the specific areas of production, even though the total sample would be small, no attempt was made to obtain a random sample of the many thousands of workers in the two plants. Instead, groups of workers were selected by skill and area of production. In AF1, where there was little power-train production, the stamping plant small and the toolrooms large, the sample of workers was taken from the unskilled and semiskilled workers in the assembly areas and the skilled workers in the toolrooms.[3] In AF2, where the power-train division was large, the stamping plant larger, and the toolroom relatively small (because of a limited division of functions between the plants), the sample included unskilled workers from the machine shops and assembly area, semiskilled workers from these two areas as well as the stamping plant, and skilled toolmakers from the tool and die area.

The interviews included questions about workers' job histories, the work performed, and wages, and also inquiries about their attitudes to wages, employment conditions, the trade unions, and political issues.[4] After the survey in AF1 the questionnaire was revised and expanded before work was begun in AF2, and for this reason there are certain areas of discussion in this chapter where information from AF2 only is presented. Few conditions were placed on me when entering the plants. I was not restricted in my access to different areas of the two plants, nor was my

[2] For a general account of auto construction, see Central Policy Review Staff, 1975:11-15.

[3] In addition, a small sample of skilled assembly-line workers—metal finishers and welders—was included, but it proved to be too small to be of general use.

[4] Within the selected groups of workers, for example semiskilled workers in the stamping plant, a random sample was taken from the clocking-in numbers.

questionnaire vetted by management. However, I did agree to keep the name of the company confidential. Therefore, it should be borne in mind that two different forms of reference will be used. When information provided directly by management and workers is being presented, the different plants in Greater São Paulo will be referred to by the codes AF1, AF2, AF3, AF4, etc. When publicly available information is quoted, the real names of the companies and plants will be used. This will undoubtedly cause some confusion, but it is unavoidable.

Theories of Segmented and Dual Labor Markets

The rapid but uneven development of the major Latin American economies in the fifties and sixties created a situation where some sectors of industry were considerably more advanced than others. The result of this uneven development was termed "structural heterogeneity." First used for the analysis of economic development, it has become a key concept in a number of accounts of the development of the working class in the postwar period. It was seen in the previous chapter that the implantation of new industries in Greater São Paulo led to the expansion of large, often multinational firms paying relatively high wages to their workers. The apparent contrast between these firms and those in the less technologically and organizationally advanced sectors has led writers to distinguish between different sectors of the working class according to the type of industry in which they are employed. Quijano, for example, has written about the contrasting hegemonic and competitive sectors of the economy. The workers in the hegemonic sectors—composed of large, oligopolistic firms—are supposed to form a stable and privileged group, marked off from other sections of the working class by their special skills, training, and cultural and psychological attitudes (1974:407-408 and 419). The workers in modern industry start with, or acquire, different attributes from those of the mass of workers, and so they are able to sell their labor in restricted markets that are immune from the general pressure of the mass of migrants in the towns.

A coherent statement of the theory of dual and segmented labor markets in Latin America can be found in Foxley and Muñoz (1977:83-87). They distinguish between jobs in the modern and the traditional sectors. Technical progress and capital-intensive processes are concentrated in the modern sectors (by definition), and so therefore is the demand for skilled and other high-quality workers. Some workers are employed who have special skills suitable for the new processes, while others are taken on because of their general aptitudes, being given the training they need on the job. The management of the modern firm invests in the workers who are trained on the job and, at the same time, wishes to retain the services of the workers who possess skills on entry because they are difficult to find in the industrial areas. Therefore, management tries to stabilize its labor force in order to reduce training and replacement costs. Because one important means of stabilizing labor is the payment of higher-than-average wages, the workers in modern industry enjoy skill, stability, and high pay. Given their secure position they can improve their wages even further by the development of strong trade unions that can extract from the employers a greater share of the modern sectors' high profits, derived from increasing productivity and monopoly power. In contrast to this, the situation is very different for workers in traditional industries. They are mainly unskilled and there is little job security: wages and productivity are low. In the course of their employment in the traditional sectors these workers can gain neither the skills nor the aptitudes that could secure them a stable high-wage job in the modern sector. For the mass of the unemployed, of course, the situation is even bleaker. The gap between the few who make it into the modern sectors and the mass of workers is great, and it is widened by both unions and the State. The unions only function effectively in the modern sector, where the pressures of the industrial reserve army of the unemployed are neutralized by the special requirements of work in modern industry. The State gives the modern sector better access to finance and government assistance (Foxley and Muñoz, 1977:86) and encourages the division of the labor market by the enactment of social legislation that protects those with jobs at the expense of those who do not have them (Miller, 1971:237). The result, according to Miller, is the creation of an elite of privileged workers:

"The development of non-competitive labour groups in urban Latin America . . . has resulted in the creation of small elite groups of workers, highly paid and secure from economic adversity" (1971:241).

The dual-labor-market notion employed by Miller and by Foxley and Muñoz is derived from Doeringer and Piore's work on labor markets in the U.S.A. The characteristics of the two types of labor market described by Foxley and Muñoz correspond to the kinds of jobs and the methods of allocation to them described by Doeringer and Piore (1971), and for this reason it is necessary to examine the analysis of the two North American authors in order to investigate more fully the creation and functioning of urban labor markets. Doeringer and Piore distinguish between a primary labor market, which consists of jobs with high wages, good working conditions, good chances of advancement, stability of employment, and equity in the administration of work rules (1971:165), and secondary labor markets, formed by clusters of jobs that lack these desirable characteristics. The formation of two such radically different types of jobs is attributed to distinct patterns of labor demand, which lead to distinct patterns of recruitment, training, and promotion within and between enterprises. The basis for distinguishing between such patterns is the fundamental concept of the ''internal labor market.'' Primary labor markets, they argue, are formed by series of internal labor markets (1971:167).

An internal labor market is defined as ''an administrative unit . . . within which the pricing and allocation of labor is governed by a set of administrative rules and procedures'' (1971:1-2). This is such a wide-ranging definition that it could apply to any deviation from the hypothetical competitive-market situation, but the discussion is quickly narrowed down to two important forms of internal labor market: (i) a ''closed'' internal labor market where entry to the firm is at the bottom of a job hierarchy and higher posts are filled through internal promotion, and (ii) an ''open'' internal labor market where jobs are filled from outside the enterprise by reference to nonmarket criteria, such as the possession of a union card. It is argued that the closed internal labor market predominates in manufacturing industry in the U.S.A.

(1971:2-3). The existence of closed internal labor markets can be related to the arguments put forward by Foxley and Muñoz. If firms need to retain skilled workers and train (and retain) semi-skilled workers, then they will use internal promotion systems and pay relatively high wages to their workers. Therefore, once it is assumed that the demand for labor in the modern sectors is either for skilled workers or for unskilled workers who can be trained on the job, then it becomes reasonable to take the evidence of relatively high rates of pay in these industries as evidence of the existence of closed internal labor markets. From here it would be logical to assume that the closed internal labor markets then form the basis of a primary labor market.

In the terms of this theory, then, there is a good case to be made for the existence of primary labor markets in modern manufacturing industry in Brazil. Wages are relatively high, as was seen in chapter two, and the development of modern industry has clearly been accompanied by a demand for skilled workers in the major industrial centers and the introduction of sophisticated systems of personnel management. In the auto industry, above all, the arrival of the large, modern firm can appear to have brought with it the modern labor practices that Doeringer and Piore have discussed for the United States. Although there have been few empirical studies of the situation of workers in the Brazilian auto industry, two discussions on the topic have tended to reinforce the notion that auto employment is a primary labor market and the workers in the industry form a privileged elite. The first is by Rodrigues and is based on a study carried out in 1963. Rodrigues provides a detailed account of the attitudes of auto workers, and in spite of occasional reservations and provisos, his main argument is that the upward mobility of the mass of workers from agricultural employment to industry and the specific experience of employment in a high-wage, modern, enlightened firm creates a labor force that is, by and large, satisfied:

> Large firm, auto firm, more agreeable firm, etc., rightly constitute for the workers synonyms for "higher wages" and "better employment opportunities." And it is in the big firms as

---

60

well that workers believe they can find better chances of promotion. At the same time the firm makes possible better training, a specialization and the acquisition of skilled trades that
often small firms cannot offer. . . . For almost all of the re-
spondents the company amply fulfills the expectation which
accompanied the search for a job. (1970:45)

At the same time, the firm's wage policy and general attitude to
industrial relations effectively neutralized the trade union, while
internal promotion offered real advancement possibilities for many
workers:

It is obvious that the wages—as well as the other advantages
that the workers value—do not appear to the group as being
the result of collective pressure or of trade union action. . . .
    In addition, partly for technical reasons and partly as a result
of its human relations policy, the auto firm attempted to promote
internally and use its own employees to fill vacancies in the
company hierarchy. The more capable and senior workers had
had, then, effective chances of promotion which did not occur
in other industries, and which may not occur in this same sector
in other countries. These chances will probably disappear when
the Brazilian auto industry reaches maturity. (1970:101-102)

The proviso at the end is significant, but it does not alter the
argument that at the time of the study the workers were reasonably
happy with their situation.[5] This view, combined with the fact
that workers in the motor industry do quite clearly earn above-
average wages, has produced a stereotype (which has been widespread in Brazil) of the well-paid, privileged, skilled auto worker.
    The second account of the situation of workers in the auto
industry is found in the work of Almeida (1975, 1977, 1978).
She argues that the structural heterogeneity of industry in Brazil

[5] Rodrigues is, in fact, ambiguous to the point of contradiction. At two points
(1970:38 and 84) he argues that he can only demonstrate that workers in the motor
industry will not adopt a revolutionary or socialist perspective, but he proceeds
to argue much more than this at other times. For example, he argues that the
firm's policy of small, frequent rises in wages had eliminated wage conflict and
had put an end to strikes.

produces a differentiation within the working class and a diversity of trade union activity:

> . . . the increasing heterogeneity of the industrial structure creates a differentiation of shop-floor workers themselves with regard to situation and conditions of work, skill levels, and wage opportunities. All this is well known. In terms of the present work it is important to stress that this internal differentiation of the factory proletariat implies a differentiation of the problems confronting distinct groups of workers, their interests and their demands. More than this, it is interesting to note how the rise and the dominance of the large modern firm within the industrial structure makes possible the emergence of new bargaining thematics, new forms of negotiation and trade union organizations, and, finally, new types of trade union activity distinct from those previously described [Populist forms]. (1978:479)

Almeida does not argue that all the jobs in the Brazilian auto industry fall within a primary labor market, but she associates the existence of limited secondary labor markets with "extremely low wages" (1978:482), while at the same time discussing the characteristics of the auto industry as a whole in terms of high wages and high productivity.[6] She states that the nucleus of high-wage, stable workers will be greater in the modern sectors than in the traditional (482), and that the characteristics of trade unionism in the auto industry will be determined by this nucleus of workers (486-487). This line of argument allows her to pose an opposition between large and small firms, modern and traditional sectors, and the newer and older industrial suburbs of Greater São Paulo, expressed most succinctly in an earlier article:

> The problems confronted by the worker in Volkswagen in the course of his daily work are necessarily different from those

[6] Although Almeida does not make any definite statement as to the prevalence of unskilled labor in the auto industry, her argument is only sustainable if such labor is in a minority. The writer she quotes on the existence of low-wage secondary labor markets, Souza, takes the same position on the proportion of unskilled labor, as will be seen in the next section.

Wages and Working Conditions

which trouble the workers in a small clothing factory in Bom
Retiro. (1977:18)

As well as implying that there is an inevitable division within the
working class resulting from the development of modern industry,
Almeida also implies that many workers in modern industry, and
in particular in the auto industry, enjoy stable, high-wage jobs
that have good working conditions and chances for advancement.
This line of argument, then, ties in with the statements made by
Rodrigues. But is it an accurate assessment of the situation of
auto workers?

Labor Markets in the Auto Industry

The basis of the argument about the existence of primary labor
markets offering good wages and working conditions is the need
for internal labor markets to train and stabilize workers. A closed
internal labor market implies the recruitment of workers from
outside the firm at the bottom of the job hierarchy and the filling
of higher posts by a process of internal training and promotion.
In the terminology of the theory, entry ports are limited and job
lines (groups of jobs between which workers can move) are relatively long. How does this correspond to the situation in the auto
industry?

The majority of workers in AF1 and AF2 were either unskilled
or semiskilled. According to the company's own classification,
29 percent of the hourly paid workers in AF1 and AF2 were in
skilled jobs, while the other 71 percent were split between 20
percent unskilled and 51 percent semiskilled. In other auto firms
similar skill distributions were found. The skilled workers were
mainly concentrated in the toolrooms and maintenance divisions,
while the unskilled and semiskilled workers were spread throughout the production areas. The proportion of skilled workers is not
low for the auto industry. Widdick cites a figure of 21 percent in
the case of General Motors in the U.S.A. (1976:8), and it seems
reasonable to assume that as the auto industry develops in Brazil,

the proportion of skilled workers will diminish rather than rise.[7] Therefore, it can be stated unequivocally that in the Brazilian auto industry skilled labor does not predominate. While this may appear a mundane statement, it is one that is often contradicted by those who wish to explain the relatively high average wages of workers in the industry.

The skilled workers mainly possessed general skills that could be found in many industries. Workers in the toolrooms and maintenance divisions required the kind of knowledge that is needed wherever tools and dies are constructed and maintenance and repair carried out. This allows the auto firms to recruit from the external labor market. Of the sixty toolroom workers interviewed in AF1 and AF2, the only ones not hired as skilled workers were seven former apprentices and two workers in AF2 who had gone to night school on their own time without any company assistance. The apprentices were employed and trained as part of the State training scheme, and other than through this scheme the company did not consider it worthwhile to train skilled workers, except for the informal training already proceeding in the toolroom (for example, the training of turners to become millers). In three other auto plants, managers were asked about training, and only the smallest plant did any training of toolroom and maintenance workers other than through the apprenticeship scheme. A third group of skilled workers—production workers such as painters, welders, metal finishers, and mechanics[8]—were recruited rather differently. In the absence of formal training systems, such workers usually receive their training on the job, but the size of the metalworking industry in São Paulo gives firms the option of recruiting them on the open market. Policies varied from company to company. In the smallest of the five plants from which information was gathered, AF5, management trained most skilled production

[7] There has been considerable controversy about the effects of technical change, and particularly automation, on skill requirements. In Brazil, the kinds of techniques likely to be introduced into the auto industry would seem to be those that will reduce overall skill levels (see Bright, 1966; Ray, 1969).

[8] These skilled production workers totaled about 5 percent of the total hourly-paid labor force in AF1 and AF2.

workers internally, but in AF4 company policy was to recruit them from outside. The policy in AF1 and AF2 was somewhere in between. Of eight metal finishers interviewed, five had entered the plant as skilled workers (four of them after having worked in a total of eleven other auto plants).[9] Similarly, five out of eight welders entered the plant after learning their jobs in other firms. Generally speaking, therefore, it can be stated that skilled workers are recruited from the external labor market. Once they are employed, they receive little, if any, training, and there is little promotion from skilled jobs to any other position. For all skilled workers the only possible promotion in AF1 and AF2 was to charge-hand or foreman, and such jobs became vacant very in frequently. This pattern of job characteristics does not correspond to a closed internal labor market. The security and strength of the situation of skilled workers derived from the general shortage of skills in the external labor market rather than the formation of internal markets.

The market for unskilled and semiskilled workers is rather different. The relatively high wages paid in the auto industry attract a wide range of candidates. The personnel departments can select and reject them according to such criteria as previous job experience, acceptance of working conditions (for the grueling work in AF5's foundry, for example, management only recruits migrant workers from the Northeast), physical suitability, and so forth. In table 3-1 it can be seen that in AF1 and AF2 approximately two thirds of the unskilled workers were recruited after having been employed in industry, while the other third came from a wide variety of nonindustrial occupations. New employees were put into unskilled jobs if they had not had the type of industrial experience relevant to the auto industry. Their work varied considerably according to the area of the plant to which they were allocated: press shop, assembly area, machine shop. Such workers could expect promotion to a semiskilled job after a period of between eighteen months and two years. However, there are three

[9] This indication of frequent change of employment within the motor industry will be taken up later in this chapter.

TABLE 3-1

Previous occupational experience of workers: AF1 and AF2 (percentages)

Group[a]	Auto industry	Other industry	Occupation prior to entering AF1 or AF2 Other[b]	Agriculture	First job	No response	
AF1							
Laborers	6	62	25	6	—	—	N = 16
Assemblers	38	42	8	4	4	4	N = 24
AF2							
Laborers	3	67	20	10	—	—	N = 30
Assemblers	44	38	13	6	—	—	N = 16
Press operators	25	50	20	5	—	—	N = 20
Machinists	27	57	7	7	3	—	N = 30

SOURCE: Interviews.

[a] Laborers are classified by the firm as unskilled, while the other groups are classified as semiskilled. Skilled workers have not been included in the table.

[b] Included in the classification "other" are commerce, services, small workshops (including mechanical workshops), and self-employment.

reasons for doubting that the recruitment and promotion of un-skilled workers constituted a closed internal labor market.

In the first place, approximately 50 percent of all semiskilled workers interviewed in AF1 and AF2 had been hired as semiskilled workers because of their previous experience in the auto industry or related industries. For assemblers, the relevant experience could be found in other auto plants, and for press operators and ma-chinists nonauto firms might also provide the kind of experience regarded as adequate by management. Therefore, internal pro-motion was not the only route to semiskilled jobs. Secondly, the difference between unskilled and semiskilled workers did not ap-pear to correspond to a real difference in experience and training. Although some semiskilled jobs certainly required the acquisition of expertise (fitting windscreens, for example), many others did not. Studies of semiskilled work in the British auto industry in-dicate that the basic training for many jobs can be carried out in a matter of days or weeks (see, for example, Beynon, 1973:118, for assembly workers and Turner et al., 1967:89, for workers in the machine shops). In many cases the jobs are so simple that even allowing for the time needed to become habituated to the task, the period of on-the-job training would not be more than a few months. Thirdly, unskilled workers in both plants often com-plained that they were performing identical or similar work to semiskilled colleagues, but receiving a lower rate of pay. The performance of identical tasks by workers of different grades was observed on a number of occasions in both plants.

Once workers reached semiskilled jobs, their chances for pro-motion were very limited. As in the case of skilled workers, only a few jobs as foremen or charge-hands were open to them, plus a small number of skilled production-line occupations. Therefore, it can be seen that for unskilled and semiskilled workers, job lines were short and entry ports relatively open. These appear to be the characteristics of a secondary labor market, and some writers have tried to distinguish between a primary market in modern industry for skilled workers and a secondary market for unskilled. Souza, for example, concludes that there are primary labor markets for skilled workers in the large, modern firm, but that these firms "participated on a large-scale in what was previously called the 'secondary labour market' in respect of some specific jobs, taking advantage of the existence of a plentiful supply of cheap, unskilled labour and notably diversifying their wage structure. This implied, of course, operating with high indexes of staff turnover in those specific jobs for which they contracted unskilled labour at very low wages" (1978:216). However, on the basis of the information presented above, it can be argued that this conceptualization does not fit at all. On the one hand, skilled workers did not participate in internal labor markets at all. They were recruited in a well-formed external labor market, and wage rates were established by intense interfirm competition resulting from an overall shortage of such workers. On the other hand, Souza's characterization of the situation of unskilled workers is completely inadequate because it can explain the existence of high wages in the auto industry (and other modern sectors) only if the workers in the secondary labor market are a minority of the total work force—as Souza himself implies in the course of his argument (1978:216). But it has been shown that the unskilled and semiskilled workers formed the *majority* of workers in the motor industry, and their wages were not low, as can be seen in table 3-2. In this table, the median wages for different skill groupings in AF2 are presented. The table shows that the workers in the middle of the spread of wages paid to unskilled workers earned two-and-one-half times the minimum wage, while the median wage for semiskilled workers was almost four times the minimum wage. These wages are well below those registered for the skilled and management groups, but they in no way correspond to the "very low wages" that Souza believes are paid to workers not protected by a primary labor market.

The full extent of the relatively high wages paid to unskilled and semiskilled auto workers can be seen through a comparison of wage rates in AF1 and those in a textile firm in the same area of Greater São Paulo.[10] In July 1980 a laborer in AF1 could earn

---

[10] It would be preferable to have more than one case for the comparison, but wage data by occupation which can be controlled for time, the dates of wage increases, and geographical area are hard to find. However, more general com-

Wages and Working Conditions

TABLE 3-2
Distribution of median wage-rates of employees by skill: AF2, 1975

Skill category[a]	Percentage of total labor force	Cumulative percentage	Median wage-rate of category[b] (Cr$ per month)	Median wage-rate in multiples of the minimum wage
Unskilled	20	20	1,037	2.5
Semiskilled	46	66	1,620	3.9
Skilled	24	90	2,459	5.9
Staff[c]	10	100	5,645	13.6
ALL EMPLOYEES			1,727	4.2

SOURCES: Skill distribution: management figures for January 1975. Wage distribution: Trade Union Contribution returns.

[a] The classification by skill is that of the company.

[b] The median wage-rate for the category is the wage earned by the worker midway up the wage distribution. For example, it is the wage earned by the semiskilled worker who earns a higher wage than half of the semiskilled workers, but a lower wage than the other half. The table has been compiled on the assumption that unskilled workers receive the lowest wages, the semiskilled the next lowest, etc. Given the company's skill classification this is reasonable for manual workers. However, some white-collar and management workers may earn less than some skilled workers. Were this to be the case the table would underestimate the median wage-rate of skilled workers and overestimate that of the staff.

[c] This category includes all white-collar workers and management at the plant. However, the plant did not contain the company's central offices.

between Cr$38 and Cr$53 per hour, and a semiskilled assembler could earn between Cr$55 and Cr$76 according to length of employment (these variations are explained in the following paragraph). In the textile plant there was a single rate for each job: laborer Cr$31 per hour, machine operator Cr$34. The differences between the two plants do not indicate the existence of a competitive interindustrial secondary labor market for unskilled workers in the area. For workers with skills, however, wages are more in alignment. In AF1 a die mounter or fitter could earn from Cr$75 to Cr$111, while in the textile plant there were three grades of machine fitters earning Cr$89, Cr$99, and Cr$106 per hour respectively. For skilled workers, then, wage rates in the two

parisons were made at the end of chapter two. I am grateful to Sra. Helena Hirata of the C.N.R.S. in Paris for providing the wage data for the textile firm. At the time of the survey US$1 = Cr$52.2.

firms appear to be roughly in line, but for unskilled and semiskilled workers there is a big difference. A theory of internal labor markets cannot explain this difference, because the relatively highly paid unskilled and semiskilled workers in the auto industry were readily recruited and easily trained.

The situation of auto workers is rendered even more puzzling by the fact that in the auto industry there were very complicated wage structures, in spite of the use of external labor markets. In AF1 and AF2 the wage structure for hourly paid workers consisted of fourteen grades, with six steps in each grade. This kind of system is common in the auto industry. In AF3, AF4, and AF5, the number of grades varied from fourteen to sixteen and the number of steps from four to six. The differences in wage rates for the different grades are presented in table 3-3, and once the reader unfamiliar with wage differentials in Brazil has caught his or her breath after seeing a top toolmaker earning over five times the starting rate for a sweeper and four times that for the basic unskilled production worker, the point to be noted is that even within the same job category the wage differentials are far from insignificant. For grades one, two, and three, the minimum period between promotions from one step to another was three months. For the other grades, the first step is the approval period of three months, and after that promotions to steps three and four come after minimum periods of six months and to steps five and six after a minimum of twelve months. While there might be some conceivable justification for an experienced top-rate toolmaker earning 40 percent more than a toolmaker who has just finished his period of approval, it is rather more difficult to explain by means of an internal-labor-market theory why an assembler with three years' experience should earn 45 percent more than a newly hired assembler, or 70 percent more than an assembly-line laborer with one year's experience.

A theory of primary and secondary labor markets cannot explain why it is that in the auto industry wages for unskilled and semi-skilled workers who required limited training were well above those paid in industry as a whole; nor can it explain why there was a complicated and differentiated wages structure when training times were short and acquisition of on-the-job expertise was

Wages and Working Conditions

TABLE 3-3

Hourly wage-rates for selected job categories: AF1, November 1974[a]

(step 1 for laborer = 100)

Grade	Skill level	Job categories included in grade[b]	Step 1	2	4	6
1	Non	Sweeper	82	88	101	116
3	Non	Laborer	100[c]	107	122	140
6	Semi	Internal driver Machine operator[d]	130	141	164	190
7	Semi	Assembler Press operator	143	154	180	209
8	Semi	Machinist[d] Trimmer	158	170	198	230
9	Skilled	Plumber Metal finisher Production painter	171	185	219	257
10	Skilled	Shaper operator Maintenance electrician	188	204	240	283
12	Highly skilled	Grinder Turner	228	247	291	343
14	Highly skilled	Toolmaker Tool & die inspector	271	296	353	421

SOURCE: Company records.

[a] The wage structure in AF2 was more or less identical.

[b] This list of job categories is merely a selection. In total there were more than eighty hourly-paid occupations in the plant.

[c] In June 1979, the hourly wage-rate for a step 1 laborer was US$0.77.

[d] The machinists interviewed in AF2 were those on grade 8.

relatively unimportant. Finally, if it is remembered that the auto industry had a largely justified reputation for high rates of turnover and job insecurity, the picture becomes even more difficult for dual-labor-market theory to explain or comprehend. Why would an employer have paid wages well above the industrial average to unskilled and semiskilled workers who required relatively little training and then have dismissed large numbers of them at regular intervals?[11] To answer this question it is necessary to examine in

[11] This allegation will be substantiated in the next section.

71

more detail wages and working conditions in the auto industry and then provide a different theory of wage levels and employment practices as an explanation. Without a different theory it will be impossible either to understand the situation of workers in the auto industry or to explain their recent militancy.

Wages and Working Conditions

To resolve the problems surrounding the employment practices of firms in the auto industry requires a detailed knowledge of wages and working conditions. Such knowledge is also essential for an understanding of capital-labor relations, workers' militancy, and the development of the Metalworkers Union of São Bernardo. This section is, therefore, the basis for the discussion in the following two chapters. It contains an analysis of wages, nonmonetary benefits, intensity of work, health and safety, labor turnover, and discipline.

WAGES

Theories of dual labor markets stress the fact that modern-sector workers earn higher-than-average wages, and it is often assumed that this also implies protection from the adversities that affect other workers. In contrast, the findings of the previous section would suggest three hypotheses about wage movements. Firstly, given that there is a very different market for skilled workers compared with unskilled and semiskilled workers, their wages might move in different directions. Secondly, the wages of both groups might well follow general wage movements, since skilled workers are recruited from an external labor market and the non-skilled groups can be recruited from a large pool of workers. Thirdly, there seems to be no reason to expect either group to be free of the problems that beset workers in general. As yet, no reason for auto workers to be treated differently from other workers has been found. The only fact established about wages so far is that they are higher in the auto industry than in most other sectors.

The construction of a reliable wage series for workers in the auto industry is complicated by the absence of industry-specific data and the high and fluctuating rate of inflation in Brazil. However, in table 3-4 wage series for the periods 1966-1974 and 1972-1977 have been matched together and then compared with wage settlements and inflation in the same overall period. This table should be considered as no more than a guide to general trends. In the period as a whole, average real wages in the industry rose by 22.3 percent of the 1966 figure, and there were rises in both the pre-1972 and post-1972 periods. Taken in isolation these figures would appear to show that auto workers were not affected by the wage squeeze after 1964 and that they did constitute a privileged group. But the picture is more complicated than this. Firstly, the available figures do not include the period immediately after the coup, when wages were greatly contained. In a sample of five large firms in São Paulo city—two auto assembly and three auto component firms—the median wage fell by 8.9 percent between 1961 and 1966 (see table 2-4). Secondly, to the extent that the average figure includes skilled workers and white-collar workers, the effect of the wage policy on the mass of manual workers in the auto industry will be masked. (This subsuming of different trends under an average figure is indicated by the work of Bacha cited in the previous chapter, but its exact effect cannot be gauged from the available data.) Thirdly, it is clearly the case that the evolution of real wages in the auto industry followed the level of wage settlements in relation to inflation. As table 3-4 shows, with only one exception (1967-1968), real wages rose when wage settlements were greater than the rate of inflation and fell when they were less. The fit is exact in the crucial period between 1969 and 1975, when real wages fluctuated considerably, rising sharply from 1969 to 1972 and then falling equally abruptly from 1972 to 1974. It was not until 1977 that the 1972-1974 fall was recouped. The period 1972-1974 deserves further investigation because it sheds considerable light on the factors determining wage movements, and it was also an important episode for the workers and unions in the motor industry.

Between 1972 and the end of 1974, the government tried to contain inflation by manipulating the official inflation index. In

Wages and Working Conditions

TABLE 3-4

Evolution of real wages of workers in the auto industry: 1966 to 1977

Year	Average annual real wage for direct production workers[a]	Real value of average hour worked[b]	Percentage by which wage increases in São Bernardo exceed or fall below the rate of inflation[c]
1966	85.6	—	—
1967	84.8	—	−8.6
1968	86.9	—	−1.3
1969	88.3	—	+1.1
1970	95.8	—	+8.9
1971	90.7	—	−4.5
1972	100	100	+6.5
1973	96.7	94.8	−8.7
1974	85.9	87.1	−14.9
1975	—	96.6	+17.0
1976	—	96.7	+3.0
1977	—	104.7	+10.5

SOURCES: See notes.

[a] This series is taken from Oliveira and Travolo, 1979:81. The definition of direct labor appears to include direct production workers, maintenance workers, and technical and administrative workers.

[b] This series is taken from *Notícias da ANFAVEA*, special issue for the Eleventh Motor Show in 1978. The accompanying text refers to "the average wage of the workers in the motor industry." The nominal hourly wage for 1972, when multiplied by 240 hours per month (rest days are paid in Brazilian industry) and twelve months per year gives a yearly figure 11 percent higher than that given by Oliveira and Travolo for the same year. The nominal wages in this series have been deflated by the Oliveira and Travolo index for 1972–1974 and by the DIEESE cost-of-living index for the lower-income strata for the period 1974–1977. Oliveira and Travolo also use a DIEESE cost-of-living index, but they do not specify which one.

[c] This column compares the level of wage settlements for the Metalworkers of São Bernardo—awarded in April of each year—with annual cost-of-living increases as measured in the rest of the table. São Bernardo has been taken as representing the Brazilian auto industry in general because of the concentration of auto production in the area.

1973, the rate of inflation was declared to be 14 percent, but three years later the government was forced to admit that it had been 26.5 percent. This falsification of the inflation index meant that wage rises were kept artificially low and real wages reduced. The impact of this can be seen in table 3-5, which compares the levels of wage settlements, inflation, and wage increases for the auto industry in São Paulo and São Bernardo. It shows that the wage settlements in the two years lagged behind the rate of inflation, and that a correct application of the wages policy, including an allowance for productivity growth, would have produced a much higher settlement. However, the impact on wages was not uniform. Skilled workers in AF1 and AF2, who were in short supply at the time, managed to obtain wage increases above the official settlement figure, while the assemblers and press operators in the two plants saw their wages tied to it. In AF2 though, even the toolmakers failed to increase their wages in line with the rate of inflation in the period.

These findings illustrate that workers in the motor industry were

TABLE 3-5
Wage settlements and wage changes: AF1 and AF2, 1973 to 1975
(percentages)

	AF1	AF
Wage increases awarded in 1973 and 1974 (cumulative)[a]	57	39
Wage increases claimed by DIEESE to be in accordance with wages policy[b]	97	86
Increase in average hourly wage-rate for assemblers (AF1) and press operators (AF2)[c]	58	42
Increase in average hourly wage-rate for toolmakers in AF1 and AF2[c]	78	57

SOURCES: Actual and claimed wage increases: *Movimento*, 24/10/1977. Hourly wage-rates: company records.

[a] The differences between AF1 and AF2 arise from the fact that they are in different unions, which negotiate at different times of year. Inflation, December 1972 to December 1974, was 66 percent (DIEESE, 1975:74).

[b] The DIEESE calculations are greater than the actual wage increases awarded because of the higher rate of past inflation, higher estimated future inflation, and higher productivity allowance used in the application of the wages-policy formula.

[c] These figures are based on actual wage-rates in January–February 1975 and estimated rates for January–February 1973 based on actual rates for July 1973. Allowances have been made for distortions arising from wage rises in anticipation of annual settlements.

not insulated from the varying fortunes of the working class after the military coup, and given the sharp fall in real wages between 1973 and 1975 it is not surprising that workers in AF1 and AF2 were not satisfied with their wages when asked to evaluate them early in 1975. With the exception of the assemblers in AF1, in all the groups of workers interviewed the number of workers assessing wages as "bad" outnumbered those saying "good." Table 3-6 shows that in AF2, in particular, where the effect of the wages policy had been more severe (table 3-5), the majority of workers thought their wages were bad. Undoubtedly, the cost of living was an important factor in these assessments: in the two factories together only one worker said that wages were rising faster than the cost of living, while 173 said the opposite. However, these responses also reflect other aspects of the wage situation, which need discussion.

When the auto industry was first implanted in Brazil, wage levels were significantly higher than in other industries for both skilled and unskilled workers, and this created the strong and lasting expectation that auto industry wages would be much higher

TABLE 3-6
"What do you think of your wages?": AF1 and AF2

Group	Response (%)			
	Good	O.K.	Bad	
AF1				
Laborers	19	38	44	N = 16
Assemblers	25	54	21	N = 24
Toolroom workers	8	55	37	N = 40
AF2				
Laborers[a]	10	40	50	N = 30
Assemblers	13	25	62	N = 16
Press operators	15	35	50	N = 20
Machinists	10	43	47	N = 30
Toolmakers	10	35	55	N = 20

SOURCE: Interviews.

[a] Two groups of laborers were interviewed in AF2—fifteen from the assembly area and fifteen from the machine shops. The responses of these two groups will only be disaggregated when significant differences emerge.

than others. In the period of the economic miracle this expectation was reinforced by the rapid expansion of the industry and its key position in the Brazilian economy. But changing circumstances prevented wage levels from fulfilling these expectations. In the first place, during the period of the "miracle," 1968-1974, real wages declined slightly, while the number of vehicles produced per employee rose by 71 percent (Oliveira and Travolo, 1979:79). It is not surprising, therefore, that 82 percent of the workers interviewed in AF2 at the beginning of 1975 felt that their firm could afford to pay higher wages because of rising output, productivity, and profitability.[12] Secondly, there was a clear narrowing of wage differentials between the auto industry and other sectors of the metal-mechanical industries in the seventies. Given its relatively high rates of pay for unskilled and semiskilled workers, the auto industry was not affected by the shortage of unskilled labor experienced in Greater São Paulo in 1973 and 1974. While many small and medium-sized firms had to increase wages to attract workers, the auto industry had no problems. This meant that wage differentials narrowed. In fact, they continued to narrow throughout the period for which comparative figures are available, 1972-1978.[13] In all the other metalworking sectors, the median and average wage rose faster than in the auto industry. This produced a feeling among auto workers that things were not as good as they had been before. As a laborer in AF1 put it: "They used to pay a lot more. In 1958 when my father worked here, they paid more than anyone else in Brazil."

The decline in interindustry differentials was particularly marked for skilled workers because of intense competition for skilled labor. In the sixties and seventies an overall shortage of skilled workers forced firms outside of the auto industry to increase their wages. The auto employers found that if they raised their own wages, this would merely provoke further increases in the other sectors. Therefore, they remained content to pay rates that were at the top end of the market, but not well above other firms; in

[12] The question of productivity will be raised again later in this section.
[13] The data is for São Bernardo and comes from the *Gúia de Contribuição Sindical*.

1973 and 1974, in particular, acute shortages of skilled labor forced wage rates up very quickly in small firms, while in AF2 the increase did not even match the rate of inflation (see table 3-5). This produced the kind of attitude expressed by a toolmaker in AF2: "The auto industry used to be better. It isn't the paradise that it used to be. It's come down a lot, and the others have come up, too. The small firms are reaching the level of the large."

This opinion was reflected in the evaluation of relative wage-rates made by skilled workers in AF2. In 1963 Rodrigues asked skilled workers to compare their wage rates with those paid by other firms, and the question was repeated in 1975. The comparison of responses in table 3-7 shows that whereas in 1963 twenty-three out of twenty-four skilled workers thought that the firm paid better-than-average wages, by 1975 only 10 percent held this opinion, while 25 percent actually thought that the firm was paying below-average wages. Workers in AF1 held the same opinions. Clearly, wages in both plants could not be said to have "amply fulfilled the expectation that accompanied the search for

TABLE 3-7
"How does . . . (AF1 or AF2) pay in relation to other firms in São Paulo?"
Comparison of results with earlier study[a]

	Response (%)			
Group	Better	Equal	Worse	
Rodrigues: Toolmakers[b]	96	4	0	N = 24
AF1: Toolroom workers	12	77	10	N = 40
AF2: Toolmakers	10	65	25	N = 20

SOURCE: Interviews and Rodrigues, 1970:46.

[a] The workers in AF2 were also asked how they rated their firm in comparison with other auto firms. Although they rated AF2 less favorably in relation to other firms than had the toolmakers interviewed by Rodrigues in the same plant some twelve years earlier, the difference was not great. This implies, therefore, that the decline in favorable responses registered in the table indicates a general downward shift in auto industry toolroom wages, relative to other industries. The evidence presented in the text suggests that toolroom workers' perceptions on this point were, in fact, correct.

[b] Rodrigues refers to his sample of skilled workers as "toolmakers." However, he describes one of them as a "final production inspector" (1970:36), and so the exact composition of the sample he took is uncertain.

a job'' (Rodrigues, 1970:45) by 1975, even if they had done so in 1963.

The general discontent with wage levels found in both plants, and in particular in AF2, was compounded by the effects of the complicated wage structure described in the previous section. While periodic incremental rises could no doubt take the edge off the effects of rising prices, the system created problems as well. The less experienced workers felt that they were being paid too little for the work they did, while the workers who had reached the top of the scale were frustrated because they were no longer cligible for further rises. A machinist in AF2 summed up the problem:

Q. Do you think that in general the firm pays its workers the wages they deserve?

A. In general, no. The laborers have to wait a long time to become machinists. And I have been on the top grade for two years now. This causes disagreements with the firm. There are a lot of people who are annoyed about it. They complain to the foreman, but he is not the one who gives the rises.

Workers felt the injustice of being paid different rates for similar work, and, at the same time, they expected the rises to come in the minimum time allowed and resented delays. Although the combination of demands for more steps and more rapid promotions can be seen as just another expression of a feeling that wages should be higher, the system as it operated in the major auto firms created its own specific discontents, as this account of it by a union director from AF5 illustrates:

They promise, for example, after a person enters the firm, they say ''after three months you'll get so many percent rise, after six you'll get so much, after one year you'll get a rise every year, and things will even out.'' But what they say will happen in three months takes six, and what happens in six takes a year. . . . So when we go and discuss the problem, they claim that this worker isn't as good as the other, and we say, ''Why not? Isn't he doing the same work as the other one?'' This creates a lot of trouble in the firm. There's a lot of conflict with the foreman because of this. Why should the other bloke, my partner, who's doing exactly the same work, get more money than me? Why? If there's a production line, then the work to be done is fixed. This, this, and this. If everyone does their job, the car is built. So, each one is doing his job. So why is this one not worth anything? But they won't see this at all.[14]

The analysis of wage movements in the period after the coup shows that, overall, real wages did not decline, but this did diffuse discontent over wages. Workers in the auto industry were not insulated from the vicissitudes of the general market for labor, and there were strong, but unfulfilled, expectations that wages should have been higher. Workers in the auto industry thought that they needed higher wages, deserved higher wages, and could be paid higher wages by the firm. Although the interviews with workers were carried out during the lowest point of wage trends in the period from 1966 to 1977, it should not be assumed that the recuperation of wage levels after 1974 was sufficient to diffuse the discontent registered at the time of the survey. Resentment about the narrowing of differentials, the failure to reward increases in productivity, and the alleged injustices of the wages structure would not necessarily be resolved by three years of rising real wages. In addition, the manipulation of the inflation index was never formally compensated, leaving a sense of injustice among the workers. They felt that they would continue to face the risk of falling wages as long as the government's wages policy remained in force. It will be shown in chapter five that these problems were important ingredients in the growing militancy of auto workers in the latter part of the seventies.

NONMONETARY BENEFITS

When the multinational firms set up plants in the fifties and sixties they established new patterns of providing nonmonetary benefits to workers. As well as setting up sports and social clubs and promoting a company spirit, the big firms established private

---

[14] This quotation is from an interview made by Werner Würtele. I am grateful to him for making this and other interviews available to researchers.

medical-insurance schemes, canteens, and transport to and from the plants.[15] It is sometimes asserted that these benefits are an important part of the workers' earnings. However, in the seventies these benefits in no way offset the workers' discontent over wages. On the one hand, many other firms had followed the example of the multinationals, and the services had become commonplace. Even in a small components-firm employing only 200 workers, a canteen and medical scheme were found. On the other hand, there were continual conflicts about the prices and quality of the services being provided. In AF2, in particular, a policy of making workers "appreciate the services being offered" by paying something toward them had created resentment among workers and controversy among management about how the situation should have been handled. At the time of the survey, a rumor went round the plant to the effect that the company was about to increase the cost of transport, and this caused considerable consternation. Because most rises in the prices of services came at the same time as wage rises, workers were often left with a feeling of being given money with one hand and seeing it taken away again with the other. Although management figures showed that the company paid for 75 percent of the cost of the company buses, many workers were convinced that *they* paid for most of it. In its negotiating platform for 1977 the Metalworkers of São Bernardo included a demand that all services have their prices fixed for the lifetime of the contract. In terms of quality, too, the services were subject to criticism. The food in the canteen in AF2 probably attracted more criticism than any other aspect of work in the whole plant, and the private medical schemes were also criticized for being too expensive, too inaccessible, and too much under the company's control. While the medical scheme was no doubt better than the State scheme, just as the company buses were a great

---

[15] These benefits can be considered as both attempts to create good will and an exercise in enlightened self-interest. The provision of a good square meal, transport, and medical services can be seen as aids to productivity if workers are undernourished, living distant from the factories, and without access to adequate medical care.

improvement on public transport, they were neither sufficient to offset discontent over other issues nor free from criticism.[16]

INTENSITY OF WORK

Unskilled and semiskilled workers in AF1 and AF2 earned three or four times the minimum wage, but they worked hard for this, particularly on the assembly lines, as the following two comments indicate:

> The wages are good. In other firms I've earned less, but you work harder here. (Laborer, AF1)

> The worker in a large firm works more. I've already worked in small firms. The first time I went to work in . . . (AF6) I was taken aback. I'm now doing the work of two men and production has only gone down a little bit. The usual thing is for the output to go up and the number of workers to remain the same. They use time and motion to force the pace. At the moment it's getting worse. Very often you can't even go to the toilet. . . . It's got worse. For example, there are people who have to work while they have their coffee. (Assembler, AF2)[17]

According to the figures supplied by Oliveira and Travolo, output per worker in the auto industry doubled between 1966 and 1974 (1979:79), and although increases tended to level off after 1974 because of the greater sales difficulties facing auto producers, the industry exerted continual pressure on workers to improve performance. Clearly, the number of vehicles produced per worker must have been decisively influenced by changes in the mix of models, improved machinery and working methods, and changes

[16] Good services can give a firm a reputation as a "good employer," but this is not enough to stop strikes, as Indústrias Villares found in 1973. As a union official pointed out at the time, the food in the firm was good, but workers' families could not eat in the canteen (*Visão* 14/1/1974).

[17] The selection of quotes from interviews is, of necessity, arbitrary. By no means all workers were as emphatic as this one, but it is reasonable to surmise that workers would have had inhibitions about making criticisms when being interviewed inside the factory. Wherever possible, claims in interviews will be corroborated. In the case of this statement, it is interesting to note that the problem of having no time to go to the toilet was mentioned by a worker in the same firm when interviewed by a newspaper one year previously.

in the ratio of direct to indirect production workers, but when output is rising rapidly managements need great efforts from their workers to maintain production in the face of the inevitable chaos resulting from a growth rate of 20 percent per year. On the other hand, when output falls there are pressures to cut costs. At the time of the interviews in AF1, there had been a cutback in production, coupled with a drive to increase profits, and this had resulted in a lot of pressure to increase the output per worker without changes being made in productive techniques, as the following description from a foreman on the assembly line showed:

> They [the workers] are working more now. One doing the job of another. I had to let another two go yesterday [dismiss them], but the work's the same. It's the management that gives the orders. Economies, there's no sense in it. Before we had timings, but not any more. Before, if they reduced the work force, we had more machines, but not any more. Nothing is altered and the timings go on falling. . . . Each manager wants to cut down even more. Work study lowered the timings and the management did the same. [To prove his point the supervisor goes to his desk and gets out two sheets of paper. He explains the figures to me. On one sheet are the times allowed for the complete set of operations for a particular type of vehicle on one section of the line, as prepared by work study and operative for the current month and four months ahead. On the other sheet are the times allocated by the management in the body and assembly plant for the same operations.] Look, here's the time from work study and there's the time from management: the management want . . . [5 percent less time on the assembly of one model and 4 percent on another]. *And* they want us to work at 102 percent efficiency.

The company had abandoned the timing of tasks and had, instead, provided its foremen with a single allowance of labor to be allocated among the different sections of the line. So, for example, if a particular model took four man-hours to produce, and one shift produced 140 units, then the number of men employed on a shift would be 560 divided by the number of hours in the shift. If the timing was reduced by a quarter-hour, then the number of men would be reduced by 6¼ percent, and it was up to the foreman to reorganize his workers' tasks to cope with the change.

Much the same situation was described by one of the production managers in AF2:

> Before we had timing. That was fair. But not any more. The times are arbitrary and lower than before. If there are ten people doing a job, they are already thinking that it's too many and that they ought to take two off. Sometimes it just won't do. Everyone leaves here nervous.

The problem seemed to affect the assembly line more than other sections of the plants. Workers were asked if they had experienced an increase in workloads since entering the plant, and while virtually no toolroom workers reported increases, elsewhere the proportion of workers reporting increases were as follows: machine-shop laborers 20 percent, machinists 27 percent (almost all of them in just one of the three machine-shop sections), press operators 37 percent, assembly-line laborers 40 percent, and assemblers 50 percent.

A further aspect of increasing the intensity of work is the expansion of overtime. Most workers in the motor industry work a five-day, forty-eight hour week, but in the miracle period a basic fifty-six-hour week was common. New workers in AF2 were expected to sign forms agreeing to work overtime when the company required it, and a refusal to perform overtime could lead to dismissal. In Brazil many leading firms have been accused of forcing their workers to work excessive hours, and workers are often willing to do it in order to supplement their wages. Although few, if any, workers in the auto assembly industry could work for the 100 hours overtime in one month (in addition to a regular forty-eight-hour week) that an examination of pay slips in a small components-firm revealed, workers in key production areas in AF2 were required to work regularly on Saturdays and Sundays.

HEALTH AND SAFETY

In chapter one, reference was made to assertions about the improvement of working conditions in Brazilian factories and the

84

decreasing importance of strikes over such matters. However, companies that try to increase the intensity of work and control their wage expenditure are unlikely to provide a fully safe and healthy working environment. Although modern factories may be cleaner and brighter than older plants and may also have proper medical services (at least during the daytime), health and safety problems are by no means eliminated. In AF1, AF2, and AF4 (the latter visited in 1979) the problems typical of large plants were immediately visible. Floors were wet and slippery, aisles were badly marked, working spaces often very crowded, and in some areas (such as body-in-white and the press shops) the noise levels were very high. These problems, along with the noxious fumes in the paint and lead booths and heat-treatment areas, were the obvious signs of less-than-perfect conditions. The need to shout to make oneself heard above the noise in the body-in-white when talking to metal finishers, and the occasional sight of workers in the paint booths not using safety equipment, were obvious enough even to the untrained eye. Although there are few serious injuries in the motor industry,[18] workers suffer from minor injuries, the general fatigue that accompanies intense work over a long period, and the more insidious effects of unhealthy working environments. Two reports made by managements in the auto industry on health and safety problems provide information on the effects of the employers' drive to increase production and cut costs.

The first report was by management in AF1 and concerned safety problems in the plant's forklift truck department. It revealed that the pressure to increase production in the miracle period had led to unsafe working conditions because output had far exceeded the plant's designed capacity. The forklifts had little room in which to move, and their paths were often impeded by component bins and machines that intruded into the aisles. At the same time, the pressure for increased productivity and the lack of adequate resources for handling materials meant that the whole department

---

[18] Fatal accidents are rare in the motor industry, although there was one in AF1 while I was there. Similarly, amputations occur only rarely.

was unsafely run. Workers overloaded the forklifts—bypassing the warning devices—and drove them at unsafe speeds in their attempts to meet output targets. Crashes and overturnings were not infrequent. At the same time, the lack of proper maintenance facilities for the fleet meant that the trucks were often operated with defective brakes, lights, and safety mechanisms. The report concluded that these problems were the result of a systematic, management-inspired pattern of operation that was solely designed to keep up production without due regard for safety.[19]

The second report was produced by a highly qualified health team working in AF3 in 1979. The result of some of the team's work is summarized by Capistrano (1980:5), who states that in various parts of the plant,

> concentrations of noxious chemical agents (toluene, phenol, acetic acid, dichloromethane, trichloroethane, metallic welding fumes, chrome vapor, fiberglass, polyester resin, among others) went well beyond the tolerances allowed for an eight-hour shift, reaching between twice and five times the limits. In seven sections studied in October 1979, the noise levels recorded varied from a minimum of 105 decibels to a maximum of 118 decibels, while the legal limit in Brazil is 85 decibels. It is not surprising that the number of workers in . . . (AF3) with serious hearing losses is calculated to be. . . .[20] None of these issues, however, concern the workers as much as the length of the working day—this always being at least ten hours—and the speed of work, both in the production of parts and on the assembly line. Physical fatigue is the number one complaint of the workers interviewed by us. The Brazilian management of . . . (AF3) is fully aware of these situations and has alternatives for each of them, classified in order of priority, to be implemented to the extent that union pressure increases.

Even in the motor plants of Europe and the U.S.A., where unions are stronger and safety consciousness is greater among the work

---

[19] This report, prepared by junior management, was welcomed by senior personnel, but it is not known whether or not it led to changes.

[20] The figure was 25 percent of the hourly-paid employees in the plant.

force, health and safety conditions are not ideal. In Brazil, where the unions are immeasurably weaker in the plants and the officially created health and safety supervisors—the Internal Accident Prevention committees and the officials of the Ministry of Labor—are largely ineffective, the situation is much worse. Even when the effects of health and safety problems do not register in the accident statistics (Brazil has one of the highest rates in the world), they affect workers in the form of premature aging and long-term illnesses. Managements are aware of many of the problems, but when the incalculable benefits of better working conditions are measured against the direct expenditures and loss of efficiency that result from better protection, the latter appear to have greater weight.[21]

LABOR TURNOVER

The policies adopted by the auto companies in the area of labor turnover were controversial throughout the seventies. The unions alleged that workers were systematically hired and fired as a means of keeping down wages. The firms denied it. The overall figures for entries and exits in the auto industry show quite high rates of turnover, as can be seen in table 3-8. For the six firms in Greater São Paulo, the annual rate of exits varies from 13.4 percent to 31.9 percent of the total labor force, and the cumulative totals for 1977-1978 vary from 33.3 percent to 54.2 percent. On their own, these figures merely indicate that labor in the auto industry is not particularly stable. What matters is to go beyond these overall figures and find out more about labor turnover and stability. Having established that significant numbers of workers enter and leave the major firms each year, it is necessary to find out if they leave of their own accord or are dismissed, whether or not only certain sections of the labor force leave each year, if only newer workers are dismissed, etc. In relation to theories of stabilization of skilled workers, the assessment of union-organizing potential,

---

[21] Certain health problems, such as those resulting from stress (whose long-term effects are only now being fully understood) would seem to be endemic in an industry with the pressure for greater productivity described in the previous subsection.

TABLE 3-8

Entries and exits of auto workers by firm: Brazil, 1977 and 1978

Firm[a]	Employment December 1976	1977 (% of total employment)			Employment December 1977	1978 (% of total employment)		
		Entries	Exits	Balance		Entries	Exits	Balance
Chrysler	3,777	21.6	25.9	-4.3	3,616	23.0	28.3	-5.3
Ford	21,808	17.7	26.8	-9.1	19,816	20.5	16.4	+4.1
General Motors[b]	17,129	11.0	25.6	-14.7	16,307	26.2	15.0	+11.3
Mercedes Benz	16,460	38.8	31.9	+7.0	17,606	18.0	13.4	+4.6
Saab-Scania	2,822	26.8	16.8	+10.0	3,104	8.0	19.1	-11.1
Volkswagen	39,057	13.6	16.9	-3.3	37,768	24.6	16.4	+8.1

SOURCE: ANFAVEA.

[a] Fiat has not been included because it was still in the start-up phase in 1977–1978. Figures for the FNM were not available. These figures are for *firms*. In comparison with the *plant* figures in table 3-9, only Saab Scania has its entire work force in São Bernardo do Campo.

[b] The figures for General Motors, as supplied by ANFAVEA, are not consistent. The figure for total employment in December 1976, less the balance of entries and exits in 1977, does not equal the total employment figure in December 1977.

and the imposition of discipline and control, the fact that (for example) 15 percent of the total labor force of General Motors left the firm in 1978 says very little. Who these workers were, why they left, and what they did after leaving, however, would be valuable information. Given that neither the companies nor the unions nor the State keep such detailed data on turnover, the evidence has to be constructed piecemeal.

The first thing to establish is whether workers were, in general, dismissed by their employers (with or without "due cause"—see chapter two) or left of their own accord. The latter case is referred to in company and union records as "asking to be dismissed." The second step is to find out how long workers were employed before they were dismissed. Some information on these points is shown in table 3-9, which gives figures from the various auto plants in São Bernardo for the numbers of workers leaving employment in the year 1978 and the numbers of workers registering the ending of their contract with the local Metalworkers Union in São Bernardo. Since workers with less than one year's employment did not have to register the recision of their contracts, it can be assumed that the differences between the figures in lines three and four and those in lines five and six correspond to workers who left employment after less than one year.

The comparison between lines six and four in the table, tabulated in line eight, shows that in four of the five firms listed more than half the workers leaving of their own accord did so without registering the ending of their contract. In other words, they had not worked for more than a year before leaving. In contrast, most of the workers dismissed from their jobs did register their contract being ended and so must have worked for at least a year. As can be seen in line seven, the proportion of workers dismissed who had worked for more than one year varies from 44.4 percent to 89.2 percent, and the average for all five firms is 78 percent.[22]

[22] These calculations are complicated by two factors. Firstly, it is not possible to be certain that all workers registered their recision of contracts with the union. Workers could register at the local Labor Office, even though the union had agreed with the employers that it should register all recisions. Therefore, the table may underestimate the proportion of workers who were employed for more than one

1

2

3

1 and 2. By day and by night the center of São Paulo is crowded with automobiles and buses. For many people, road transport is the only mode available. There is only one fully functioning subway line, and the suburban rail links are limited and extremely overcrowded.

3. The government has invested a lot of money in prestigious road projects such as the rebuilt Avenida Paulista, seen here in the late afternoon. The implementation of bus lanes, restricted left turns, and phased traffic lights has not stopped heavy congestion in the rush hour.

4

4. The nine lanes of the Via Anchieta—viewed here in São Bernardo—link São Paulo to the sea. Alongside it lie the auto plants belonging to Chrysler, Ford, Mercedes, Scania, and Volkswagen.

5. An auto transporter carries the three main Volkswagen models available in 1979. The front automobile on the top deck is the classic "beetle," now exported from Brazil to markets in Asia, Africa, and Latin America. Behind it is the Passat model, and at the back is a hatchback model derived from the "beetle" by Volkswagen engineers in Brazil. The Rabbit model has since been brought into production in Brazil.

6. Ford and General Motors sited their first plants by the railway running from São Paulo to Santos. Here a trainload of Chevrolet Opalas heads into São Paulo.

5

6

GENERAL MOTORS DO BRASIL S. A.
VAGAS MENSALISTAS

GENERAL MOTORS DO BRASIL S. A.
VAGAS HORISTAS

7

7. At the General Motors plant in São Caetano a notice board advertises vacancies for six manual jobs. All of them are for skilled workers.

8 and 9. Some parts of auto production are dirty, strenuous, and unhealthy. In the first picture a worker with full protective clothing applies sealant to the underside of the body. In the second, metal finishers use grinders to smooth the body shell. In the body shop, one of the noisiest parts of the plant, conversation is almost impossible.

8

9

10

10 and 11. While auto work can be dangerous and unhealthy, large firms are generally better in their provision of
protective equipment than small firms. In photograph 10 a
worker in a small auto-components plant is wearing no overalls,
safety boots, glasses, or gloves. He is working at a foot-oper-
ated press without any guard to prevent his hand entering it. At
his side, a half oil-drum with jagged edges serves as a component bin. In photograph 11 an auto worker operates a hand-acti-
vated press and wears overalls, safety boots, and gloves. The
component bin has smooth edges. In some auto plants the
worker would have added protection from the compulsory wearing of safety glasses and a protective grill around the press.

12. The workers in this plant are producing components for
the auto industry. They work within one mile of two auto plants
employing 25,000 workers. Their wages would be between 25
and 40 percent below the average rate for a laborer in AF2.

11

12

TABLE 3-9
Exits and registered exits by plant: São Bernardo, 1978

		Chrysler	Ford	Mercedes	Scania	Volkswagen
(1)	Number of workers employed, January 1978	2,254	11,854	17,191	3,104	33,928
(2)	Total exits as a percentage of (1)[a]	22.2	14.3	12.9	18.4	16.2
(3)	Number of workers dismissed	360	1,173	1,776	511	4,070
(4)	Number of workers requesting to leave	140	518	450	59	1,422
(5)	Registered dismissals	160	1,047	1,467	445	3,046
(6)	Registered requests to leave	41	219	207	40	604
(7)	(5) as a percentage of (3)	44.4	89.2	82.6	87.1	74.8
(8)	(6) as a percentage of (4)	29.3	42.3	46.0	67.8	42.5

SOURCES: Lines (1) through (4): ANFAVEA. Lines (5) and (6): Metalworkers Union of São Bernardo do Campo.

[a] These figures do not include the small number of workers (under one percent) dying or retiring in 1978. This accounts for the differences in exits for Scania between this table and table 3-8. For the other four firms, the existence of plants outside of São Bernardo (even for Mercedes, though it is very small) makes a direct comparison of the figures impossible.

Over three quarters of all workers dismissed had been employed for more than one year. In fact, 59 percent of all workers leaving the five factories in 1978 had been dismissed after having worked for more than one year. This is a clear indication that labor turnover did not affect only the newly recruited workers. As can be seen in table 3-8, 1978 was a year of lower turnover than 1977, and it is reasonable to expect that when overall turnover declines the ratio of dismissals to workers leaving of their own accord will also decline. The year 1978 cannot be considered in any way "bad."

---

year prior to their recision of contract. Secondly, the payment of compensation for dismissal "without due cause" encourages workers to force their dismissal when they want to leave a job. Therefore, the relation between voluntary exits and dismissals is probably distorted by the figures. However, firms try to stop workers from doing this by dismissing them "with due cause," which disqualifies them from compensation.

98

The information from table 3-9 supports material from other sources indicating that a large number of workers are affected by a deliberate policy of hire-and-fire. A survey of 500 workers dismissed by Ford in 1977 showed that of the total group 250 had worked in the plant for more than four years.[23] At the same time, the survey also showed that 29 percent of the 416 workers for whom information was available (those with one year's service or more whose recisions of contract were registered with the union) were skilled workers. This is roughly in line with the proportion of skilled workers in the plant. In general, sackings provoked by fluctuations in output did affect the assembly areas more than the toolrooms and maintenance, because the number of workers needed in the former is more directly linked to sales and production. In AF1 in December 1974, for example, a sharp fall in sales led to a slump in production, resulting in a cutback of over 20 percent in assembly-area workers. The cuts fell most heavily on the unskilled production workers, cut back 42 percent in one month alone, but they also fell on semiskilled assemblers, cut by 21 percent, and the skilled production-line workers such as painters, metal finishers, and trimmers, cut by between 18 and 29 percent.

Further limited information is available from the job histories of the workers interviewed in AF1 and AF2. Of the 166 semi-skilled and skilled workers interviewed in the two plants, fifty had been employed in at least one other auto plant prior to their current employment. The average length of employment in these previous auto industry jobs was under three years, and of the thirty-three workers who had moved directly from an auto plant to their current employment twenty-one had been dismissed. The figures were roughly similar for toolroom workers and semiskilled workers, once again indicating that skilled workers were far from exempt from the rotation of labor. This information points to the generality of the rotation of labor, giving no support to theories

[23] This information is taken from a survey commissioned by the Metalworkers of São Bernardo, whose results were published in the *Tribuna Metalúrgica*, July 1977.

that see bad working conditions (including insecurity) as being confined to very limited groups of workers.

The reasons for the rates of turnover will be discussed fully in the next chapter, but it should be said now that it was greatly resented by workers, who faced the threat of a serious loss of income and possibly unemployment. The survey of Ford workers showed that most of those dismissed had failed to secure a new job that paid equal or better wages, and many of them had had either to refuse jobs or to accept lower pay. In many cases the workers had been forced to move out of the metalworking sector altogether in their search for employment.[24] At the same time, the workers felt badly treated by their employers. They reasoned that they cooperated with the auto firms, doing excessive hours of work, for example, in the periods of boom, and then found that they—or their brothers—were dismissed when there was a downturn in sales. When large numbers of workers are dismissed, there is no possible element of "justice" in the decision, because the firms are forced to dispense with workers whose records are unblemished, and this further heightens the sense of injustice and resentment. When asked about the rotation of labor, workers in AF2 were often indignant about the apparent callousness of a firm that would seem to be quite willing to expose good employees (and their families) to the hazards of unemployment. This topic probably aroused more heated feelings than any other discussed in the questionnaire.

DISCIPLINE

Given the previous description of the situation in the auto plants, it should come as no surprise that discipline, control, and fear were pervasive in both AF1 and AF2. This does not mean that there was a climate of permanent tension and anxiety. On the contrary, when asked about conditions in the plants, workers who had previously worked in AF3 and AF4, in particular, compared their current employer very favorably. The intensity of work was generally considered to be less than in AF3, and workers com-

---

[24] This finding matches that of Nun (1978) for the Argentine auto industry.

mented upon the arbitrariness of the foreman in AF4. Indeed, workers usually said that they had a good employer and that the atmosphere at work was good. Generally speaking, they had good friends and there was time to talk while doing most jobs. Certainly, there was no obvious signs of the intense control exercised by Henry Ford at the height of his reign, when even speaking to another worker was an offense (Beynon, 1973:30-31). However, this apparently easygoing atmosphere functioned within well-defined limits.

The discipline in the background was seen most clearly when workers were asked about the role of the foreman. In both factories the workers were rather complimentary about their foremen, stressing that in contrast to certain other factories (AF3 and AF4) the foremen did not stand over the workers all the time but just left them to get on with it. At the same time, foremen in AF1 and AF2 had only a limited participation in the decision to promote a worker, and this limitation was favorably compared with the system of patronage in AF4, where promotion was very much under the foreman's control.[25] However, the absence of close supervision was clearly dependent on the fulfillment of production targets. Even in the toolroom this point was made by many workers. When asked, "What's the foreman like? Does he keep a watch all the time?," all but two of the toolroom workers in AF1 answered "no," but many of them followed up this reply with comments like "if we do what we're supposed to do," or "they're pretty liberal, as long as everyone's doing their job." In the toolroom, job allocations were flexible enough for this to be a relatively unonerous imposition, but in the main production areas specific tasks determined by either the speed of the line or hourly quotas had to be performed. Even when workloads were reorganized, as described by the foremen quoted earlier, the work had to be done. A worker on the assembly line summed it up:

[25] It might be the case that some workers were more willing to make criticisms of previous employers than current ones. However, there was some basis to the distinctions made. In particular, allegations of favoritism by the foremen in AF4 were confirmed in 1979 by a senior Industrial Relations executive, who said that this had been a problem in earlier years.

> The work we have to do is too much. Each one of us on our own has a lot to do. What was being done by two or three is now being done by one or two. It's harder now, more work for us. The foremen don't force us. Here, what comes along has to be done. The work has to be done. (Assembler, AF1)

While some workers complained much less than others, the rapid reorganization of tasks on the line following cutbacks in production and personnel must have created uneven workloads. In spite of this, everyone had to carry out the allotted tasks.

The foremen had a lot of power. They could recommend that workers be sacked, for example, and there were no appeals procedures. More importantly, they were the ones who selected workers to be dismissed when cutbacks took place. The criteria they claimed to use included such factors as time keeping, absenteeism, and ability to do the work, but when big cutbacks were made, such as in AF1 in 1974, the foreman's power of decision was considerable. Workers would be anxious not to displease someone with so much power over them. Similarly, they would be reluctant to complain about their workloads or overtime if this could be taken as a sign of inability to do a proper job. When workers in AF2 were asked about what would happen to a worker who did not like doing overtime and did not do it when asked, a quarter of the assembly-line workers and approximately half of the workers in the machine shops and press shop said that such a worker would be sacked "when the next cutback comes." Between a third and a half of all the groups of workers answered that either promotion would be withheld (via the foreman's recommendation) or that "the foremen don't like it," without specification of the results. The "next cutback," the *facão* (literally "big knife"), was frequently mentioned in both plants. It was considered a real threat at the time of the interviews, and the relatively high wages paid in the auto industry made dismissal something to be feared by most workers.

In some other firms the situation was much worse, as illustrated by this description of a plant in São Bernardo:[26] "In the toolroom,

[26] The plant in question had a bad reputation for its discipline and its use of security guards.

the regime is very much hard-line at the moment. It's enough for two workers to be caught talking together for both to be warned or even suspended. . . . The foremen forgive nothing" (*Tribuna Metalúrgica*, November 1975). Similarly, it was noted in chapter two that when conflicts did occur, management was willing to use the force of the State. By means of the threat to call in the State security forces, the companies' own internal guards, and the large amount of power wielded by the supervisors, workers in these plants were kept under control, fearful of losing their jobs. Even in AF1 and AF2 fear pervaded the attitudes of many of the unskilled and semiskilled workers. The assembly-line foreman quoted above observed: "The workers don't complain because the situation outside is bad. They don't ask for their cards and they don't ask to be dismissed—they are scared of losing their jobs. But the situation [the increase in workloads on the line] is certainly too much. Welders, painters, metal finishers—if other firms are looking for workers, they leave. They can't stand the production."

This concern about employment also inhibits strike action. When some of the machinists in AF2 stopped work in 1974 (an occasion to be discussed further in the next chapter) workers in other parts of the plant did not, and some of them were asked why in the course of the interviews.[27] Their answers sum up the situation:

Some men in the press shop wanted to, but others didn't. They were scared. If everyone stopped, they wouldn't sack anybody, but they're still scared. . . . I'm not going to speak out on my own. Saying "Let's stop" gets you marked out. You don't go very far like that, you know. (Press operator, AF2)

In our section we weren't united. But, on the other hand, I think it was fear that did it. The sack. That's why I didn't stop. (Machinist, AF2)

While some workers would certainly not approve of strike actions, others were inhibited by the fear of dismissal. This fear was exacerbated by both the general insecurity of employment and the

---

[27] This question was rather delicate in the circumstances and for this reason it was only asked of workers who appeared confident and cooperative.

lack of a union organization in the plant, which made collective action difficult. The skilled workers were, of course, less inhibited because of their better position in the labor market, and management knew that they were more difficult to deal with, as one of the personnel-department managers in AF1 acknowledged: "The toolmaker has a greater awareness. He knows his value. He's more difficult to deal with. He knows that he is indispensable."

CONCLUSION

The characteristics of a primary labor market—stability of employment, equity in the administration of work rules, a healthy environment—were not found in the auto industry in Brazil at the time of the study. Instead, wage levels fluctuated in accordance with the influence of the State and external labor markets, health and safety were far from ideal, employment was unstable for significant groups of workers, productivity was increased without improved techniques, and the supervisory staff wielded considerable power, often in an arbitrary manner. This evidence is sufficient to justify the rejection of theories that claim that workers in the auto industry are by and large satisfied with their situation and that they participate in a primary labor market. However, the employment practices described need to be analyzed further and explained. Why should management adopt policies that appear to create so much resentment among workers? Having rejected one theoretical approach it is necessary to substitute a different explanation, and then to examine its implications for management strategy, industrial relations, and workers' resistance.

4

Employment Policies and Industrial Relations in the Auto Industry

SO FAR, THE DUAL-LABOR-MARKET approach has been criticized by means of, firstly, an examination of recruitment, training, and promotion policies, and, secondly, an account of wages and working conditions. But a critique of the dual-labor-market approach alone merely leaves a number of puzzles. Why were turnover rates so high? Why did the auto industry employers pay higher-than-average wages to nonskilled workers and then sack many of them at regular intervals? Why was there a complicated wage structure if it did not correspond to training and promotion policies? To explain these phenomena a different theory will be advanced in the first section of this chapter. It will be argued that the labor market and political conditions existing in the seventies allowed the employers to develop a specific system of labor use and control. Relatively high wages, a complex wage structure, and the rotation of labor were combined in a coherent system that was able to increase productivity and control labor costs. However, this sytem was dependent on more than the control of labor at the factory level. It was made possible by State control over unions and rank-and-file militants, and it functioned within the official system of industrial relations, which reinforced it. In the second section of this chapter, the operation of the official industrial-relations system will be discussed. The third section examines the points at which the overall system of labor control was vulnerable to working-class resistance.

Auto Industry Employment Practices

Much of the discussion about dual or segmented labor markets is derived from attempts to explain the high wages and other characteristics prevailing in much of the manufacturing sector of the U.S. economy after the Second World War. However, in order to explain the characteristics found in the Brazilian auto industry, the prewar period in the U.S.A. provides a better model. Before the Second World War, high wages and job instability were often combined. McPherson describes the auto industry as follows: "During a period of some thirty years [prior to the unionization drive in the thirties] . . . the industry had been conspicuous for its high hourly wage rates, sharp variability of employment, speed and efficiency of operations, insecurity of job tenure, and resistance to unionization" (1940:3). This could be a description of the Brazilian auto industry in the seventies. McPherson adds that the great majority (90 percent) of U.S. auto workers were in unskilled jobs requiring less than one year's training (1940:8).[1] This labor system was made both possible and necessary by the introduction of the assembly line to the motor industry in the early part of the century. The effect of the moving chain was to reduce the level of skill required, divide work tasks, and integrate the performance of work in a new way. With the subdivision of jobs, management gained a much greater control and specification of tasks, and the interchangeability of workers. Workers no longer integrated and coordinated production, but instead management organized the line and regulated the flow of its attendant supplies.

High wages were part of the control and organization of labor that accompanied the assembly line. As Braverman has pointed out, Henry Ford introduced the famous "five-dollar day" at the River Rouge plant in Detroit because otherwise workers would not accept the increased discipline and effort required by the new assembly-line production (1975:147-149). Workers were leaving the River Rouge plant because of the intensity and monotony of the work, and they would not work harder at the Rouge for the same wages they could get elsewhere. The introduction of the

[1] In the prewar U.S. motor industry, some major skilled tasks—tool and die, and body work, for example—were often subcontracted from the assemblers to specialized firms. In the postwar period, and in all modern auto industries, these jobs are now carried out by the assemblers. For this reason, the proportion of skilled workers in the assembly sector is higher now than in the thirties.

Employment Policies

"five-dollar day" did not mean that employment was stabilized in the Ford factories, but it did mean that it was Ford, not the workers, who decided who entered and who left. A large number of workers wanted to earn the high wages, and Ford was able to pick and choose among the candidates. Those who were admitted to the plants had to reach the standards of behavior set by Ford—both inside and outside the plant—and those who failed to do so were either fined or dismissed (Beynon, 1973:22-27). Ford could easily replace unsatisfactory workers precisely because the new assemby line required little skill or training. The vast majority of his workers were unskilled operatives whose jobs were exactly specified and quickly learnt. The role of high wages was to secure an adequate supply of replacement labor and to obtain a labor force that would submit to the rigors of assembly-line production.[2] Henry Ford himself, when talking about his wage policy for unskilled workers, expressed the strategy succinctly:

One frequently hears that wages have to be cut because of competition, but competition is never really met by lowering wages. Cutting wages does not reduce costs—it increases them. The only way to get a low-cost product is to pay a high price for a high grade of human service and to see to it through management that you get that service. (1926:43)

[2] The misinterpretation of the role of high wages in the auto industry is not confined to writers on Brazil and the postwar U.S.A. Gramsci, for example, saw Fordism as a policy of creating a highly paid, stable labor aristocracy, and he related this to their training and experience: "It would be uneconomic to allow the elements of an organic whole so laboriously built up to be dispersed, because it would be almost impossible to bring them together again, while on the other hand reconstructing it with new elements, chosen haphazardly, would involve not inconsiderable effort and expense. This is a limitation on the law of competition determined by the reserve army and by unemployment, and this limitation has always been at the origin of the formation of privileged labour aristocracies" (1971:312-313). This argument mistakenly asserts that work in the auto industry involves an organic unity that requires labor stability. In fact, the unity of auto production is achieved through the coordination by management of divided tasks, and there is little need for the workers to be stabilized at all. They are dispensable and replaceable.

High wages allow the employer to attract the most suitable workers and subject them to a rigorous discipline.

The effect of high wages, therefore, was not to create a labor force protected from the competition of the industrial reserve army, as Gramsci supposed, but on the contrary to expose the labor force to such competition. As can be seen from table 4-1, very few workers in AF1 and AF2 thought that there were firms which paid higher wages for their type of work, with the exception of the toolmakers. In particular, it can be seen that for the workers on the assembly line, who received the biggest differential over what they could expect to earn in other industries, the only way they could have hoped to earn equally high wages would have been in another auto firm. Given the comments they made about other auto plants, this would not appear to have been an attractive option. For this reason, they accepted the discipline of assembly-line production, even when it entailed the rigors described in the previous chapter. For the other groups of unskilled and semiskilled workers in the plant, much the same situation applied. High wages allowed management to impose the discipline on workers that

TABLE 4-1

"Are there firms that pay higher wages for your type of work?" If yes, "What kinds of firms pay more?": AF1 and AF2 (percentages)

Groups	No	Yes		
		Auto firms	Auto firms and others	Other firms
AF1				
Laborers	75	25	—	—
Assemblers	71	29	—	—
Toolroom workers	13	9	9	67
AF2				
Laborers, assembly line	93	7	—	—
Laborers, machine shop	33	56	7	7
Assemblers	69	25	—	6
Press operators	65	20	—	15
Machinists	40	37	3	20
Toolmakers	25	—	15	60

SOURCE: Interviews.

would have been impossible in low-wage firms. This point was noted by two foremen in a small components-firm who had previously worked in the motor industry. They complained that with the level of wages in their firm they could not impose an adequate discipline, because their workers would leave. In the auto industry, by contrast, leaving is not an attractive option. Given high wages, workers put up with all the problems outlined in the previous chapter and still regarded an auto plant as a desirable place to work.

Given that high wages were neither a device for stabilizing the labor force nor a concession to union power, they could be combined with other policies that were less attractive to workers. For example, wage cuts took place because the auto industry's wage policy was concerned with differentials, not absolute levels of pay. And the high wages in the industry provided a basis for a higher-than-average intensity of work, which also had an impact on health and safety in the plants (as was seen in the case of the forklift division in AF1). High wages were not an indication that other aspects of employment were satisfactory.[3] In addition, high wages did not imply that the auto firms were unconcerned about the level of their wage bill. It has been argued by some analysts that in modern industries the generally high levels of capital investment and productivity reduce direct labor costs so much that firms are willing to concede wage rises because they do not have a great impact on total costs. The existence of higher-than-average rates of pay is often taken as proof of this. However, if high wages are part of a specific employment policy, the argument does not hold. Large firms in the auto industry may be able to concede wage increases with less difficulty than smaller and less profitable concerns, but they may also take steps to contain wage costs. In fact, the control of wage costs was at the center of two puzzling features of the employment policies in the auto industry: the wage structure and the rotation of labor. In the criticism of the dual-labor-market theories made so far, it has merely been shown that

---

[3] In dual-market theories, high wages are taken as a sign that all the primary labor-market characteristics are present.

the patterns of labor use in the auto industry did not necessitate the stabilization of labor. At this point, it is necessary to go further, and explain how auto firms used their wage structures and rotation policy.

In chapter three a complicated wage structure of fourteen grades and six steps was described for AF1 and AF2. The use of fourteen grades was designed to give wage planners maximum flexibility, so that each job could be given the wage that corresponded to the "market rate" as perceived by the wage planners. For semiskilled and unskilled workers the market rate was that paid by other auto companies, and it was calculated in relation to these firms and other large companies. For skilled workers, the market rate was closely related to the general rates of pay in the surrounding area and the adequacy of labor supply to the needs of the firm. When there were shortages of skilled labor, in 1973 for example, AF1 readjusted wage rates in the toolroom. For turners, who were in slightly short supply, the category was moved from grade eleven to grade twelve. For grinders, who were in very short supply, the category was shifted from grade eleven to grade thirteen. Given that wage differentials between unskilled and skilled jobs were so large in Brazil, a large number of grades were needed to fill the intervening space and ensure optimum rates for each job category. Erikkson's analysis of wage structures in Argentina and Brazil in the early sixties demonstrates this. In the Argentinian auto industry the ratio of a toolmaker's basic wage to that of a janitor was about two to one, compared with three to one in Brazilian auto firms. Argentinian auto firms had between five and seven grades of jobs, compared with between ten and fourteen in Brazil (Erikkson, 1966:137-141).[4]

The reasons for having four, five, or six steps in each job category were rather more complex. It can be assumed that with the exception of skilled workers in times of severe shortages the initial wage-rate (step one) was sufficient to attract enough suitable

[4] It should also be noted that the ratio of 3:1 between toolmakers' and janitors' basic pay is not significantly less than the ratio of 3.3:1 found in table 3-3 (for 1974), in spite of the evidence of a widening of differentials in the early seventies.

applicants.[5] Certainly the personnel departments in the auto firms
had long lists of nonskilled applicants waiting to be called up for
a job. But if this was the case, why should AF1 increase wages
in a series of steps, resulting in a step-six unskilled worker earning
40 percent more than a step-one worker in the same job (see table
3-3)? One reason was that workers were attracted to the plants
by the prospect of future increases in wages, and that the system
of rises according to merit or length of employment was included
in the workers' calculations when they applied for jobs. A second
reason was that the incremental increases in wages allowed management to retain control over workers who were gaining experience that might have been marketable. This effect is seen in
table 4-2. For the machinists—the most stable group of workers
interviewed—there were few opportunities of securing a new job
at a wage equivalent to the one they were earning. Twenty-nine
out of thirty machinists thought it would be difficult to find such
a job, even though 60 percent thought that there were firms which
paid higher wages (table 4-1). Because of their relative stability,
twenty-six out of thirty machinists were on steps five or six. Thus
long-service workers were made dependent on the company by
this wage structure in spite of any experience they might have

TABLE 4-2
"If you were sacked or asked for your cards, do you think that it would be
easy or difficult to find another similar job paying the same wage?": AF2
(percentages)

Group	Difficult	So-so	Easy	Don't know
Laborers, assembly line	80	7	7	7
Laborers, machine shop	60	7	27	7
Assemblers	69	—	25	7
Press operators	80	—	15	5
Machinists	97	—	3	—
Toolmakers	30	15	45	10

SOURCE: Interviews.

[5] In AF1 and AF2 workers were being admitted to the toolrooms in 1974-1975
on steps three or four because step one wage-rates would not attract sufficient
applicants.

acquired. The firm could keep hold of the workers it really wanted and dispense with those it did not, dismissing them and bringing in replacements at the bottom of the pay scale. A third reason advanced by some managers in favor of the step system was that it offered workers frequent rises, and although it was seen in the previous chapter that these rises and the consequent differences in wage rates were the subject of a certain amount of discontent, it is possible that they did blunt the edge of workers' feelings about pay.[6] Finally, it should be said that the system could divide the labor force, and workers were sometimes encouraged to remain secretive about their wages. In the toolroom in AF2, for example, a revision of the top scales for toolmakers had been introduced in 1973, but only some of the eligible workers had received the new rise. The others did not even known in 1975 that the wage structure had been altered. Clearly, managers and foremen can use the wage structure as part of their general system of control. Whatever the reasons behind the introduction of the pay steps, management in the auto industry felt that it would be impossible to abandon the system without raising the wages of the newer workers up to the rates paid to the workers with more experience. In other words, in spite of the availability of adequate supplies of most types of labor at the prevailing starting rates, management felt that a transition to a unitary wage system, or a compression of steps, would only lead in the direction of higher average wages.[7]

The system as it stood provided both flexibility and control over wage costs precisely because it was combined with a high degree of labor turnover. In the auto plants, wage bills were strictly controlled by the Finance departments, who produced targets for the plant as a whole and for specific sections. Plant management and the Industrial Relations departments then had to meet the

[6] This was the opinion of a manager in AF5, but it was flatly contradicted by a manager in AF4 who argued that the system only caused resentment among workers.

[7] This attitude may have stemmed from the fact that a modification of the system was usually discussed in response to increasing workers' agitation against wage policies and employment practices. Firms did not appear likely to modify the system in any other circumstances.

financial targets, which were of two kinds.[8] Firstly, wage costs were not allowed to exceed a certain proportion of total value-added. Therefore, if there was a downturn in production then wage costs had to be reduced in line with it. The firms matched output to sales quite closely, holding stocks low, and so employment was closely tied to the fluctuating level of sales. This caused the periodic rises and falls in employment that were noticeable in the industry. Secondly, there were target figures for the average wage per worker. Given that rates of self-dismissal were low, the tendency would be for workers to remain in their jobs and gradually move up the wage structure, from step one to step six. This would raise the total wage-bill as more and more workers reached the top steps. To stop this happening and keep the wage bill in line with some notion of what the total wages should be, management had to dismiss longer-service workers with relatively high wage-rates and replace them with newer workers earning the initial rate. By controlling wage costs in this way, the Finance departments forced plant and Industrial Relations management to adopt a permanent policy of rotating labor. This policy accounts for the simultaneous hiring and firing that was noticeable in the industry. Given the generally high level of wages offered to unskilled and semiskilled workers, the companies had no trouble in finding adequate replacements for the workers dismissed.

The rotation of labor was the subject of a lot of controversy in Brazil in the seventies. The unions often alleged that firms deliberately adopted hire-and-fire policies to reduce their wage bills. The information presented here supports this claim. However, the effect of labor rotation on wage bills should not obscure an equally important consequence. As Henry Ford pointed out, high wages could be recouped by high productivity, as long as management

---

[8] This description of the effect of financial targets was given to me by a very senior executive in one of the companies in 1979. Apart from providing an insider's view of the system of labor rotation, it reinforces the findings of Lobos, whose analysis of management structures in the auto industry showed that the Industrial Relations departments ranked equal last in a hierarchy of importance (along with Research and Development), while Finance was one of the two most important of the six general management areas he surveyed (1976:198-201).

ran the plants efficiently. One of the bases for such efficiency is the power of command and control, and this was reinforced by the policy of labor rotation. If workers are secure in their jobs, then high wages are not an incentive to work hard and submit to discipline. But if workers know that they can be dismissed at any time, and that at some point in the future the foremen will be selecting workers for dismissal, then the potential loss of employment at high wages becomes a real threat and constraint. It was this threat that was noted in the previous chapter. The two policies together—high wages and rotation—enforced a high degree of discipline and control in the plants.

The Formal System of Industrial Relations

The control exercized by management in the plants was backed up by, on the one hand, the control of the State over unions and rank-and-file activists, and on the other, the legally constituted industrial-relations system in Brazil. Within the authoritarian system of labor use and control described above, there was little room for negotiation. Workers' grievances (of the type discussed in chapter three) were, by and large, suppressed rather than resolved. This was partly achieved through the operation of the formal industrial-relations system. Although four main channels of negotiation were potentially available to resolve grievances, it will be shown how they effectively reinforced management control.

The first channel was the use of government legislation either directly to alter a given situation or to provide the means whereby alterations might be made. From the discussion in chapter two, however, it should be obvious that the unions had virtually no influence on legislation after the coup in 1964. Indeed, as far as the unions were concerned, many of their problems emanated from postcoup legislation such as the restriction on the right to strike, the introduction of the FGTS, and the wages policy. For the employers, on the other hand, the State was extremely helpful, and it is alleged that the change in the financing of compensation for dismissal "without due cause" in the FGTS was in response to the wishes of the auto firms. Similarly, modifications introduced to the wages policy in 1979 were developed by two wage planners from major auto firms. The close liaison between the employers and the State made this potential form of grievance resolution almost totally ineffective for the unions after 1964. A second avenue that could have been used by workers and unions was the machinery of the Labor Courts and the Regional Labor Office. The unions had some successes with this approach, particularly over the inclusion of payment for habitual overtime in the calculations for dismissal compensation, holiday pay, and the end-of-year bonus, but its use was limited. The mechanisms of the Labor Courts and the activities of the Labor Offices did not enforce much of the legislation: in some cases there were not enough enforcement officials to check on firms, while in others the penalties were too small to have a deterrent effect.[9] There was widespread violation of the laws limiting overtime and Sunday working, and although the CLT regulated hours of work and rest, shift systems, and work on Sundays, the legal provisions were ignored by large and small firms alike. As was noted in the previous chapter, the fifty-six- and fifty-eight-hour week was a regular practice, and in some of the large firms twelve-hour shifts and regular Sunday working were common.[10] In other areas, such as equal pay for women, no attempt had ever been made to enforce the principle that had been laid down in the CLT in 1943. As well as inadequate enforcement of the law, the unions were faced with the problem that many of the matters about which they had grievances were perfectly legal. The wages policy, rotation of labor, and intensification of work all fell within the bounds established by law. At the same time, given that the Labor Courts were designed to resolve disputes between employers and individual employees, unions could only take up issues on behalf of

[9] In one small components-firm the plant manager informed me that the company had been regularly fined for working excessive overtime, but this had not been enough to prevent the firm continuing with it. Working hours were only cut down after management decided that long hours were causing declining productivity. They came to this conclusion after a worker had fallen half asleep at a press and damaged his hand. This accident was made possible by a combination of fatigue and inadequate safety provisions—gloves, guards, and safety buttons.

[10] See, for example, complaints against Firestone, Pirelli, and Indústrias Villares on these issues (OESP, 11/7/1974 and 23/8/1975).

individual workers. Therefore, the Labor Courts were of very limited help.

Collective contracts and the regulation of all matters concerning wages and working conditions were, however, negotiable *in principle* during the annual contract negotiations between unions and employers. Along this third channel, at least, the unions were guaranteed a role and a voice. In theory the annual contract could cover any aspect of wages, working conditions, and procedures for conflict resolution in the periods between negotiations. However, after 1964 such general contracts were rarely negotiated. The employers were content to declare a "failure to agree" at the initial stages of negotiation and then allow the Labor Courts to institute compulsory arbitration. The Courts' decisions on wage settlements were bound by the wages policy, and thus one major area of negotiation was removed at the outset. On other matters the unions could only request that the Labor Courts judge in their favor, but this happened only rarely. In the words of one executive in the auto industry, the Regional Labor Court in São Paulo "always used to make its decisions within the narrowest possible parameters," which favored the status quo. In most cases, the annual "negotiations" involved no negotiation at all. The employers, content with the government's wages policy and feeling no pressure to concede any of the unions' other demands, allowed the negotiations to be a formality.[11] The major union gains would appear to have been the introduction of pay slips for all workers and some provision of boots and overalls.

The final avenue open to unions and workers was that of direct negotiation with the employers. Once again, however, this channel was little used after 1964. Although on some occasions managements set up plant committees to discuss problems—for example in the Cobrasma plant in Osasco up to 1968 (Weffort, 1972:87-88) and in the Saab-Scania plant in São Bernardo do Campo in 1977—the general position of the employers was to oppose such developments. In 1969, when the Metalworkers of

[11] The Labor Courts could be flexible in certain situations. It was noticeable that in 1968, and again in 1978 and 1979, established norms could be modified in the face of mounting workers' unrest.

São Paulo put forward a demand for "joint internal committees of employers and employees in firms to discuss problems emerging in the place of work" (OESP, 20/12/1969, the employers refused to accept it, and they were supported by the Labor Court. Given the control exercised in the places of work by management, there was no reason to develop plant bargaining. It was not needed to secure flexibility in production, as was the case in Spain, for example (Amsden, 1972:146), and the control of the unions by the Ministry of Labor obviated any tendency that might have existed before 1964 to use plant bargaining as a means of isolating workers from the unions and weakening the centralized labor movement.[12] Given the success with which management was able to control labor, there was little need for any formal negotiation procedures at all. In AF1 and AF2 the only formal worker-management committees were the Internal Accident Prevention Committees required by law, and even here managements dominated the proceedings. When managements were forced to negotiate directly with workers they used informal channels and the unions were more or less excluded from any participation at plant level. Managements resisted union attempts to represent workers either through the narrow framework of official arbitration or outside of it.

For most of the seventies, management in the auto industry was based on command, not negotiation, and the channels outlined above were allowed to fall into disuse. When not a matter for the police, labor relations were controlled by the Finance departments. However, this system of labor control could only operate as long as the labor market and political conditions remained favorable, and even at its period of greatest effectiveness there were certain limitations.

Labor Resistance in the Auto Plants

The system of labor control, and the pattern of industrial-relations practices associated with it, had two major points of weakness.

[12] Sellier gives this as one of the reasons for the development of plant bargaining in Italy after the Second World War (1971:143-145).

The first of these was in the control of skilled workers, whose scarcity and importance gave them a stronger position in relation to management than most other groups of workers. They were less easily replaced and less threatened by being dismissed, because they could get other jobs. The second was the threat to authoritarian control posed by workers' organization. Although the rotation of labor and the control exercised by the State made such organization both difficult and precarious, the size and concentration of the auto industry favored the development of groups of militants in the plants. Labor control was never perfect, and in some instances managements were forced to negotiate and conciliate. But as the next section will show, the development of workers' opposition was kept in check by the State, which controlled both the unions and rank-and-file activists. In this section, two incidents of workers' resistance will be discussed—the case of the toolroom workers in AF1 and AF2, and the case of the machinists in AF2. These case studies illustrate the weaknesses of the system of labor control and show how certain groups in both factories provided the bases for more generalized opposition to it later in the seventies.

THE TOOLROOM WORKERS

The toolroom workers in AF1 and AF2 displayed rather different characteristics from the majority of workers in the two plants. They were less subject to the threat of dismissal, although it was not unknown for toolroom workers to be sacked. Because of this they were more experienced than other groups of workers. In the two plants, the average length of employment for the sixty workers interviewed in the toolrooms was about six years, compared with 3⅓ years for assemblers in both plants and 4⅓ for the press operators in AF2. Perhaps more importantly, 68 percent of the toolroom workers in AF1 and 90 percent of the toolmakers in AF2 had worked in the plants for more than five years, compared with 25 percent and 19 percent for the assemblers in the two plants and 35 percent for the press operators in AF2. This length of employment gave a certain security, and also gave workers a stronger collective identity. Toolroom workers were generally considered to be the source of union support in the auto industry, and in AF2 the rate of unionization was higher in the toolroom than in the press shop and on the assembly line. In AF1 (where the workers were in a rather inactive union, different from that in São Bernardo), the toolroom workers were much more critical of its lack of force than other groups of workers. They stressed that the union had no power, or made comments such as "it used to be better" or "we lack unity" when asked to evaluate it, and this was in marked contrast to the assembly-line workers in the plant. Toolroom workers would have preferred a more active labor organization.[13]

In the previous chapter, some grievances were outlined. In spite of the scarcity of toolroom labor, the differentials between the auto industry and other employers had narrowed substantially, and in the case of AF2 the average wage-rate for toolmakers had not kept pace with inflation between 1973 and 1975.[14] Because of their relatively long periods of employment, the majority of skilled workers in the toolrooms were at the top of the wage scales. With few chances of promotion to charge-hand or foreman available, there was considerable feeling about the "*teto*," the top point of the wage scale. In addition to the discontent surrounding wages, the toolroom workers were also affected by the general discipline of the plant, and although they were not subject to the same rigorous control as workers in the main production areas, they were required to reach definite work norms. At times of high toolroom activity they were also expected to work a sixty-hour week, according to the toolroom management in AF1, and refusal to accept overtime was regarded as a sign of a worker's

[13] On the basis of interviews in 1975, the position of toolroom workers was ambiguous. In AF1 they complained about the weakness of the union and in AF2 they wanted more union action on wages, but in AF2 the toolmakers were less in favor of direct negotiations with the employers and extending the right to strike than certain other groups (see Humphrey, 1977:184-193). I concluded then that toolmakers might be content to pursue their demands through action solely at plant level. In fact, they played an important role in the development of militancy at the end of the seventies, as will be seen and discussed in the following two chapters.

[14] See tables 3-5 and 3-7.

wanting to be dismissed. Given their relative security, workers in the toolrooms could try to resolve such grievances without having the same fear as those working in other sections of the plants.

The problems in the toolrooms came to a head in 1973. The squeeze on wages resulting from the misapplication of the wages policy was combined with acute shortages of skilled labor. The auto employers found that they could not attract enough skilled workers, and smaller firms were "poaching" them with offers of higher wages. At this time skilled workers in the smaller firms were moving around in search of higher wages, as this quote from a turner in a small components-firm illustrates:

> I worked in a factory just by the zoo, larger than this, with about 1500 workers. I fixed up two jobs before leaving—this one and one in another firm. It was easy. At that time [1973] all of them were looking for people, and one firm would take workers from the other. Everyone was complaining. A friend and I asked for our cards, and seven others left at the same time. A lot of people left there.

But if workers in smaller firms were content to move from firm to firm in the search for higher wages, the workers in the large firms were not. Instead of leaving, the toolroom workers wanted to stay in AF1 and AF2 and secure better wages at the same time. Therefore, they used the scarcity of skilled workers as a weapon against management. Some of the workers threatened to leave, and they brought in notices to the plant which advertised wage rates higher than those being paid in AF1 and AF2. When this failed to secure rises, the workers in AF1 started to work "without enthusiasm." The management was left in no doubt that it needed to raise wage rates, and this was done. The top rates for skilled workers were increased by between 11 percent and 38 percent according to the scarcity of labor in different categories.

At this time the skilled workers were in a very strong position. The labor market was very favorable to them, and they would have had no difficulty in obtaining new work had they been sacked. They were almost forcing management to adjust its wage rates in line with its own interests (obtaining an adequate supply of skilled workers). In spite of this, the skilled workers in some other plants were obliged to force harder for their rises. In AF3, for example, there was a well-organized overtime ban that led to a sharp reduction in output in the plant. After more than a week of declining production, management conceded rises. However, these successes were only gained because of the combination of labor-market scarcities and a strong demand for vehicles. Managements did not concede higher wages without a great deal of reluctance, and their determination to control wage costs was seen in the following year. Once again in 1974 accelerating inflation and a low wage-settlement in April began to bite into wages, and in the latter part of the year workers began to agitate again for rises. But this time the situation was a little different, because the market for autos had stagnated and the overall demand for skilled workers had eased a little. In a number of plants, including AF2 and AF3, stoppages and demands for higher pay were insufficient to extract concessions from management. The kind of action adopted by toolroom workers, involving limited mobilization and opposition, was only effective when the general situation was very favorable.

THE MACHINISTS

The machinists occupied a unique position in AF2. Their work was classified as semiskilled, but they were a very stable group. The average length of employment was 8¼ years, and 93 percent of those interviewed (twenty-eight out of thirty) had been employed by the firm for more than five years. This resulted from the nature of their work and the management problems affecting the plant. In three of the four machine shops the machinery was quite old: the conditions for working were not good, and even with regular overtime taking place when other sections of the plant were doing none, output was barely sufficient to match demand. In some cases, workers on vital machines worked a seven-day week to keep up with production targets. The machine shops were the bottleneck in the plant's productive activities, and, of course, essential to them. For various historical reasons, the central company management had less than full control over the

121

management of the machine shops, and the foremen, too, were considered with some suspicion as being a law unto themselves. For these reasons, normal company policy was not applied in this area. Unwilling supervisors were not forced to adopt the rotation-of-labor policy, and management did not wish to apply it to a group of workers whose knowledge of the aging machinery was essential to keep the plant running. In spite of its disapproval of the situation in the machine shops, central management felt that it would be better to leave well enough alone and hope for continued production. This put the machinists—the most experienced operatives in the machine shops—in an exceptional position. Unless a new machine shop was built, central management was faced with a problem that could only get worse. The machinery was getting older while output was expected to rise.

Faced with the same pressure on real wages as other workers, the machinists could not adopt the same tactics as the toolmakers. They could hardly threaten to leave: twenty-nine out of thirty machinists thought that it would be difficult to find another job at the same wage as they were earning at the time of the interviews (table 4-2). Nor could they wait for promotion or further rises in pay according to length of service: in January 1975 there were 601 machinists and only six charge-hands, and of this group of 601, 90 percent were on the top two steps of the wage scale, with no possibility of training or promotion to other job categories. Nor could they lower their work rates by working "without enthusiasm," because they were tied to hourly production schedules. Therefore, decisive action was needed to force the firm to pay higher wages. As a result of their stability of employment the machinists were the most cohesive group in the factory. They had by far the highest rate of unionization (80 percent in the sample), and they were regarded as the backbone of the union in the plant. It was this strength they had to use against the company.

In September 1974 there was a short, unsuccessful stoppage in the machine shops in AF2. Workers halted production for a number of hours and demanded a 20 percent wage rise to compensate for inflation. It started with just a few workers making it known that they were prepared to stop work, through talking to people on the bus and writing slogans in the washrooms. Given the general discontent over falling wages, this was sufficient to provoke a stoppage, and once one section stopped work other sections were brought to a halt by workers moving around the machine shops encouraging them to stop as well. But this low level of organization was not sufficient to prepare the workers for a serious confrontation with the company. Management tried to defuse the situation by promising to consider the workers' demands and asking for a return to work until this could be done. When there was no resumption of work after lunch, the supervisory staff put great pressure on one particular worker, an elected union director, to restart his machine. After he did this the rest of the workers resumed production as well, and the stoppage was over. In the following week the firm announced that no increases could be given to workers because of the government's wages policy.

In the face of management pressure, there had not been enough preparation and determination to carry through the initial act. Many workers interviewed six months after the event said that they had been unsure of the reasons for the stoppage and not at all clear what demands were raised when it took place. The lack of preparation was often cited as a criticism of the stoppage and its failure, but success would have been hard to achieve in the circumstances. Even at the height of the boom, semiskilled workers had difficulty in securing wage rises in the larger firms. In one components firm, for example, a go-slow which lasted for some time in 1973, and then a stoppage by workers on the night shift involving a parade around the factory, was needed to force a rise in anticipation of the following wage settlement.[15] Although workers were willing to oppose the firm—some of the workers in the machine shop in AF2 saw the stoppage very clearly as a chance to "get back" at the company and express their discontent—it was difficult to translate these general sentiments of discontent and opposition into an organized resistance that could withstand the considerable pressures that management brought to bear. To oppose the employer when the labor market and product

[15] This information is taken from interviews with workers in the firm.

market are unfavorable requires a degree of determination and preparation that can rarely be achieved and sustained when the organization and activities of workers are curtailed by the employers and the State. Because of this, in both AF1 and AF2 the underlying discontent expressed at the time of the interviews was contained and isolated.

THE CONTAINMENT OF RESISTANCE IN THE MID-SEVENTIES

The characteristic feature of the protests that took place in the mid-seventies was their precarious nature. They were both difficult to organize and difficult to generalize. They aroused a considerable interest at the time because they were the first signs of workers' activities following the severest period of repression at the beginning of the decade, but they never turned into a general movement that threatened the State or the employers. This was because of the high rate of attrition of militants. While relatively unorganized protests were common in 1973 and the first part of 1974, longer-term organizing was considerably more hazardous. The case of Indústrias Villares, a large engineering firm in the Greater São Paulo area, is illustrative. In November and December 1973 the workers in the machine shops stopped work on a number of occasions and demanded a 10 percent wage rise, a revision of the grading structure, free transport, and a lowering of prices in the canteen (OESP, 14/12/1973). In preparation for this, militants linked to the Catholic Church had been working for over a year in the plant. They discussed with workers the advantages and disadvantages of industrial action, the justness of their claims, and the chances of winning a dispute. The dispute was pursued first through the acceptable channels—requests to foremen or small meetings with management—in order to exhaust the legitimate recourses of the workers, and when this produced little result, short stoppages began. The management offered increased wages to skilled workers, in accordance with market conditions, but the workers pressed for a more general increase, applicable to all grades. The dispute was widely reported, and after it had continued for some time the local union, the Metalworkers of São Paulo, was called in to mediate between the workers and the management. In the end, no general rises were conceded by the firm.[16]

There was a price to pay for this degree of organization. After the stoppages and negotiations, about ten of the leading militants in the plant were dismissed. Even when workers do not openly organize stoppages and participate in negotiations, their activities can be noted by the employers: in some auto plants it was alleged that there were networks of informers. The threat of dismissal was reinforced by the threat of direct repression, and in the seventies the army and the police were a regular feature of labor-management relations. Even apparently minor protests could put workers in trouble, as the following newspaper extract indicates:

> They [the bus operators in Sao Paulo] are so dissatisfied that they have not yet given wage rises to the majority of their 25,000 drivers and 12,000 conductors. Ten of these drivers, who work for Viação Intercontinental, all failed to turn up for work on one day last week. . . . By the end of the morning these drivers were taken to the *Delegacia de Ordem Política e Social*—"to help with inquiries," according to an official of the Transport Department. (JT, 3/6/1974)

In other cases, the forces of the State can be used when there are problems at the workplace, as this report suggests:

> Yesterday troops of the Army Police occupied the installations of the General Electric factory in the Rua Miguel Angelo in Maria da Graça. The movement of forces of the Army Police was part of maneuvers for industrial security.[17] There were 52 cases of intoxication by tear gas among local people who watched the exercise. (JB, 13/4/1976)

In these conditions workers may have been reluctant to enter into protests that could end in trouble.

The existence of the State's repressive apparatus also served to isolate struggles. Within companies, the difficulties described above

---

[16] This account is based on newspaper reports and interviews with one of the militants who participated.

[17] The term *seguranca* can mean either "safety" or "security."

limited protests to small sections, and in 1973 and 1974 there were virtually no cases of stoppages affecting the whole of major plants. Coordination from one plant to another was even more difficult since it required an organization and network of militants that went beyond the confines of the workplace. In the early seventies, the Trade Union Opposition in São Paulo was particularly badly hit by successive waves of imprisonments, and the blacker side of this repressive activity was revealed by the publicity surrounding the death of Manoel Fiel Filho, a metalworker, in January 1976. As the respected daily, *O Estado de S. Paulo*, reported:

> The imprisonment of workers is no new thing for the trade union leaders in ABC, who up to last night did not know what had happened to Manoel Fiel Filho. From the end of 1968 up until yesterday it is calculated that more than 800 workers from the region had been taken prisoner, and there had been allegations of several deaths, although it is impossible to give a precise number. . . . In ABC the imprisonment of workers intensified after the victory of the MDB in 1974. Soon after the elections, more than 200 workers at Volkswagen were put into jail at one time. There have also been innumerable imprisonments of workers at Mercedes, Phillips, and other factories in São Bernardo and São Caetano, mainly of metalworkers. (OESP, 20/1/1976, quoted by Frederico, 1978:132)

The toolroom workers at Volkswagen had been quite active in 1973 and 1974, and these arrests and the rooting out of cells of political militants set back the organization in the plant.

In this situation, the union might have been expected to give some kind of lead to the workers, but union activities were also severely circumscribed. In AF2, for example, one union director was of the opinion that if the union had called the stoppage in the machine shop discussed above it would have been followed by the mass of workers and could have been successful. But this was not possible. Although the Metalworkers of São Bernardo had some influence in the major plants at that time, they were unable to support the stoppages directly: the Ministry of Labor was watching for any sign of union involvement and had threatened intervention. The same kind of vigilance by the Ministry also prevented the union from taking a strong lead in the fight for better working conditions. It was allowed to raise demands for better wages and conditions and the introduction of direct negotiations with the employers, but when, for example, active steps were taken in advance of the 1975 pay negotiations to conduct negotiations independently of the other trade unions of the Interior of the State of São Paulo, the Ministry of Labor again threatened intervention. This kind of intimidation, coupled with the imprisonment of active trade union leaders (for example, leaders of the Textile Workers in São Paulo and the Metalworkers in São Caetano), restrained some unions from mobilizing their workers and from giving direction and organization to the largely spontaneous protests that emerged in 1973 and 1974.

In these conditions there were clear limits to the general power of rank-and-file organizations, but within certain plants the potential for resistance was clearly demonstrated. The employment policies adopted by the auto firms could not contain all conflicts, particularly when there were shortages of labor. At the time of the survey of the two plants, resistance was contained by the use of the repressive organs of the State and the control over the unions exercized by the Ministry of Labor. The workers in the two plants were not on the verge of outright revolt, but the degree of discontent on a wide range of issues was great enough to provide fertile ground for activists and on occasion to provoke industrial action. From this it can be concluded that the workers in the auto industry could support a more militant form of union activity if the general political conditions allowed it. But before the period of open resistance is discussed, it is necessary to examine the development of the union that represented most workers in the auto industry, the Metalworkers of São Bernardo.

5

Trade Unionism in the Auto Industry

ALL BRAZILIAN TRADE UNIONS faced problems in providing effective representation and protection for their members following the coup in 1964. Even in the Populist period the unions had been hampered by a labor system which granted them funds to finance extensive bureaucracies and welfare services, but left them with small active memberships and little or no organization in places of work. These problems were made worse by the military regime, which greatly restricted union activities. In the late sixties and early seventies those few unions which attempted to overcome their inactivity and ineffectiveness suffered repression from the Ministry of Labor and the security forces. The Metalworkers Union of São Bernardo do Campo and Diadema was in the same general situation as other unions, and yet it was able to develop its policies and organization to such an extent that by the end of the nineteen-seventies it was one of the most militant and effective unions in Brazil. The reasons for its success lay in the exceptional policies pursued by its leadership and the receptivity of workers in the area. In this chapter the bases of the union's strength and the development of the overall political and union situation in the seventies which allowed this strength to become manifest will be examined.

The New Trade Unionism in São Bernardo do Campo

The history of the Metalworkers of São Bernardo is inextricably linked to the growth of the auto industry. In 1950, the industrial census registered only 4,030 workers in manufacturing industry as a whole in the *município* of São Bernardo do Campo, but with the implantation of the auto industry in the fifties employment in the region expanded rapidly. The new auto firms—Mercedes,

Trade Unionism

Scania, Simca, Volkswagen, and Willys Overland—built green-field plants on or near the main road linking São Paulo and the port of Santos, which ran from the city of São Paulo through São Bernardo and then down the coastal escarpment to the sea. By 1960 there were 20,039 workers employed in São Bernardo,[1] and in the following year the Metalworkers Union of São Bernardo was established. Up until 1961 the metalworkers of the area had been represented by the Metalworkers Union of Santo André, but the rapid expansion of the auto industry made a separate union viable. Such was the industry's growth that by 1970 there were 75,118 workers employed in São Bernardo, compared with 50,372 in Santo André; just twenty years before there had been six workers in Santo André for every one in Sao Bernardo. Of these 75,118 workers, 55 percent worked in the transport materials sector—in effect, auto components and auto assembly—and a further 18 percent were employed in the metallurgical, mechanical, and electrical industries. São Bernardo was not without reason called the Detroit of Brazil. It was a one-industry and one-union town. In 1970, 73 percent of all workers in manufacturing industry were represented by one union, and over half of the workers in it worked in the five large auto plants.

Between 1961 and 1964 the union was controlled by left-wingers, but following the military coup the leadership was deposed by the Ministry of Labor.[2] When elections were called in the following year, the union was in such disarray that neither the ruling group appointed by the Ministry nor the old leadership was able to secure victory. Instead, the two groups formed a joint leadership which held office for the periods 1965-1967 and 1967-1969. In 1969 the two groups contested the election, and the one linked to the team appointed by the Ministry of Labor in 1964 emerged as the winner.[3] In many unions the Ministry-appointed

---

[1] The dates of the censuses were January 1, 1950, and December 31, 1959. The definitions and sources can be found in the notes to table 2-2. The Metalworkers Union in São Bernardo also covers the small, neighboring *município* of Diadema, which is not included in the figures presented here.

[2] The information is taken from Almeida, 1978:485.

[3] Union elections are contested by slates which contain candidates for all the

slates won elections by fraud and manipulation, and their continuation in office was usually associated with unrepresentative, inactive, and often corrupt leadership. In 1969 the outlook for the Metalworkers of São Bernardo could not have appeared to be promising.

The situation was made worse by the events of 1969 (see chapter two) and the clampdown on union and political activities following the passing of Institutional Act Five in December 1968. Trade union leaders and rank-and-file activists were subject to severe pressure, and in the Greater São Paulo area strike activity came to a virtual halt until 1973. Even if the slate linked to the pre-1964 leadership had been elected in 1969, it would probably have suffered the harassment, arrests, and Ministry of Labor intervention experienced by other unions. However, the group which won the 1969 election in São Bernardo differed markedly from both of the two major tendencies found in Brazilian trade unionism at that time. It was neither radically opposed to the government nor content to run an inactive and unrepresentative union. The São Bernardo leadership was antipolitical and antileft (particularly anticommunist), but it favored rank-and-file activism, organization in the plants, and giving priority to the defense of the immediate interests of the category.[4] This corresponded to the notion of "authentic trade unionism," free from political influence and concerned solely with "union matters," which had been expounded without success by Jarbas Passarinho when he was Minister of Labor (see OESP, 7/5/1967 and 11/8/1967).

The new leadership's antipolitical stance, combined with an emphasis on the resolution of workers' problems by direct contact

vacant posts. All candidates must be paid-up members of the union. Votes are cast for slates, not individual candidates. The CLT (Article 531) states that the winning slate must poll at least 50 percent of the electorate. If no one slate polls 50 percent, then a second ballot is required, in which the winning slate has to poll 50 percent of the votes cast. The elected candidates hold office for three years (two years until 1969).

[4] The term "category" refers to all the workers represented by the union. In the case of the Metalworkers of São Bernardo, this means all the metalworkers in São Bernardo and Diadema. This is not the same as union members, who are metalworkers who affiliate to the union and pay a subscription.

between union and employers, led to a strategy that was in some respects similar to that found in modern-sector unions before the coup. Although the union could not ignore the State—and, indeed, it expressed a strong opposition to the State's role in union and industrial-relations matters—it sought to avoid State interference wherever possible. One way of achieving this was to look for local, sectional solutions to workers' problems, solutions which could be achieved by direct negotiation with the employers. In doing this the union reflected quite closely the feelings of workers in the big plants and their ambiguities about how grievances should be resolved.

In the area of wages, for example, the union claimed a right to special treatment. It demanded that the employers and the State take into account the exceptional conditions prevailing in the auto industry, and pushed for the abolition of the wages policy and higher wage-increases on the grounds of excessive rises in the cost of living. The demand for exceptional treatment is seen clearly in the following report:

> The workers in the auto industry are going to demand collective contracts independent of the rest of the metalworkers, according to the President of the Metalworkers of São Bernardo. The claim of the metalworkers who work in auto plants is that their sector is much more profitable and has higher productivity. "The auto industries," says Paulo Vidal, "have their own particular circumstances which make them different from other metalworking, mechanical, and electrical-goods factories." Because of this he claims that the 18% wage rise obtained by the metalworkers of the Interior . . . has left the workers of the seven car plants in his *município* discontented. (OESP, 10/5/1974)

However, three months later the Metalworkers of São Bernardo were willing to join with the Metalworkers of Santo André and São Caetano (the three areas known collectively as ABC) to demand higher wages on rather different grounds: "The metalworkers of ABC are going to ask the firms in which they work and the Ministry of Labor for a recovery of wages equal to 28%

to compensate for the difference between wages received and the rise of the cost of living—46% between April 1973 and now, according to a study done by the Departamento Intersindical de Estatística e Estudos Sócio-Econômicos (DIEESE)'' (JT, 21/8/1974). This early statement of the need for a ''wage recovery'' (*reposição salarial*)[5] to compensate for the low level of wage settlements in 1973 and 1974 (discussed in chapter three) was based upon cost-of-living criteria that could have applied to all workers.

But while the wages policy was unjust, the Metalworkers of São Bernardo thought that it was particularly unjust to them because of the special conditions of productivity and profitability prevailing in the auto industry. The same newspaper report quoted a document sent by the Metalworkers of São Bernardo to the Ministry of Labor, which said: ''In the case of the wages policy . . . a similar phenomenon occurs, it being merely observed that it has never met the needs of the people since it was implanted. But, in regions such as ours, marked by the rapid transformations caused by unprecedented development, the current wages policy has shown itself to be inadequate and obsolete. Our modern firms, constituted by the auto and related industries, have very notable levels of profitability and productivity'' (JT, 21/8/1974). The union was quite willing to pursue two different lines of argument at the same time: all workers need more money because of falling real wages, but auto workers deserve extra rises because of the high productivity and profitability in their industry. The union was also willing to address both arguments to both the employers and the State, as the above quotations illustrate.

A similar amalgam of general and specific approaches, addressed to both the employers and the State, could be seen in the union's attitude to labor turnover and the hire-and-fire policies pursued by the auto companies. In the Declaration of São Bernardo issued at the union's First Congress in 1974, it was argued that

[5] There is no simple translation of the term *reposição salarial*. It means a readjustment of wage levels outside of the normal settlement procedure, and in the text it will either be left in Portuguese or translated by the term ''wage recovery,'' which is used by the translators in *Latin American Perspectives* (1979:91).

the rotation of labor had its "principle cause in the existence of the FGTS," and in line with this the Declaration called for the abolition of that legislation. But in the face of a refusal by the government to countenance such a change, and given the pressing need for some alleviation of the problem, the union tried other tactics as well. At the annual negotiations in 1977 it introduced the idea of a "substitute clause," which specified that no worker could be hired to replace another at less than the wage earned by the worker being replaced. If effective, this would have eliminated one of the causes of rapid turnover in the auto industry, but it would also have been much more sectional, because the clause would only have been valid for the metalworkers in São Bernardo (in the first instance, at least).

Interviews reveal the same kind of ambiguity among the attitudes of workers in AF2 as was found in union strategy. On the one hand, they agreed strongly with the statement that workers as a whole should benefit from the growth of the country, and they supported the idea that wage disparities should be evened out by means of workers on low wages obtaining larger rises than workers on higher wages. A number of workers also expressed sympathy for the plight of the lower-paid and the unemployed. However, balanced against this was a strong feeling that the high productivity and profitability of the auto industry entitled them to higher wages. This was particularly true for the unskilled and semiskilled workers, whose wages were higher in the auto industry than they could have expected to earn elsewhere.

The willingness to countenance and press for limited, sectional gains was a distinctive feature of the program of the Metalworkers of São Bernardo, and in the early seventies some currents of opinion in the labor movement and some writers on the working class thought that the union was heading in the direction of accommodation with the government and the pursuit of totally sectional and divisive policies. Almeida implies this by her identification of the union's strategy with the "business unionism" of North America: "Summing up, it would appear that the ideal of this new current in the unions would be something close to the 'business unionism' of North America: combative, 'apolitical,' solidly implanted in the firm, and technically prepared to confront and resolve the general and specific problems of the workers it represents'' (1975:73). Such a union, it was argued, could only be of interest to workers in the modern sectors of industry (1975:71).[6] In effect, modern-sector workers were supposedly running the risk of acquiescence to the military regime by pursuing the lure of a strictly economistic and sectional trade union strategy based on the advantages of working in large, modern firms.

In practical terms, however, the direction taken by the São Bernardo union clearly depended on the feasibility of an economistic and sectional strategy. Almeida's assessment derives its plausibility from the assumptions about labor-market segmentation and modern-sector workers criticized in chapter three. A ''business union'' strategy could only work if, firstly, labor markets were sufficiently segmented for modern-sector workers to be in a strong bargaining position and, secondly, employers were willing to collude in the payment of high wages and the guarantee of privileged working conditions. These are the assumptions made, for example, by Foxley and Muñoz (1977:83-87). As a result of making similar assumptions about auto workers, Almeida is willing to emphasize just one aspect of the program of the São Bernardo Metalworkers, and to assume that it would develop in a divisive and sectional manner.[7]

In the light of the information and analysis presented in the previous two chapters, a radically different assessment of the effects of the union's strategy can be made. A union prepared, in Almeida's words, to ''confront and resolve the general and specific problems of workers'' would need to mount a major challenge to both the employers and the State. In relation to the

---

[6] A fuller discussion of union policies that might be found in the ''traditional'' and ''modern'' sectors will be undertaken in chapter nine. At this point the evaluation of union strategies will be made solely in terms of their implications for the immediate situation.

[7] The reader may feel that no one other than Almeida has written about Brazilian auto workers. In the early seventies she was virtually the only person writing about the current period, and given the clarity of the line of argument she presents and the widespread acceptance of the kind of position she argues, her work is taken as a basic source for a discussion of the Metalworkers of São Bernardo.

employers, the system of labor use and labor control in the auto plants was predicated upon the use of relatively highly paid unskilled and semiskilled workers whose replaceability and lack of security allowed the employers to impose a strict discipline. For the workers and for the union, the "general and specific problems" arose in large part from the employers' labor system and the more general framework of industrial relations which reinforced it. The union's demands for better wages, stability of employment, and, above all, union representation in the plants directly challenged the basis of the employers' system. As has been emphasized in chapter four, the payment of higher-than-average wages to auto workers in no way indicated a willingness on the part of firms either to stabilize labor or to lose control over wage costs. While the labor system was not immutable—and the type of changes that could be made to it will be discussed in chapter eight—there was no evidence in the mid-seventies that the auto employers would countenance such changes except under considerable duress.

The union's demands also ran directly counter to the State's policy for the working class. The union wanted the abolition or major reform of laws relating to restrictions on the right to strike, wage bargaining (the wages policy), and the stability of labor (the FGTS). It also sought to reduce or eliminate the Ministry of Labor's control over the unions and to replace the CLT by a restricted Labor Code. The union could not avoid confrontation with the State if it pursued its policies seriously. It sought to circumvent these laws in practice by developing direct relations with the employers, but the employers would look to the State for assistance if the union were successful.

A serious attempt to promote authentic trade unionism, linked to the rank and file and concerned with the immediate interests of the category, would have had to involve a direct and sustained confrontation with the employers and the State. Accommodation with the employers would not be possible until they had been forced to accept the need for change, and in the mid-seventies there was no sign of that. For this reason, the basis on which to evaluate the performance and policies of the union can only be the seriousness and effectiveness of its struggle to achieve the desired reforms. Almeida's evaluation, based on a segmented-labor-market model, leads her to mistake completely the impact of the union's demands, and also to group together two distinct currents within the trade union movement: "It is possible to affirm that the leadership of the Metalworkers of São Bernardo do Campo, *jointly with the metalworkers leadership in São Paulo*, constitutes the embryo of a new current within the Brazilian trade-union movement, formulating an organizational, political, and union project that is more in line with the interests of the 'modern' sector of factory wage-earners" (1975:71, emphasis added). The extent to which this was an erroneous conflation of two distinct union leaderships became evident later in the seventies, but the differences between the Metalworkers of São Bernardo and the Metalworkers of São Paulo (often referred to as the Metalworkers of the Capital) were evident in 1975. To understand why the Metalworkers of São Bernardo became a powerful force in the late seventies and broke with the immobilism that characterized trade unionism in Brazil after 1968, it is necessary to look at both the conditions in São Bernardo which favored "authentic" unionism and the efforts of its leadership to establish a network of representatives in the major plants.

Organizing Workers in the Auto Industry

The development of the Metalworkers of São Bernardo cannot be attributed solely to either the grievances of auto workers or the strategy pursued by the union's leadership. The conditions of auto workers were no worse, and probably better, than those of workers in many other sectors. Although it has been demonstrated that they did not form a privileged elite, it would be incorrect to see their militancy and organization in the seventies as stemming solely from the strength of their grievances. If deprivation and grievances were the cause of militancy, then the most militant workers would be found among the least-organized sections of the working class. At the same time, the development of the union cannot be taken as being an effect only of its leadership's decision to pursue a policy of "authentic trade unionism" based on the mobilization of the rank and file and opposition to State control. Although union leaderships do not merely reflect the categories of workers they represent, as Torre has argued (1974:18-19), they do develop in response to specific situations, and the success or failure of their strategies will depend on the terrain upon which they are put into practice. While the adoption of "authentic trade unionism" by the post-1969 leadership can be attributed to the ideology of that particular group and the mechanisms that allowed it to come to power, the impact of that strategy and its modification and development in the course of the seventies need to be explained. In this section, attention will be focused on the conditions in the large auto plants which facilitated union organization and the role played by the union's directors. The next section will turn to an examination of the equally important overall union and political situation in the mid-seventies.

THE CONCENTRATION OF THE AUTO INDUSTRY

As has been noted already, the large auto plants dominated industry in São Bernardo. The overall concentration of workers in large establishments in the metalworking category can be seen in table 2-6, which shows that in 1978 two thirds of all metalworkers in São Bernardo were employed in firms with more than 1,000 employees. In that same year 48 percent of the workers in the category were employed in just three large plants employing among them over 60,000 people—Volkswagen, Mercedes, and Ford.[8] Earlier in the decade, in 1972, these three plants had accounted for 54 percent of all metalworkers in the area. This concentration is in marked contrast to the situation in the city of São Paulo. Although the metalworking category was much larger in the Capital than in São Bernardo (see table 2-6), it was dispersed over a far greater area and number of firms. The largest forty-one firms employed only 21 percent of the category in 1976, and

[8] The source of this information is the same as for table 2-6. The reader is reminded that in the sixties Willys Overland was taken over by Ford, and the parent companies of Scania and Simca were bought by Saab and Chrysler respectively.

even the top 100 firms employed less than one third of all met-alworkers in the city. In all, there were over 10,000 metalworking establishments in São Paulo, and the major industrial zones were scattered about, making communication very difficult. Unlike São Paulo, then, the metalworking industry in São Bernardo was dom-inated by a few large firms, closely grouped together and pro-ducing similar products. Contact between the plants was facilitated by the hire-and-fire policies that forced workers to move between them. This concentration had two distinct impacts on the nature of trade union activity in the area.

In the first place, the proximity and importance of the major firms meant that the union's leadership was closely linked to the militants in them. The union's headquarters were close at hand, and the leadership was overwhelmingly drawn from the big plants. In the union elections of 1972, for example, both contesting slates of candidates drew heavily on the three biggest auto plants. Each slate had twenty-four names: fifteen members of the incumbent slate and fourteen of the opposition slate were drawn from the three plants. Given that only seven of the twenty-four elected officers worked full time in the union, the other seventeen formed part of the ruling group in the union but continued to work in the plants. In São Paulo, by contrast, the much greater dispersal of plants and workers made direct communication between union directors and most plants very difficult, and the size of the Capital meant that many factories were extremely remote from the union's headquarters in the center of the city. In this situation, the union could be much easier prey to clientalism and corruption.

A second effect of the concentration of workers in a few very large plants relates to their inclination to stay in their jobs and fight for improvements rather than leave and look for work else-where. It was noted in chapter four that toolroom workers in the auto industry preferred to force better wages by means of collec-tive action in 1973, whereas skilled workers in small firms often improved their situation by changing jobs. For unskilled and semi-skilled workers, the alternatives to work in the auto industry were much less attractive. Insofar as they were able to protest at all, these workers, too, were pushed into collective action. Individual protests about wages and working conditions were ruled out. The rotation-of-labor policy made such common forms of registering discontent as absenteeism, bad time-keeping, and substandard work extremely unattractive, because workers would immediately face the threat of the sack. At the same time, the size and bureaucratization of the large plants ruled out individual solutions for workers' problems. In Brazil, paternalism has been an important element of social control in the workplace, but in the auto industry the massification of labor in giant production complexes broke down paternalistic employment practices. The bureaucratic administration used in the large plants left little room for the development of personal ties between management and workers. Although the foremen had considerable power and discretion in the application of rules—such as in the selection of workers for dismissal and the allocation of overtime—they were constrained by promotion structures and the rotation-of-labor policy. These policies were unpopular with workers, and their effects led them to be very disillusioned about the benevolence and goodwill of the company. In both AF1 and AF2 it was noticeable that workers who had had experience of two or three auto plants took an extremely cynical view of their employers. The supervisory staff could favor some workers at the expense of others, but it was not possible to pursue a properly paternalistic policy which individualized treatment and matched submission with reward. Given the application of general rules, workers were forced to consider collective attempts to change them.[9]

The union's ability to take advantage of this potential for collective action was enhanced by two further factors. Firstly, the motor industry gave the union a large base from which to develop. Between 1972 and 1978 employment in the auto assembly sector in São Bernardo grew at an annual compound rate of 6.8 percent, which was less than the 8.3 percent for the metalworking sectors as a whole, but still high. Membership of the union must have

[9] There is an extensive literature on workers' militancy and strikes in large firms in general and the auto industry in particular. On the effects of bureaucratization, two extremely interesting studies are those of Gouldner (1954) and Crozier (1967).

grown even faster because the rate of unionization in auto firms increased in the period. This rapid rise in membership no doubt strengthened the union's hand. Secondly, the relatively high percentage of skilled workers in the auto industry gave the union a strong base from which to organize, because the skilled workers had more security than other workers, as well as better education and greater opportunities for discussion and movement around the plants.

The workers in the auto industry earned higher wages than workers in most other sectors, but they were far from satisfied with their situation in the mid-seventies. The "success" of the auto industry had largely been achieved at their expense, and yet rising productivity and profitability had been accompanied by the squeeze on wages between 1972 and 1974. Auto workers' expectations that they should benefit from the economic miracle were not met, and they were left with a sense of grievance and strong feelings that their employers could afford to provide better wages and working conditions. Given the nature of their employment they had strong incentives to channel their frustration into collective action. The aim of the union's leadership was to become the institution through which discontent and resistance could be expressed and organized.

THE UNION DIRECTORS

In the early seventies the problem for the union was to translate this desire into practice. In the previous chapter the constraints on the union and the limitations of the mechanisms open to it for the resolution of grievances were outlined. Brant has argued that even in the area of enforcement of legislation and the denouncing of bad working conditions the unions were largely ineffective when faced by the big employers (1980:41). To establish a union presence in the big plants was even more difficult. Whereas before 1966 the workers with a guarantee of stability of labor (after having worked for ten years in the same company) could form the nucleus of union activists, the substitution of the Lei da Estabilidade by the FGTS meant that even long-service workers had no protection against dismissal. In the seventies, the only workers with protection from dismissal "without due cause" were the elected union officers, who were granted provisional stability of employment from the date of nomination until one year after ceasing to hold office.[10] The full membership of the union executive was seven full-time directors, three members of the Inspection Committee, and two delegates to the Federation, and their twelve deputies. If all of these officers and deputies were considered to be covered by the protection of the CLT, then the Metalworkers of São Bernardo had seventeen directors employed in the plants enjoying stability of employment. Not only this, the law also stated that employees elected to union office had certain rights. An elected official cannot be "impeded in the exercise of his (her) functions, nor transferred to a place or duty which would make the performance of his (her) union functions difficult or impossible. . . . The time in which the employee absents himself (herself) from work in the performance of the functions referred to in this article will be considered as unpaid leave, unless agreed to by the firm or by contractual agreement" (CLT, Article 543). The Metalworkers of São Bernardo attempted to push this legal provision to the limit. They claimed the protection of the CLT for all the seventeen workers elected to union positions but still working in the plants, and where possible they attempted to use the officials as plant activists. Because the functions of the union and the officials were defined quite broadly in the CLT, there was adequate room for demanding, or merely assuming, a fairly wide brief.

Establishing the rights of union delegates,[11] and in particular their right to stop normal work to deal with grievances, was not easy. In AF2, the management was hostile, and according to one of the delegates: ". . . (AF2) thinks that we should do the same

[10] This meant that union officers could only be dismissed if they commited a serious fault that could be proved in the Labor Court (CLT, Article 543, para. 3).

[11] The term "delegate" was a common description in 1974-1975, but because the union had also demanded elected delegates in proportion to the numbers of workers in each plant, the union officials were referred to as *diretores de base* by 1979.

work as everyone else. It's one of the firms that fights against us most in the plant. I was almost sacked with due cause. I have to fight to be able to leave my section to see about problems—complaints about the washrooms, the food, safety, etc. In the past it was much easier. At one time you could spend the whole day on union work'' (plant director interviewed in 1975). In spite of these problems, the union directors were making some headway in AF2 by 1975. Workers were asked about their knowledge of the delegates, and their responses are presented in table 5-1. Inevitably, given the restrictions on their activities, knowledge about the union directors was greatest in those areas where they worked. The machine shop had had two delegates at one time, and the press shop had had delegates working in it. Although a majority of workers in the other areas either did not know about the delegates or could not say what they did, a significant minority could give some description of their activities. Generally, they referred to the recruitment of workers to the union, the distribution of notices about union meetings, and information about the union's campaigns. But some of the machinists also said that the union director could be used as a line of communication with management and as someone who might be able to resolve workers' problems of varying types: he could defend workers facing disciplinary charges and give advice about personal problems.

In some other plants the directors had won more freedom. In AF6, for example, management allowed the full-time union directors access to the plant, which AF2 did not permit, and the directors working in the plant had freedom to discuss matters with management at any time. In AF5 the directors had a considerable role, as this description by one who worked in the plant while a director between 1972 and 1978 illustrates: "Up to May 1978 I worked in the firm, and there was a lot of flexibility. When there was a problem I tried to resolve it. Even when there were things that would have given the firm the legal right to fire the worker without any right to compensation, I used to go along there, chat, start a dialogue and try to resolve the matter without the worker losing out. . . . When I used to go and talk to the management, I was well attended. He would deal with the matter at once. . . .

Trade Unionism

TABLE 5-1

"Is there a delegate or representative of the union in your section?"
If no, "Are there any in other sections?" If yes to either question,
"What does he do?": AF2 (percentages)

	Response		
Group	No/no response (first two questions)	Yes, but no information about what he does	Yes, and some description of what he does
Laborers, assembly line	67	13	20
Laborers, machine shop	33	20	47
Assemblers	38	31	31
Press operators	35	10	55
Machinists	7	17	76
Toolmakers	45	10	45

SOURCE: Interviews.

NOTE: The information in this table is not reliable. In all the interviews there was a problem of gaining the confidence of workers, who were far from convinced about who I was and why I was asking this question. In the case of this particular question, the union director quoted above told me shortly after the interviews had been completed that one worker had come to him, worried that he might be called for an interview. He asked what he should say if he was asked about the activities of the union director. The director answered, "Say, 'nothing.' "

They didn't force me to stay at my job. They gave me full freedom to deal with matters. I used to leave the section and the foreman never said a thing" (interview by Werner Würtele).

The importance that the union attached to plant organizing and the activities of the directors paid dividends. Even in 1975 the difference in union penetration between AF2 and AF1 was striking. In AF1, which lay in the area covered by the Metalworkers of São Paulo, very few workers had bothered to join the union. As can be seen from table 5-2, the rate of unionization for each category of worker interviewed in the plant was very low, and the union had clearly failed to capture potential members who had been in a union at some time previous to the interviews. More striking than this was the lack of any union presence in the plant. The few workers who were in the union related to it as individuals, paying their dues to the union offices in the city and not necessarily knowing who the other union members in the plant were. There

TABLE 5-2

Rates of current unionization and past membership: AF1 and AF2, January to March, 1975 (percentages)

	AF1		AF2	
Group	Union member	Not unionized, but has been in the past	Union member	Not unionized, but has been in the past
Laborers, assembly line	12	12	7	20
Laborers, machine shop	—	—	27	13
Assemblers	12	30	31	38
Press operators	—	—	20	30
Machinists	—	—	80	10
Toolroom workers[a]	16	36	40	10

SOURCE: Interviews.

[a] In AF2, toolmakers.

seemed to be very little attempt made to increase membership. In fact, one labor lawyer connected with the union alleged to me that it deliberately discouraged workers from joining because the dues new members paid were usually less than the cost of the services they used.[12] In AF2 the situation was very different. Rates of unionization for the semiskilled assemblers and the toolroom workers were higher, although there were still a considerable number of workers not in the union. The overall rate of unionization in the plant in December 1974 was 27 percent according to the union, and this estimate is matched by the figures in table 5-2.[13] By December 1978, just four years later, the union had increased its membership in the plant to 43 percent of the work force.

The contrast between São Paulo and São Bernardo was also evident in the relationship between the militants in the plants and

[12] For an analysis of the Metalworkers of São Paulo in this period, see Souza Martins, 1979.

[13] Taking the percentages in the table as averages for the different skill categories in the plant—that is, 40 percent for skilled workers, 25½ percent for semiskilled workers and 17 percent for unskilled workers—and taking the machinists as a special case, the estimated overall unionization rate is 30 percent for the hourly-paid workers, who constitute 90 percent of the total number of employees in the plant. This is very close to the union's figure of 27 percent.

144

the elected leadership in the two areas. In São Paulo the elected leaders were largely divorced from the plant-based militants. The latter made repeated attempts to organize an effective rank-and-file movement and an effective opposition to the leadership in the early seventies, but their attempts foundered because of the repression of the State and the enormous difficulties facing any group trying to organize such a large number of workers spread across a huge city. There was more or less permanent combat between these opposing groups within the union in the seventies. In São Bernardo, such a division did not occur to anything like the same extent. Although there were often groups in the plants which opposed leadership, its attempts to organize in the plants were sufficient to disarm the opposition and attract it into the union's leadership in the course of the decade. By 1978 the opposition was fully integrated into the leadership. Even in 1975 the opposition was weak, and the election in that year marked the beginning of a new phase in the union's development, when it countenanced a greater willingness to mobilize workers and force confrontation. At this election a former turner at Indústrias Villares, Luis Inácio da Silva, "Lula," became President after having been a full-time director for six years.

THE UNION'S PROBLEM

In many respects the union was potentially quite strong by 1975. Although it did not have a strong base in the plants—the directors were far too few to constitute an adequate network of militants—it had begun to gain the support of the plant militants. This meant that there were no challenges to its claim to be the legitimate representative of workers in the area. There was little internal opposition seeking to displace it, and neither the State nor the employers were concerned with making serious attempts to rival its claims. Both the employers and the State were content to hamper the union and contain its power, but not to challenge its claim to represent the workers.

The union's chief problem at this time was its continuing low level of penetration into the plants and its own lack of credibility when trying to oppose the State and the employers, who were in a strong position. Given a decade of repression, the workers in the plants were often unaware of what a union was, or could be, and they did not look toward it as their natural recourse when disputes arose. This was a serious problem for the union, but it should be stressed that it was a very different one from that discussed by analysts of the trade unions in the Populist period. Most studies of workers in the fifties and early sixties indicated that the workers either were not interested in unions or saw them exclusively as providers of welfare services. Rodrigues' study of AF2 in 1963 produced results that justified the following conclusion: "Initially it must be taken into account that, in line with other studies, *the majority of those interviewed see the union primarily as a welfare organization, whose job is to provide its members with medical resources and legal assistance*" (1970:106-107). These kinds of conclusions have been challenged for the period in which they were made because of the assumptions they contain about workers' attitudes and the derivation of such attitudes from general structural characteristics of the working class (theories of migration, rural values, etc.), but they can be questioned on more specific grounds. Rodrigues asked the workers in AF2 such questions as "Why are you a member of the union?" or "Why are you not a member of the union?" and "What are the advantages that the union really offers to the workers?" (1970:107-109). However, the answers to them tell us more about the objective state of the union than the workers' general attitudes toward trade unionism. If the union was weak on combativeness and strong on welfare services, then workers would join it because of the latter and rate it highly on that basis. This would not indicate what kind of union the workers would prefer.

In 1975, workers in AF2 were asked to say what they thought of the union and to give a reason for their evaluation. The results, presented in table 5-3, show that most workers who had an opinion rated the union as either "good on welfare" or "bad on wages." A substantial minority offered no opinion at all. This indicated a failure of the union to impress these workers with its effectiveness, but it does not necessarily mean that such workers would be unreceptive to the activities of the union, were it to become more

TABLE 5-3

Evaluation of the union and criteria used: AF2 (absolute numbers)

Group	The union is good on:				The union is bad on:			
	Welfare	No response	Strength[a]	Union O.K.[b]	Welfare	No response	Strength[a]	Don't know[c]
Laborers, assembly line	4	1	—	1	—	—	—	9
Laborers, machine shop[d]	4	—	3	1	—	1	1	6
Assemblers	4	1	1	1	—	1	1	7
Press operators	3	1	1	4	—	1	3	7
Machinists[e]	12	2	1	2	—	3	8	4
Toolmakers[e]	4	—	1	3	—	—	6	7

SOURCE: Interviews.

[a] The term "strength" refers to the ability of the union to obtain wage rises. Such comments as "it used to be better" and "it can't do anything" are included in this column.

[b] Workers who responded to the first question with "O.K." were not asked to give a reason.

[c] The workers not giving an evaluation of the union came disproportionately from nonunionized workers who had never been in a union.

[d] One machine-shop laborer said the union was good on both counts. Both replies have been tabulated.

[e] Two machinists and one toolmaker gave the dual response of "good on welfare and bad on wages."

effective. When workers were asked the question "What, in your opinion, should a good union do?," 80 percent or more of all the groups except the assembly-line laborers included wages as one of the areas with which a good union should concern itself. In a question that allowed multiple answers, only between one third and a half of the workers in the different groups mentioned the provision of welfare benefits. This indicates that they could envisage a union that was more active in the field of wage claims. Clearly, however, a great deal of work was still necessary to mobilize these workers and convince them that striking, for example, was both possible and effective. On the question of the right to strike, the workers' opinions are tabulated in table 5-4. Being such a sensitive issue, the responses have to be treated with some caution. They show that, overall, workers were rather evenly split on the question. The press-shop and machine-shop workers were generally in favor, while the assembly-line and toolroom workers were against. The question generated a certain amount of confusion because some workers distinguished between a stoppage (or down-tools) and a strike, and for others the term "strike" was linked to notions of pickets, armed police, arrests, and stonings. At the same time, a number of workers regarded themselves as the inevitable losers in conflicts with the firm. All these types of answers point to the conclusion that one successful, peaceful strike would probably be dramatically effective propaganda for the union, and although some workers would never be happy

TABLE 5-4
"Do you think that in order for the trade union to have more strength it is necessary for the government to allow it the right to strike?": AF2
(percentages)

Group	Yes	No	Don't know/ refusal to answer
Laborers, assembly line	20	67	13
Laborers, machine shop	54	39	7
Assemblers	44	56	—
Press operators	70	30	—
Machinists	60	37	3
Toolmakers	45	55	—

SOURCE: Interviews.

about it, there could well be enough workers in AF2 with the opposite view to make a strike action of some sort possible.[14]

The union had developed considerably in the difficult period for trade unions following Institutional Act Five in December 1968, but further progress depended crucially on being able to break out of the bonds described in chapter four. Unless the union could gain more freedom, any credibility it could obtain through its policies and its organizing efforts would be dissipated by its failure to achieve notable victories over the State and the employers. Instead of holding back from participation in plant struggles—as it had done in 1973-1974 because of the threat of action by the Ministry of Labor it needed to take them up and lead them. But this only became possible a little later in the decade when broader political transformations in Brazil produced a more propitious climate for activity.

The Impact of Liberalization

During the period of rapid economic growth and industrial expansion, from 1968 to 1974, political life in Brazil was narrowly circumscribed. After Institutional Act Five there was an immense centralization of power in the hands of the President. Congress was closed and then only reopened as a rubber stamp for presidential decisions, and other aspects of political life were kept in check by censorship of the media and repression by the armed forces. The government of President Médici embodied the ideal of the authoritarian, technocratic State, where rapid economic development could be fostered without the hindrance of political debate and rivalry. For some analysts the Médici government was the full expression of the model of economic development adopted

---

[14] At this point the reader may feel that all the analysis has been adjusted with the benefit of hindsight. In defense I can only say that when I wrote very similar things in 1976 and 1977 (see Humphrey, 1977), before the strikes started in May 1978, I sometimes wondered if I was engaged in an exercise in wishful thinking. The major error in the analysis made then was to fail to perceive the importance of skilled workers in the struggle. Taking such indications as table 5-4, I argued that they might well stand apart from the main struggles of auto workers. The reasons for the incorrectness of this evaluation will be discussed in chapter six.

in the fifties and sixties: the authoritarian State, closely tied to international capital and ruthless in its repression of the masses. In the early seventies this regime appeared to be very secure. It had managed to eliminate radical opposition, and the fruits of economic growth gave it solid support from the middle classes. However, this period of "exception" in terms of the suspension of normal congressional and judicial practices was also exceptional in the sense that it was a limited interlude in the history of the military regime. In spite of its apparent solidity in the early seventies, there were two factors which led to change. Firstly, as Cardoso has pointed out, the Brazilian military were never fully committed to an antidemocratic State, and even within the Médici power block there were supporters of the previous "liberal-conservative model of authoritarianism" (1980:176-177). Although the Médici government marginalized politicians and the political process to a much greater extent than had been the case during the presidencies of Castelo Branco and Costa e Silva, they were not completely eliminated. When Ernesto Geisel became President, attempts were made to reintroduce a controlled political process, starting with the congressional elections in 1974. The manipulations and frustrations of 1974-1978 reproduced the difficulties experienced between 1964 and 1968, when the military regime attempted to control and utilize elections, Congress, and political parties.

Secondly, the Brazilian economy was unable to sustain its rapid economic growth beyond 1974, partly because of the stresses imposed by rapid growth itself and partly because of the world recession in 1973-1974. Even if by international standards the Brazilian economy continued to expand fairly rapidly after 1974, there was a definite downturn. This imposed economic strains, which had effects of considerable importance. The slowdown in growth and the problems experienced with external debt forced the government to reconsider economic priorities (Munck, 1979:25). The issues raised in the reappraisal of economic strategy carried out in 1975-1976 included the role of the State in manufacturing, measures to encourage the development of basic capital-goods industries, the reorganization of priorities in the transport sector, and measures to promote (or force) the export of manufactured products. The State was forced to propose a shift in policy which was far from popular among its own supporters, and the dominant classes were deeply divided about what measures should be taken. At the same time, faced with the need for tough and controversial decisions, the government found itself without valid mechanisms for developing policy and establishing agreement even among those groups who supported it. In the terms of Souza and Lamounier (1980) the regime was suffering from "decisional paralysis" brought on by an excessive concentration of power. Although it had managed to maintain some mechanisms for the expression and temporary resolution of conflict within the military circle itself (Cardoso, 1980:177), much more open channels were needed for the debates arising out of the economic crisis. The "need for politics" was expressed by one São Paulo industrialist in 1977:

> In the golden years of the Brazilian economy, from 1972 to 1974 for example, the businessman did not talk about politics and was not interested in the subject, but not because there was or there was not censorship, but just because the economy was going well. . . . The lack of interest in political questions was seen not only in public pronouncements but also in private conversations among businessmen. Political discussion only started in effect when economic perspectives for the near future were lacking, which was the consequence of a very incipient and ill-defined economic, financial, and industrial policy. (Luis Eulálio Bueno Vidigal Filho, President of the Auto Component Employers Union and future President of the Federation of Industries, OESP, 4/9/1977)

The demand for more participation in decision-making inevitably involved both a criticism of government policy and a call for more open debate on economic issues. Pressure for this undoubtedly strengthened the position of the new President, General Geisel, who favored some limited and controlled liberalization.[15]

[15] The Brazilian political vocabulary at the time was *distensão* (relieving or relaxation) under Geisel, and *abertura* (opening) under Figueiredo.

151

The return to relatively free elections, the reinforcement of the party system, the relaxation of controls on the press, and the reining in of the security forces provided opportunities for the unions and the working class to express their discontent. Indeed, the expression of such discontent was so strong at times that the process of *distensão* itself went through a series of convulsions as hard-liners in the regime reacted to the successes of the opposition. Some of the events mentioned in previous chapters, such as the death of Manoel Fiel Filho in 1976 and the mass arrests of Volkswagen workers in 1975 arose from the uncertainties of this period of transition. There was a protracted process of establishing the boundaries of acceptable activity.

In spite of the uncertain progress of liberalization and in spite of the fact that freer debate and freer elections did not necessarily translate into freer union activity in this period, there were gains for the unions and workers. In the first place, there was a noticeable relaxation of the wage squeeze. As was seen in table 3-4, wages in the auto industry rose in 1975, in large part because of the much higher wage-increases granted by the government. Wage increases remained above the rate of inflation in 1976 and 1977 as well. Secondly, as Moisés has argued, political relaxation can lead to increased institutional space for the unions (1979:58). The limits of this space were uncertain, but generally unions were allowed to *say* a lot more, even if their activities were still constrained. In the case of the Metalworkers of São Bernardo, for example, the difference was seen in the official reaction to its congresses in 1974 and 1976. At the First Congress in 1974, business was conducted under some pressure in the presence of a strong and unfriendly police contingent. Two years later the Congress was attended by the head of the Regional Labor Office and the Governor of the State of São Paulo, both of whom were subjected to questioning during discussion (*Tribuna Metalúrgica*, October 1976). More generally, relaxation allowed a wider debate about the need for and desirability of union reform. Discussion of reforms and suggestions for them were not limited to the metalworking sectors, as is shown by the following list of demands presented to the government by the Presidents of the Confederations of Workers in Agriculture and Credit Establishments:

Revision of the trade union structure transplanted from Italian fascism and, therefore, inadequate for a democratic society. An end to the restriction of trade union freedom by factors such as the Trade Union Contribution and principally by the link between union organizations and the Ministry of Labor.

Participation of workers in the fixing of wage increases. Permission for free and direct bargaining between workers and employers, which current legislation impedes in practice. That official wage settlements be set as minima, rather than as the only possible level. Reformulation of the FGTS, ''the real AI-5 [Institutional Act Five] of the workers.'' Liberalization of the right to strike as the worker's ''final recourse.'' (*Movimento*, 24/10/1977)

Discussion about union reform was not confined to unionists. The government began its own review of labor legislation, and in 1977 industrialists, too, began to consider such matters as the right to strike and greater freedom for the unions.

However, discussion alone does not lead to great transformations, and perhaps the most decisive advance was seen in 1977 with the campaign over the ''wage recovery'' (*reposição salarial*). In 1973 and 1974, the Inter-Trade Union Research and Statistical Department (DIEESE) in São Paulo had claimed that government calculations of inflation in 1973 and 1974 had been unrealistically low, and that this had meant wage increases below the rate of inflation. (An expression of this position was quoted at the beginning of this chapter.) In 1977, the government responded to inquiries from the International Monetary Fund about the rate of inflation in the period by admitting that inflation in 1973 had been 26 percent, not 14 percent as originally claimed. This was partly a government maneuver to criticize the previous administration and cast doubt upon its record of success, but in the new climate of liberalization the unions quickly took up the matter with vigor. DIEESE carefully entangled the issue of inflation rates in 1973-

1974 with the correct application of the wages policy. By demanding higher allowances for improvements in productivity than the government had calculated and providing a cumulative figure for the two years together, DIEESE calculated the wage increase necessary to compensate for the misapplication of the wages policy in 1973-1974 as being 34 percent.[16] The government argued that the "mistake" had been compensated by the wages-policy settlements in 1975-1977, but the unions were not satisfied. Although it is true to say that wages in the auto industry, at least, rose by 4 percent between 1972 and 1977 (see table 3-4), for workers in the industry 4 percent was little compensation for the increases in productivity registered in the same period.

As the unions attempted to mount a public campaign in support of the 34 percent demand, the government "maintained a certain tolerance," according to Moisés (1979:51). The unions were allowed to talk and declaim, but they did not attempt to do much more than this. On the one hand they did not have the organization to mount a campaign of mobilization, and, on the other, they were wary of the State's tolerance, unsure of how far it would extend. But the Metalworkers of São Bernardo were willing to mount a more effective campaign, and because of their previous history of organization they were able to do so. In addition to the use of the union directors in the plants, the union had patiently pursued a policy of attempting to negotiate with the major employers, and some limited successes had been achieved. In 1975 Ford negotiated with it over changes in medical insurance, and in 1977 the same firm attempted to negotiate a four-day working week as an alternative to redundancies. In 1977, Saab-Scania negotiated the introduction of a "trade union commission" of ten workers, who were guaranteed provisional stability of employment. But it was the campaign over the wage recovery that provided the impetus to move to a new level of mobilization. The union's President at the time, Lula, has provided a description:

> I remember from the beginning that we were discredited by our fellow union leaders. They were saying that we were going to

[16] The calculations can be found in table 3-5.

pull a rabbit out a hat and just simply go blah-dah-blah, which wouldn't get anywhere. We talked with the workers in meetings and through the union's paper and said that the most important thing was not the 34 percent, but rather to get rid of what had caused the theft in 1973 and 1974—the lack of trade union freedom. So, by means of the struggle over the *reposição* we had a way of openly combatting the wages policy and the trade union structure and of making workers aware of the issue. (Interview, *Cara a Cara*, 1978:55)

In September 1977, 5,000 workers in São Bernardo met and demanded that a 34 percent rise be given in compensation for what should have been conceded in 1973 and 1974. The meeting decided that negotiations with the employers (not the State) should be started. As well as supporting the dissemination of information and propaganda for the campaign, the meeting voted in favor of creating groups of workers in factories to help the mobilization, and it further decided to consider strike action at a future date if appropriate (*Movimento*, 24/10/1977, and JB 3/9/1977). What for many unions was a campaign restricted to declarations and appeals to the government was for the Metalworkers of São Bernardo a golden opportunity to develop a mass awareness of the problem and further stimulate the union's presence in the plants. The message to workers was that using the legal channels provided by the State would not resolve their problems: "It was a campaign of practically five months, showing the worker that he could only recoup this money if he got tough. And when we workers use this language of 'getting tough,' we don't mean start fighting; it simply means stopping the machines" (Lula, interview, Cadernos do Presente, 1978:73). The solution, according to the union, was in the factory at the machine.

The impetus provided by the *reposição* campaign was taken forward by the union's refusal to participate in the 1978 wage negotiations. It was argued in chapter four that the annual negotiations provided no platform for the unions to engage in serious discussions with the employers. The Metalworkers of São Bernardo had tried to use them for propaganda purposes. From 1973

to 1976 the union attempted to withdraw from the collective negotiations with the Metalworkers of the Interior[17] so that it could
present its own list of demands without having to have them
accepted by the other unions and the Metalworkers Federation of
São Paulo, which were unsympathetic to the aims of the São
Bernardo union. It secured the right to do this in 1976, and in
that year and the following year an extensive series of demands
was put to union meetings for approval, discussed, and then taken
to the "negotiations" at the Regional Labor Office. While the
union did not hope to gain concessions on important issues, it
tried to use the negotiations as a way of making propaganda points,
drawing workers into the union's debates and raising consciousness about what needed to be changed.

In 1977 the union presented thirty-two demands to an assembly
of members for discussion, including the following eight items:

1. No rise in the cost of fringe benefits in the life of the contract.
2. An eight-hour day with two hours overtime maximum, except when twelve-hour shifts are absolutely necessary.
3. A "substitute clause" such that workers hired to take the
   place of dismissed workers cannot be taken on at a lower
   rate.
4. Priority to workers dismissed during a crisis period when
   the firm starts rehiring.
5. Formalization and regulation of disciplinary procedures.
6. Inclusion of habitual overtime in the calculations for holiday
   pay, the thirteenth-month bonus, dismissal compensation
   (FGTS), and rest days.
7. Provision of day-care facilities on factory premises or within
   one kilometer in firms of more than fifteen female employees
   aged sixteen or over.
8. The right for the union to have factory delegates in all firms,
   the number to be proportional to the size of firm, and pro-

[17] The unions in the city of São Paulo, Osasco, and Guarulhos negotiate in
November. The other thirty-or-so metalworking unions, referred to as the Metalworkers of the Interior, negotiate in April.

tection against dismissal for such delegates. (*Tribuna Metalúrgica*, February 1977)

These demands were directly concerned with the immediate problems confronting workers in the area, and the background to them has been analyzed in chapters three and four. They encapsulate the issues which the union had been unable to resolve by other means, such as direct negotiations or attempts to enforce the law. In this sense the list of demands is a guide to the union's impotence.

The strategy of using the annual wage negotiations for propaganda purposes had one serious drawback. It confirmed the union's lack of power, because in the Labor Court there was no prospect of winning any concessions from the employers. The *dissídio coletivo* took the form of arbitration, not negotiation, and the union ran the risk of giving it prestige by taking it seriously.[18] As has been argued, the union's main problem was a lack of credibility among workers, and particularly among militants in the plants, because of its inability to resolve their problems. To cope with this problem the union adopted a very different stance during the runup to the 1978 *dissídio*. Taking advantage of the new political climate, the union decided on a strategy of nonparticipation, which would have been extremely incautious earlier in the decade. Instead of struggling within a system designed to frustrate its ambitions, the union decided to expose the annual settlement as a farce—a pantomime in which the outcome was fixed before the start. As the union President, Lula, put it:

This process [of raising workers' consciousness] had another phase, which I think was the really crucial point, when the union decided to show the metalworkers of São Bernardo and Diadema that everything that had been done up to then by way

[18] The term *dissídio coletivo* was translated as "wage decision" in *Latin American Perspectives* (1979:92), which is misleading. The *dissídio* is a particular form in which negotiations take place, and the translators confuse this form with the question of how specific levels of wage increase are determined. The *dissídio* should be contrasted with the "collective contract," which would not be subject to arbitration by the Labor Courts.

of the wages campaign had been a farce. . . . We tried to show the worker that it did not matter very much if he took part in union assemblies about wages . . . because the attendance at assemblies would have little influence on the determination of the figure decreed by the government. (Interview, História Imediata, 1978:73)

The message to workers was that higher wages would have to be obtained by more direct means in the short term, and by changes in the whole system in the long term. In spite of its nonparticipation in the *dissídio*, the union got the same rise as the other unions.

By means of the *reposição* campaign and the refusal to participate in the 1978 negotiations, the union was able to establish stronger links with workers in the plants. Its message was clearly that unless workers took action in the plants their problems would not be resolved. As a result of its earlier history of plant organization and commitment to active unionism, the Metalworkers of São Bernardo was better equipped than most other unions to take advantage of the liberalization that occurred in the mid-seventies. By doing so, the union increased its own credibility and managed to draw to it the majority of the militants. When the union elections came round early in 1978 the president put forward a slate which incorporated the militants active in the *reposição* campaign (Frederico, 1979:147), and his prestige was so great that no one opposed him. The union was preparing for a period of further mobilization.

In spite of the successes of 1977-1978, the union was still far from effectively mobilizing and representing the 125,000 metalworkers in the area. Early in 1978, when the satirical weekly *Pasquim* asked 112 workers at the gates of four factories in São Bernardo just who Lula was, only one quarter could give the correct answer (*Pasquim*, 24/3/1978). However, the union had a nucleus of strength in the major plants, and it has been argued that in AF2, at least, the situation could have been transformed by one successful strike. After ten years without major strikes and with the labor movement still uncertain as to just how far the liberalization of political life would extend, the strike was unknown territory; but the leadership in São Bernardo was thinking about this course of action, as this interview with Lula, published in March, indicates:

> "But you can't bring the factories to a halt."
> "We can't to some extent. Let's wait a little longer to see if we can or can't. I don't see any other way. Talk to the bosses? We've already talked. Talk to the authorities? We've already talked. No one cares about the worker. . . . We've given everything for the good of Brazil. And what do we get in return? Nothing. So let's just wait a little bit. The time is coming, I feel." (Interview, *Pasquim*, 24/3/1978)

In these circumstances the fact that in May 1978 a stoppage by workers in the Saab-Scania plant in São Bernardo quickly spread to other major auto plants and then to the rest of the metalworkers in the southern São Paulo industrial belt is hardly surprising.

6

The Auto Workers Take On
the Employers: 1978

THE STOPPAGES IN THE AUTO INDUSTRY in May 1978 opened up
a new period for the working class in Brazil. After ten years of
tight control, new parameters were established for workers and
trade unions. Suddenly strikes became acceptable, and the Metalworkers in São Bernardo rose to national prominence. The main
focus of the analysis in this chapter remains the auto industry,
and it will be shown how the stoppages and their aftermath related
to material conditions in the workplace. This approach has the
merit of firmly grounding the events of the time in their objective
context, but it also has two drawbacks. Firstly, the development
of the Brazilian labor movement in this period involved more than
the Metalworkers of São Bernardo, even though this union played
a leading role. The account presented here is limited by its concentration on the workers in one sector at the expense of the
broader but less defined canvas of the labor movement as a whole.
This restriction of scope inevitably obscures understanding of the
general framework in which the union in São Bernardo was operating. Secondly, the strategy of taking the workplace and the
union as a point of departure entails a corresponding weakness in
discussing the role of the Church and political movements within
the labor movement.[1] At the time of the surveys of the plants in
1975, study in these areas would have been difficult and unre-
warding, and it has not been possible to supplement this deficiency
at a later stage. Instead, the analysis presented in this and the

[1] For some reference to the role of the Church and political groups in the period
before the strikes, see Moisés (1979:62-65). Little other material is available in
English, but in Portuguese there are some interesting collections of material and
opinions on the strike movement in 1978. See for example Cadernos do Presente,
1978; História Imediata, 1978; and the journal *Cara a Cara*, 1(2), 1978.

following chapter is focused on the auto industry, with particular emphasis being placed on union and management strategies in the new situation and the question of control in the plants.

The May Strikes

The strike started from a spontaneous decision by the day-shift workers in the toolroom. The night shift was leaving when the day shift entered and did not start up the machines. No one started working. Not the slightest noise was heard in the factory. It was seven in the morning on May 12. A Friday. (A worker at Saab-Scania interviewed in História Imediata, 1978)

In one sense the strike was spontaneous. It happened at a certain time and in a certain factory, and neither could have been predicted exactly. But it was not, in retrospect at least, a big surprise. The first major stoppage in Brazilian industry for a decade started in the auto industry, in a factory where the Metalworkers of São Bernardo had negotiated the setting up of a ten-person trade union committee in the previous year, and in the toolroom, where the workers were most able to resist management authority. The timing was also unsurprising. In the previous eight months the union had mounted a campaign over the *reposição* and refused to participate in the annual wage negotiations. On May 10 the workers received the first wage packet to include the annual wage increase decreed in April. The increase was 39 percent on top of the April 1977 wage, which meant an effective rise from March to April 1978 of only 20 percent, because the workers had already received rises of 10 and 5 percent earlier in the year in anticipation of the settlement. These were discounted from the annual rise. The development of the strike, too, took not unexpected lines. Instead of being restricted to one section of the factory, it spread in the new liberal climate to the whole of the Scania plant, with the workers standing by their machines refusing to work. After Scania, the stoppages spread to other auto plants—Mercedes, Ford, Volkswagen, and Chrysler—and then to other metalworking plants in the southern industrial belt. Within the first two weeks over 45,000 workers had downed tools in pursuit of wage rises, and within a month the weekly magazine *Movimento* had compiled a list of sixty-nine firms in Greater São Paulo in which stoppages had taken place (*Movimento*, 12/6/1978). The pent up grievances of workers and the sudden demonstration that striking was both possible and effective quickly created a mass movement that marked the beginning of a period of considerable conflict.

In most factories the skilled workers made the first move, although in AF2, significantly enough, the machine shop was the first to stop work. The skilled workers were not immune to the problems of workers in the auto industry—as was shown in chapters three and four—and they provided the first basis for opposition to the employers. For them striking was less hazardous, as a skilled worker in Volkswagen commented: "We fight for the others, and we even understand why it takes time for them to join us. It is difficult for the head of a family earning Cr$4,000 [approximately U.S. $200 per month] to take a decision to stop work. He is frightened, and he has a right to be" (quoted in *Veja*, 31/5/1978). In the freer conditions in 1978 it was easier to spread the stoppages from the skilled areas to the other parts of the plants. In AF2, as in other plants, the area most under the control of management, the assembly line, was the last to stop work. Although the union did not give the order to stop, it was a powerful influence, and it provided a focus for the workers. The stoppage in Saab-Scania was disciplined and total. In Ford, which stopped the following Monday, the mass of workers were very determined and the few newer workers (still in the three-month trial period) who resumed work were quickly dealt with by the strikers. In Mercedes, and later in Chrysler, the story was the same. The workers went on strike, but they reported for work each day, taking the works bus, eating in the canteen, and in some cases even staying in the factory during the normal overtime period. But they did no work.[2]

[2] The information in this chapter is collected from three sources: accounts by workers involved and people in the labor movement; accounts by employers and industrialists; and published accounts and interviews, both at the time and later. A particularly useful source has been the interviews published in História Imediata (1978) along with the reports in the June 1978 edition of *Tribuna Metalúrgica*.

In spite of the buildup to the strike, it was still a surprise to everyone when it finally happened. It was only in retrospect that even union leaders could reflect on the development of an atmosphere conducive to the idea of a strike. Striking was still a great unknown: no one knew what the government or the employers would do when the factories came to a standstill for the first time in a decade. In this situation, it was reasonable for management either to have ignored what signs there were in advance or simply to have assumed that in spite of the changing situation nothing would happen in the end. Taken by surprise, its response was based on what it had done in the past. After fifteen years of largely untroubled industrial relations, there were no procedures or structures to deal with the new situation. As was seen in chapter four, management had had no need for direct communication with the workers as a collective body, and even when stoppages had occurred earlier in the seventies a tough line had often been enough to get production going again. Therefore, management's initial step was to instruct the foremen to get the men back to work. When this failed, and when management realized that it was failing, the next step was to announce that there would be no negotiation until work had been resumed. Then it would try more intimidation.

In Saab-Scania the management's response was to refuse to consider the workers' demand for a 20 percent wage rise until after a return to work. It put pressure on the union director working in the plant to call for a return and asked the President of the union to do the same. When this failed, and when the intervening weekend failed to bring the stoppage to an end, management offered to consider the workers' demands provided that they work in the meantime, and give an answer by the following Friday (again at the weekend, in the hope of demobilizing the stoppage). The firm offered 6½ percent, and the combination of this small rise, renewed pressure on workers, and the resumption of work in the intervening period were enough to divide the work force in the plant. Some sections accepted the offer and started work again while others did not, and the uncertainties were sufficient to obtain a full resumption. In the case of Ford, one of the union's strongholds, the stoppage was more disciplined and effective. It started on the Monday after the initial stoppage in Scania, and management at first met it with a refusal to negotiate. Then, as at Scania, the firm requested a return to work and promised that the workers' demands would be considered. When this was ignored, the foremen started to threaten workers with dismissal, while the activists argued that it was impossible for the firm to sack everyone. On the fourth day of the stoppage, management stepped up the pressure, declaring that the strike was illegal and instructing the foremen to start up the machines. But when even this failed to break the strike, it was forced to start negotiation. In contrast to the situation in Scania, the Ford workers refused to return to work while the negotiations took place, and it was only on the following Monday, after a full week on strike, that they agreed to a return while the company considered the possibility of a 15 percent rise.

At this time there were also stoppages in Chrysler and Mercedes, although they were more limited. The only major auto company in São Bernardo that managed to contain the stoppages and prevent a complete halt to production was Volkswagen. Its factory is so big, over 30,000 workers, that it is hardly a single factory at all. There are over 2,000 toolroom workers, concentrated in a number of large and small toolrooms, and communication is difficult within the plant. The toolroom stopped on a Monday, returned to work pending an offer at the end of a week, and then went out on strike the following Friday. But the union had only made a limited penetration, mainly among skilled workers, and it proved impossible to bring the main production areas to a halt except for very short periods. When the stoppage in the toolroom resumed, the firm isolated the toolroom workers and the union representatives. The internal telephones were cut and armed security personnel were placed at the entrances to the main production areas and the toolrooms. Then the firm ordered workers not willing to start their machines to go home. When the toolroom workers entered the plant on the following Monday and still left the machines silent, even though they had promised to work so that they could enter the plant, the company decided to start dismissing workers "with due cause,'' and picked out twenty-eight workers as an initial step. The union representatives, whose own movements had been severely restricted by the security personnel, were then faced with the task of negotiating the return of the twenty-eight. It was finally agreed that the twenty-eight should be readmitted, and the firm would offer whatever increase was negotiated generally in São Bernardo. Even after this agreement, there were some continued protests in the plant, but the main resistance ceased.

In Volkswagen more than in the other auto plants, the management took a tough line, but even here they were forced to concede. Not only had the managements been taken by surprise, but they had also been left without the traditional support of the State. The government confined its participation to stressing to the auto firms (and to other employers when affected) that wage concessions could not be passed on in the form of higher prices. Faced with a series of protests and the threat of further problems, the auto employers decided to try and resolve the issue by making an agreement with the union that would apply to all auto workers in São Bernardo. At the beginning of the stoppages the union had restricted its formal role to that of intermediary between specific firms and specific groups of workers, but it later took on the role of negotiator, which led to the first collective contract in the Brazilian auto industry. The agreement provided for two rises of 5½ percent—one immediately and one in October 1978—and three further rises which would be discounted from the April 1979 wage settlement. These would be 4½ percent each. The deal was a good one for the workers in most plants, who had either negotiated rises of 6½ percent overall or no specific rise at all, although it was not so good for the Ford workers, who thought that the firm had promised them 15 percent, only to find that the figure was 11 percent in total.

The stoppages did not cost the employers a great deal in monetary terms. The losses in production were unfortunate at a time when the market was quite competitive, but neither the lost production nor the limited increases in wages were a serious threat to profitability in a year that saw a big rise in auto production and more than one million vehicles produced for the first time. The loss to the employers was more by way of ending a period of "normality" in the plants. They had been forced to negotiate a collective contract directly with the union. The workers had "stopped the machines and negotiated" as the union had been encouraging them to do in the previous year, and the result had been a success. Taken by surprise and quite unprepared, the employers had been forced to concede a principle and a precedent that was more important than money. Moreover, there was every likelihood that the situation would get worse in the following months. The first steps taken by the auto workers of São Bernardo led to many other stoppages.

The next areas to be affected by stoppages were other metal-working sectors in the southern industrial belt. Phillips, General Electric, Pirelli, Brastemp, and many others were forced to concede a 10 percent wage rise or more as workers clocked into the plants and refused to work. Quickly the strike spread from the main concentrations in São Bernardo (twenty-four firms affected according to *Movimento* 12/6/1978) and Santo André (twenty-three firms) to São Caetano (where the workers received virtually no support from the union), Osasco, and to the city of São Paulo itself. In some plants the workers stood at their machines, while in others they merely entered the factory. In some places the union was called in to represent the workers, while in others the union was so distrusted that it was not used. Where the workers did not see the union as a valid mediator, they formed factory committees and unofficial groups. Management sometimes did not know with whom to negotiate even when they could predict trouble. For example, in one large auto components firm in São Paulo, the managers were well aware that there would be a stoppage, but because of the atrophy of channels of communication they were unable to find legitimate workers' representatives. As one senior manager put it, they could hardly go to the shop floor and say "Would you like a rise?" They had to wait for the machines to stop, and then negotiate with fifty workers who came as a deputation. The rise was conceded and production resumed.

In the first four months of the strike movement it is estimated that 280,000 workers in over 250 firms stopped work, and that the number of workers affected directly or indirectly by the wage settlements resulting from these stoppages exceeded one million (*Veja*, 20/9/1978). From the dynamic industries and the industrial centers the strike movement spread. There were strikes in the schools, hospitals, banks, and other public-service sectors as the grievances of more than a decade were unleashed. Even the workers in the pottery industry in the small city of Itú, in the Interior of the State of São Paulo, went on strike in August, and 2,000 workers in twenty-seven firms stayed out for over two weeks until the Pottery Union of the State of São Paulo negotiated a 15 percent rise for all its workers (OESP, 11/8/1978). That the strike wave should arrive in Itú was an indication that the political and union situation had indeed changed: henceforth all employers would have to come to terms with a rather different environment.

Responding to the New Situation

Management in the auto industry was not prepared for the strikes in May 1978. Nor was it used to the idea of bargaining. Even if some senior executives were perhaps more inclined to accept the change, the general readiness and the management structures necessary to deal with the new situation were lacking. In the hurried negotiations that produced the settlement for the auto industry, management made a number of mistakes, as it later acknowledged.[3] Firstly, allowing the workers to remain in the factories without working was considered an error because it gave them the opportunity to communicate with ease and allowed the strike to remain low key. Forcing workers out into the street would have been much more serious for the strikers. Secondly, once the negotiations started, management allowed the union to negotiate on behalf of white-collar workers, even though they had not been involved in the strike. For management it would have been better to make a deal with the manual workers and then extend it to the white-collar workers by its own decision. Thirdly, and worst of

[3] These mistakes were part of an evaluation of the events by one of the senior Industrial Relations managers in AF2.

all from management's point of view, it agreed to pay the workers for the days of the stoppages. Looking back on the events of May, top managers could only feel that they had been badly outmaneuvered.

If lack of preparation was the diagnosis, then clearly management had to prepare for the next round of negotiations. But prepare for what exactly? The first remedial steps were clear enough. In the factories it was necessary to stop giving the union free rein to represent the workers and to start trying to attract them back to management. The labor system described in chapters three and four presented the union with many opportunities to defend workers and appear as their one legitimate representative, and Industrial Relations personnel quickly realized that in the new situation this merely strengthened the union. Therefore, in a number of the big auto plants management started to try and resolve small problems before they were taken up by the union. Foremen were given courses on aspects of their job that had been neglected up to that time, such as listening to the problems of workers. Staff from Industrial Relations departments were put onto the shop floor to detect problems and try to resolve them. However, given that the overall system remained fully intact, these changes in the plants could be regarded as "full control and authority with a human face," designed more to weaken the union than to resolve problems. At the level of the industry as a whole, the first result of the strikes was for management to strengthen its coordination through the auto assembly employers' union, SINFAVEA, so that a united front could be worked out and maintained in future negotiations. A negotiating committee and a "logistic support" committee were set up. Having been badly caught out once, management laid plans to prevent the same thing happening again.

These immediate adjustments could not provide a long-term strategy for the employers. They had to choose between two basic options. The first of these was to accept that there was no long-term viability in the system of industrial relations that had served them so well for more than a decade and that the union would inevitably grow in strength as the process of democratization proceeded. Therefore, it could be argued, changes would have to be made. Faced with the possibility of increasing union strength and the declining effectiveness of the systems of control employed in the past, it could be better to try and integrate the union into a stable system of industrial relations and to encourage the tendencies toward "business unionism" on the North American pattern that some researchers had discerned within the Metalworkers of São Bernardo. The second option was to dig in and try to weaken the union. This could be seen as either a strategy that looked for a renewal of State support or an attempt to forestall the inevitable changes in industrial relations until such time as they could be carried out on terms more favorable to the employers. Both options could be supported on grounds of political conviction—the desirability or undesirability of democratization and the union liberalization that would probably accompany it—or merely on purely pragmatic grounds—the viability of different industrial-relations systems in different political contexts. Support for both options was found in management circles, and within the auto industry both currents of opinion were represented. The great uncertainty about both the intentions of the government and the real strength of the Metalworkers of São Bernardo left ample margin for disagreement. A full discussion of the employers' attitudes will be left until chapter eight, and at this point attention will be concentrated on the short-term dynamic of industrial relations in 1978. Given that two basic courses were open to the auto employers—acceptance of a greater role for the union or continued resistance to it—it is necessary to explain why the first of these options was, to some extent, feasible, but at the same time unrealizable in the short term.

The "co-option" strategy can be seen as an attempt to develop a type of "business unionism," which if not exactly following the North American (and perhaps the German) model, would provide the same advantages for management. The reasoning behind the preference for such a system was that if unions were to become a fact of industrial life in Brazil as a result of the democratization program, then it would be preferable to have a union which would seek economic goals and not subordinate its activities to wider political aims, which would adopt a responsible position during negotiations that recognized the need for management to manage and the importance of maintaining profitability, and which would be able to control the rank and file and force it to adhere to agreed procedures. This kind of orderly unionism was contrasted in the management mind with the dual threat of a union leadership that sought political ends and a rank and file that accepted no discipline or procedures. Both of these specters threaten the predictability of workers' activities and the possibility of resolving disputes through orderly negotiations at the firm or industry level. If either type of threat materializes, management is no longer fully in control. If the "business union" system operates, on the other hand, then management is in control, even when forced to make concessions. It can be argued that in the auto industry, control and predictability at the point of production is more important to management than wages.[4] Hard bargaining once a year (or even less frequently), confined mainly to questions of wages and the minimum conditions of employment stability and work regimes, would be far preferable to irregular stoppages, sabotage, and political conflicts. Given that the strength of the Metalworkers of São Bernardo was greatest in the auto industry, the auto employers might have been the first to recognize the need for coming to terms with the union's new power and seeking a new relationship.

For some managers, the characteristics outlined in the previous paragraph defined the ideal union—willing to live with capitalism and strong enough to avoid anarchy on the shop floor. They saw the union as an inherently moderating force essential for the running of a large plant (at least if the workers were free to organize). In Brazil as a whole there were some reasons for seeing the Metalworkers of São Bernardo taking on this kind of role with more ease than other unions. Firstly, the union had shown a fairly consistent suspicion of politicians and had often criticized the political orientation of the Populist unions. Instead it had empha-

---

[4] This does not imply that wage levels are not important in the motor industry. The evidence from chapters three and four suggests the contrary. However, it was also shown that control over the workers was a vital factor, and this could be worth concessions on wages.

sized issues of direct relevance to workers in the plants. Secondly, there was no doubt that the union was becoming an authentic representative of the workers in the category, who accepted its leadership. In a period of rising class struggle and workers' mobilization, some less representative unions had found themselves bypassed by the rank and file. This left management with the problem of not being sure with whom to negotiate. One of the features of the negotiations in São Bernardo had been their orderliness, even though in the initial stage the union had acted only as the mediator between workers and employers. Management must have been particularly impressed by the performance of the union at Kubota-Tekko after the May strikes. When the workers went out on strike for a further rise after the general agreement for the auto industry had been signed, the union made it clear that a settlement had been signed and that they should go back to work. Thirdly, the union appeared to be a reasonable negotiator. Its demands in May had been tolerable and a settlement had been reached that was above the 6½ percent offered in Scania but below the 20 percent originally claimed. The negotiations had been fairly straightforward, with none of the political maneuvering that management associated with some of the more conservative leaders such as the Presidents of the São Paulo Metalworkers and the Federation of Metalworkers.

For these reasons, the development of a new relation with the unions appeared to have more chance of success in the auto industry than in other sectors, but in practice the situation was more complicated. Important sections of capital were opposed to any concessions being made, and this group included some of the auto firms. Even some firms more favorably disposed to a conciliatory line were worried about making concessions and then finding themselves put in the role of the "target" firm for the union. More important, however, was the degree of change that would be necessary to make possible the transition from the old system to the new. The model for such a change is clearly Henry Ford's reluctant recognition of the United Auto Workers as the legitimate representative of all Ford workers. In 1941, in the face of massive resistance by the workers, Ford recognized the union, stopped trying to eliminate it physically from the plants, gave it full bargaining rights, and introduced the union shop. The UAW's former greatest enemy decided that it should build up a working relationship with it, and the results were not disastrous for the company. As *Business Week* saw it: "A third benefit which Ford apparently expects is of a negative variety—a freedom from the labor troubles which beset companies like all the other auto manufacturers, not operating under an agreement which makes union membership compulsory. In positive terms, *it is 'union protection,' a kind of plant policing by the union for the company*" (quoted in Beynon, 1973:38, emphasis added). But the U.S.A. in the thirties was not the same as Brazil in the seventies. Although it has been argued that there were similarities in the labor systems, the general political and union situations were very different. Henry Ford decided to go with the tide and stop opposing the New Deal, which had looked for cooperative arrangements with the unions. In Brazil in 1978, such a move toward union recognition would have meant a complete break with the established trade union system and the forms of industrial relations laid down by the State. This would have created major conflicts within the Employers Federation as well as serious political problems.[5]

From the union's point of view, any transfer to a new relationship needed to involve a lot more than just direct negotiations over pay. The union had shown that by stopping the machines it was possible to force negotiations with the employers, and in May 1978 it had won an 11 percent rise. But 11 percent was not very much compared with the 34 percent demanded in the *reposição* campaign, and all the other issues outlined in chapters three, four, and five remained unresolved. The union wanted the elimination of State control, not merely the temporary suspension of some of its features. Most of all it wanted delegates in the plants so that it could increase its rank-and-file organizing. Finally, the union was learning rapidly about the need for trade union unity and political reform. The issue of democratization had been part of

[5] This may imply that the Fordist strategy will be adopted at a later stage in the democratization process, a possibility that will be discussed in chapters seven and eight.

the union's stated platform in 1977, but it became linked to other political demands in the latter half of 1978, such as amnesty for political prisoners, agrarian reform, the Constituent Assembly, and controls on the multinationals (*Tribuna Metalúrgica*, September 1978). At its Third Congress the union also emphasized the importance of unity and the preservation of the "single union" (*sindicato único*) for each category of workers.[6] By the end of 1978 the Metalworkers of São Bernardo were at the head of an increasingly influential current of "authentic" union leaders, and their activities in São Bernardo had an impact on the labor movement as a whole and on the national political situation. There was little chance of the auto industry either buying peace through recognition or being allowed to change the system in São Bernardo when it would so obviously provide the precedent for changes elsewhere. In this situation, even those firms inclined to favor a more cooperative relation with the union put the transition into abeyance.

The development of the union's political awareness and its commitment to strengthening its position in the plants reinforced the attitudes of those in management who preferred to take a much harder line after May. They were almost certainly the majority from the outset. The firms wanted to recoup their losses, and the chances of doing so appeared to be quite good. Although the workers had had the element of surprise, their victory had been partial, and it was only in Ford that they had demonstrated a serious unity of purpose and determination. Therefore, with adequate management preparation a different outcome could be expected in 1979. This preparation included the weakening of the union's base in the plants by both a modified management strategy toward the workers and a determined assault on militants. Because of this, relations between employers and the union deteriorated in the second half of the year. In Saab-Scania and Mercedes management tried to control the activities of the union directors in the plants, requesting that they not carry out any union activities

---

[6] The President of the union, Lula, had declared himself to be in favor of union pluralism in March 1978 (*Pasquim*, 24/3/1978), but he shifted position in the course of the year.

in normal working hours. Saab-Scania argued that the directors were spreading a "climate of intranquility in the work environment" and generating "conflicts between the supervisory staff and the employees, with an evident deterioration in the relation between foremen and their subordinates."[7] At Mercedes, the management also wrote to the union protesting about the activities of directors in working hours, and in this case explicit mention was made of the possibility of dismissal "with due cause." The union felt that it had established by custom and practice the right of directors to carry out union business in normal working hours, even if the right was not fully guaranteed by the CLT. The sudden shift in management attitudes looked like a persecution of union directors.

The climate worsened when union militants and participants in the Third Metalworkers Congress (held in September 1978) were dismissed from the Volkswagen plant, and although the company claimed that the workers had been sacked as part of the company's normal labor turnover, twelve of the twenty workers attending the Congress were dismissed within a few months. The union regarded this as a direct attack on its organization in the plant. Further confirmation of the harder management line came in November 1978 when a circular from the São Paulo Employers Federation fell into the hands of the union. The circular, which was published on the front page of the union's newspaper, instructed members of the Federation to deal with stoppages by forcing workers out of the factories, suspending workers who enter the factories but do not work, and not in any circumstances paying the days lost through stoppages. A company should "in the last instance dismiss a certain number of people with due cause after having asked jointly with the supervisor in the area affected by the stoppage that the workers perform a determined task (a refusal can be characterized as an act of insubordination). This situation creates insecurity among workers. Generally after this is done the workers or the union will ask for a suspension of the dismissals, proposing a return to work" (cited in *Tribuna*

---

[7] Letter from the management of Saab-Scania to the union, November 1978.

Metalúrgica, November 1978). These proposals clearly delineated the growing influence of a "hard line" within the employers' group, and the union began to think about tactics to counter it.

As the negotiations for the April 1979 wage settlement began to get under way late in 1978, the prospects for an easy transfer to a "business union" approach had almost vanished. The direct relations between the employers and the union in São Bernardo had turned sour. In the course of the year, union membership in the major auto plants had risen by between 10 and 27 percent. The union's influence and activity had grown, and it wanted to press ahead and make progress on the many demands that it had raised. The employers, on the other hand, were anxious to regain what they had lost. They knew that they had given ground in May, and they looked to the 1979 negotiations as a way of discrediting the union and claiming back what had been conceded. At a more general level, the Metalworkers of São Bernardo were hoping to consolidate their growing importance within the union movement generally, while the employers were seeking to undermine that advance and bring the São Bernardo union firmly down to earth.[8] By the time the negotiations opened, the lines of division were fairly clearly drawn. Although both sides entered the 1979 negotiations with good intentions, each was anxious to gain at the expense of the other. Not only did each side intend to gain major concessions, but both sides thought they could win. The negotiations had assumed a symbolic importance for both the employers and the union movement, as well as for the State; and so they were regarded as the opening episode of the most serious labor conflict in over a decade.

[8] In fact there were complex power struggles within both camps. The union wanted to consolidate its position within the State Metalworkers Federation, while the Employers Federation was in the early stages of a hotly contested battle for the presidency which involved various groups participating in the negotiations in March 1979.

7

The Auto Workers Take On
the State: 1979

THE SITUATION SURROUNDING the 1979 negotiations was much more complicated than in May 1978. The May strike and its settlement had been the first experiment in strikes and collective bargaining, and the government had left the employers to deal with the situation alone. Free bargaining, largely unhampered by the State or political considerations, had been a possibility. But by 1979 there was more at stake than merely the size of the wage packets of workers in the metal-mechanical industry. The success or failure of the leadership of the metalworkers' union in São Bernardo meant a great deal to both the established powers in the trade union movement and the government. For the *pelegos*, the "new unionism" in São Bernardo was a threat to their control of the labor movement.[1] The May 1978 stoppages had created a new climate in which rank-and-file mobilizations were rife, and in the city of São Paulo the old union leadership had faced serious opposition during the annual wage-settlement negotiations in November 1978. The new leaders wanted to undermine the power of the pro-government elements in the unions even further. For the government, the annual negotiations would be a test of the degree to which democratization could be kept under control. President Figueiredo was due to take office in March 1979, and he had a clear commitment to pursue a policy of democratization. However, the plans of the government did not include the widespread mobilization of workers and the disobedience of the existing labor legislation. As Cardoso has put it, liberalization was "not a rupture of the authoritarian order, but a transformation of

[1] *Pelego* is a term used to describe union leaders who are subservient to the State. The term originates from the Estado Novo period.

it'' (1980:184). The government wanted to keep the new unionism in check, whereas the unions wanted to translate the climate of liberalization immediately into tangible institutional gains for the working class. They had no desire to return to the straitjacket of the *dissídio coletivo* after having experienced the triumph of negotiating the collective agreement which settled the May strikes. But whereas the 1978 agreement was negotiated outside of the formal procedures laid down by law, a repeat in 1979 would require the suspension of these procedures and their abandonment by the government. Although there was some scope for flexibility, the general context of the negotiations did not augur well.

The March Strike

The 1979 negotiations were more extensive and complicated than those conducted by the Metalworkers of São Bernardo in 1978. Many more parties were involved. The employers' side consisted of the auto employers' union, SINFAVEA, and twenty-one other employers' groups (the twenty-two known collectively as "Group 14" of the Employers Federation, FIESP). These twenty-two employer unions represented all the different sections of the metal-mechanical industries. Negotiating for the workers were the thirty-four unions of the Interior of the State of São Paulo and the Federation of São Paulo Metalworkers.[2] These unions contained the most varied currents within the labor movement. In addition to variations in the employment situations of the workers represented by the different unions, the smaller unions of the Interior were dominated by the President of the Metalworkers Federation, Argeu dos Santos, who was resolutely opposed to the style and influence of the metalworkers of the southen industrial belt. The latter were deeply suspicious of the *pelegos*, but they could not afford to be isolated. Therefore, they agreed to a common platform for the negotiations, with the main demands being a significant wage rise and the introduction of delegates in the plants.

[2] Most metalworking unions negotiate together in advance of an annual settlement date in early April. The metalworkers of the city of São Paulo, Osasco, Guarulhos, and Santos (the COSIPA steel plant) negotiate at other times.

After a long period of negotiation, most of the unions, led by the Federation of São Paulo Metalworkers, accepted an offer of a 63 percent wage rise for workers earning up to three times the minimum wage, 57 percent for those earning between three and ten times the minimum wage, and the "official" wage increase of 44 percent for those earning more than ten times the minimum wage.[3] This wage deal was good for the metalworkers of the Interior. The smaller unions representing workers in areas away from the major industrial centers had neither the strength nor the will to obtain major concessions from the employers through their own efforts, and yet they were offered both a relatively good wage rise and a minimum wage for the industry (*piso salarial*) some way above the rates many of their workers were earning. However, for the metalworkers of the southern industrial belt, the agreement was much less attractive. There were four main reasons for this. Firstly, wage levels in the auto industry were relatively high, and they were also relatively high in many other metalworking firms. Therefore, most auto workers, and many metalworkers would receive only the 57 percent because they would be earning more than three times the minimum wage. In March 1978, one year before the settlement, only 31 percent of all metalworkers in São Bernardo earned less than three times the minimum wage.[4] Secondly, for the same reason, the workers earning relatively high wages would not benefit from the increase in the minimum wage-rate payable in the industry—to 1.4 times the official minimum wage. Thirdly, the gains made in May and June 1978 were to be discounted from the increases of 63 and 57 percent. In the 1978 collective contract the employers had agreed that the two rises of 5½ percent would not be discounted from the April 1979 settlement. However, they argued that this commitment only meant that the workers would not receive less than the officially decreed increase, which was 44 percent. Therefore,

---

[3] This figure of 44 percent was not significant. Few workers earned more than ten times the minimum wage, and such workers would not have had the officially negotiated rise applied to their wage rates.

[4] Fifteen percent of auto workers and 51 percent of other metalworkers earned less than three times the minimum wage in March 1978.

178

the employers reasoned, they could discount the 11 percent. This reduced the rise for most auto workers (and for many other metalworkers who had negotiated rises of 10 percent or more in May and June 1978) to 41½ percent above the wages they had earned in June 1978.[5] Irrespective of the exact calculations, which were the subject of some dispute, this interpretation of the previous year's settlement left those workers who had gone on strike and gained rises in 1978 no better off than workers who had not. In fact, most workers in the auto industry would be earning only 57 percent more than their April 1978 wage in April 1979, whereas for the lower-paid worker the increase would be 63 percent. Fourthly, there had been no concession by the employers on the question of union delegates in the plants, which had been one of the priority demands of the unions of the southern industrial belt.

As a result of this settlement and its acceptance by thirty-one of the unions of the Interior, the metalworkers of the southern belt were placed in a difficult position. They were faced with a choice of either refusing to accept the terms of the settlement or going out on a limb and taking strike action in isolation from the other metalworking unions. Both choices appeared to be unpalatable. Acceptance of the settlement would signify an economic and political defeat for the Metalworkers of São Bernardo. Economically, nothing would have been gained from the strikes of the previous year, and the employers would have taken back what they had been forced to concede when the workers had "negotiated with the machines stopped." Politically, going along with the unions of the Interior would have meant a subordination of the Metalworkers of São Bernardo to the leadership of the President of the Metalwokers Federation, Argeu dos Santos, who was resolutely opposed to the "new" unionism. The emergent leadership of the union in São Bernardo would have been checked at a crucial stage. Lula, the leader of the Metalworkers of São Bernardo, had never been willing to accept such subordination and in private had declared his intention to break with the unions of

[5] The union calculated 57 percent on top of the April-1978-wage-plus-11 percent, which equals 41½ percent. The employers argued that the rise was 57 percent less 11 percent, making 46 percent.

the Interior and seek a better deal even before the negotiations had started. For these reasons the Metalworkers of São Bernardo, supported by three other union leaders, decided to take strike action, but this choice, too, appeared to be rather unpalatable. Some employers, including some firms in the auto industry, believed that the union was incapable of sustaining an all-out strike, and they wanted to force it into strike action in order to inflict a defeat. The maneuvers between the unions of the Interior and São Bernardo appeared to give the employers the victory they desired, but events turned out rather differently.

The union in São Bernardo was prepared for strike action, although it did not know what would happen once a strike was called. In advance of the negotiations, the union had held meetings in factories and developed a degree of organization and coordination. It had tested the use of pickets during a ten-day strike at a large components-plant in February, and it was aware that President Geisel would leave office on March 15, thus causing some hesitation in government circles. At midnight on March 13, hours after the unions of the Interior had accepted the employers' proposal, the first factories in São Bernardo stopped work. At once, the strike took on its own dynamic. In Ford, the workers on the night shift began to face severe pressure from the foremen to start work again, and in the early hours of the morning they walked out. The workers were on the streets, not in the plants. At 5:00 A.M. a small picket was sent to the Volkswagen plant—the weakest link in the union's chain of resistance—and in a few hours a euphoric picket of thousands of workers blocked the main entrance and brought the factory to a standstill. Other major plants stopped at the same time. Two small unions in the Interior that had supported the call for a strike found it impossible to sustain, but workers responded to the strike call in Santo André, in São Caetano, where the union had signed the agreement, and in large firms in Campinas and São José dos Campos[6]—Mercedes, General Electric, Cobrasma, Embraer, and others. However, the strike

[6] Outside of Greater São Paulo, the districts of Campinas and São José dos Campos have the highest average size of establishment in manufacturing industry, according to census data.

movement was only sustained in ABC—the southern industrial belt. From the beginning, the strike was centered on São Bernardo, and above all on the large auto plants.

Although strikes take on their own dynamic as conflicts become condensed and clarified and the excitement of a major confrontation raises feelings on both sides, they are also fairly accurate reflections of what has preceded them. Just as in 1978, when the plants and groups of workers most actively involved in the stoppages were explicable, so in 1979 events moved in unforeseen but not inexplicable ways. The use of pickets on the first day was not part of the union's original plans, but it was clear that Volkswagen was the key plant. After the May 1978 strikes, it was the symbol of management intransigence and also the most difficult factory to stop. In 1978 the company had successfully persuaded four of the six union directors in the plant to abandon their union activities, which had weakened the union and increased its bitterness toward the management.[7] After initial success in bringing "the holocaust" (as the plant was sometimes called in the union's newspaper) to a standstill the situation became more difficult for the strikers. That evening the police were called in, and the activities of the union pickets were increasingly curtailed. One account of the events estimated that the full police contingent for the São Bernardo area for the strike, 2,000 armed police along with dogs, lorries, horses, and armored cars, was stationed in the Volkswagen plant. To counter this, the pickets moved farther away, stopping the works buses on the roads leading to the plant and even moving into the areas where the buses started to pick up workers. By the end of the first week, the plant was still virtually paralyzed.

While it was impossible to stop all the small firms working, the large firms in Santo André and São Bernardo were at a halt. Ford, Volkswagen, General Electric, Pirelli, Alcan, Phillips, and others remained out, in spite of the propaganda campaign on television and radio and the use of the police to intimidate pickets.

---

[7] The exact circumstance of the withdrawal of these directors from the union is not clear. It appears that some form of inducement was offered by the company.

181

In some cases, management tried to keep the factories running with the few workers who attended and the white-collar staff, but production was minimal. The pressure of the employers and the State was not enough to prevent the strike continuing. The strike's momentum was kept up by mass meetings of workers and the activities of the union directors and Comissão de Salários (Wage Committee). Well aware that a stay-at-home strike would lead to demoralization because of inactivity and state-controlled media coverage (which included false reports about the development of the strike, emphasis on its illegality, etc.), the unions organized regular mass meetings. Tens of thousands of workers attended them, particularly on the first weekend of the strike, which was considered the period of greatest potential demobilization (as it had been in 1978). There were also frequent meetings at union headquarters, and this reinforced the preparations made before the strike. The Wage Committee, a group of thirty to forty militants, organized pickets and meetings and helped the union directors. A strike fund was organized to provide food for workers in financial difficulties, and this both gave workers practical assistance and illustrated the support being offered by other unions and the public in general. The use of the various meetings, the pickets, and the strike fund allowed the union to impress on workers the solidarity of the strike and gave its leaders a chance to gauge the level of support.

In contrast to the continued solidarity and determination of the workers, the dynamic of the strike tended to fragment the employers. Many firms had not expected a strike at all. Even in the auto industry there had been no attempt to build up stocks in preparation for a long stoppage, and for the smaller firms the costs of the strike were not easy to bear. One owner of a small firm expressed the following opinion after the first week of the strike: "The multinationals and the big firms can enjoy the luxury of being intransigent because they have the capital and the sources of credit. But we small and medium firms cannot sustain this strike any longer" (*Movimento*, 26/3/1979, quoting from FSP). Many employers wanted a rapid resolution of the strike, but there were differences about how this should be done. Whereas some businessmen were against State intervention because they saw it as further complicating a difficult situation, others looked to the State for a solution, either because they felt themselves unable to pay the wage rise demanded by the union or because they saw the strike as an opportunity to teach the union a lesson. For some employers, the most important issue in the strike was the future of the Metalworkers of São Bernardo, not the size of any possible wage increase to be negotiated, and this led to pressure from some quarters for State intervention to bring the union under control. Even industrialists who had favored a more open, democratic regime began to show concern for the application of law and the establishment of order.

Within the government, the Labor Minister, Murillo Macedo, favored a peaceful solution, but only with strict limits on the final pay award. In effect, this meant a solution on the employers' terms and a capitulation by the unions. Negotiations continued throughout the strike, and after ten days, with the threat of intervention hanging over them, the union leaders agreed to put forward a proposal for a return to work pending further negotiations over a forty-five-day period. When this offer was rejected by mass meetings of over 90,000 workers in the three unions, the Ministry of Labor took direct control. The headquarters of the three unions were occupied, their funds fell into the hands of the intervenor appointed by the Ministry, and the unions were denied the right to carry on their mass meetings. Lula, the President of the Metalworkers of São Bernardo, went into temporary seclusion. It appeared that the hard-line forces in the government and among the employees had won the day and that the union had suffered a major defeat. However, in spite of the loss of printing facilities, cash, and meeting places, the strike movement did not come to an end. On the day after the intervention, Saturday March 24, an estimated 20,000 people gathered in the center of São Bernardo and serious clashes were only narrowly avoided by prudent police action. The workers still had widespread sympathy, and the Church began to provide support for the deposed leaders. The intervention had not immediately ended the strike, and the situation appeared to be getting out of hand. Another of the standard recipes of the post-1964 period for dealing with workers' unrest, intervention by the Ministry of Labor, was less effective than before.

In this situation, some liberal industrialists managed to arrange a truce between the Metalworkers of São Bernardo and the State. Neither side was gaining much from the intervention: the union's situation had been made extremely difficult, while the State had not secured the immediate return to work that it had anticipated. According to one of the industrialists responsible for the truce arrangement, the São Bernardo union had been incorrect to refuse the original settlement, and it had shown itself to be indulging in a blatant political strike aimed at securing a victory over the Federation of São Paulo Metalworkers and its President, Argeu dos Santos. In this situation it was right, he argued, for the employers to refuse any further improvement in settlement terms because this would penalize the unions of the Interior and reward the unions and the strikers who had negotiated jointly and then refused to accept the agreement. However, this attitude was tempered by a feeling that the police could not resolve an industrial-relations dispute and that the transition to democracy needed union leaders of Lula's type. The need to preserve the more representative São Bernardo union, combined with fears about the short-term and long-term consequences of resorting to force to resolve the dispute, led this industrialist and some others to arrange a compromise whereby the workers would return to work on the same conditions as had been rejected at the mass meetings and the Ministry of Labor would end its intervention in the three unions within forty-five days. On the Monday following the intervention, the workers of São Bernardo accepted the compromise because of the difficulties they were experiencing in carrying on the strike. After two weeks the strike was over. The potential conflict over payment or nonpayment of the strike days was left ambiguous, but the unions were offered a promise of no dismissals for sixty days.

The strike ended without any immediate gains for the union, and it was now forced to negotiate "with the machines running," in contrast to the rallying call adopted in 1978. The employers, too, had not won a victory. As the strike had gone on, the issue of wages had become secondary to the question of the future of the union and its President. At one time, the management of one of the major auto firms was jubilant at the government's intervention in the union and the thought of deposing Lula, but the final truce foresaw his return, and the union had not been broken by the strike. In fact, the union maintained its strength. The return to work did not lead to a complete ending of workers' resistance, and the negotiations in the forty-five-day period were not a formality. The employers and the government had expected the negotiations to result in an agreement identical to that rejected by the union leaders before the strike started, but the union negotiating team still had some cards to play. The deposed leaders had called for an overtime ban in the plants until the intervention was ended, and this had some effect. In some plants, attempts to dismiss workers within the sixty-day period were met with further stoppages—including one at Indústrias Villares where 2,500 workers went on strike. In spite of having no legal position, the deposed leaders continued to act as the workers' representatives in these situations, and in the case of Villares even the company called in Lula to discuss the problem (*Isto É*, 2/5/1979). On May Day, the union managed to upstage the official celebrations completely by organizing a rally of 150,000 people in São Bernardo. This was a clear indication of its continuing popularity.

The employers could have expected the workers to be demoralized and the union to be preoccupied more with the return of its elected officers than with the minutiae of the wage settlement, but as the end of the forty-five-day period came closer the situation became tense. In spite of warnings by the government about the dire consequences of not accepting the terms offered by the employers, the union not only refused to accept them but also insisted that any agreement would have to go to a mass meeting for approval. Early in May the issue was resolved quickly as a result of the auto workers' taking action. The Ford management had decided to deduct 10 percent of the total amount of pay lost during the strike from the May wage packet, and the Ford workers went out on strike. They were so determined not to lose the money that even when Lula and one of the directors obtained a reversal of the company's decision, the workers stayed out until the following day, when the deducted money was paid to them. This event seems to have broken the nerve of the auto employers. The other firms, which make their monthly payments the day after Ford, canceled plans to deduct the 10 percent. The auto companies broke with the Employers Federation and offered a wage increase of 63 percent for all workers earning up to ten times the minimum wage—an increase of 6 percent over the March settlement for most workers in the industry. The question of the deduction of pay for the days lost in the strike was left uncertain: 50 percent would be deducted and 50 percent would be negotiated further. The auto employers then forced this settlement onto the other twenty-one employers' unions in Group 14. The settlement was accepted by the three workers' unions on May 13, and two days later, some two months after the strike had started, the Ministry of Labor's intervention in the union was lifted and the situation returned more or less to normal.

The Effects of the March Strike

THE EMPLOYERS

The failure to win a decisive victory even with the full help of the State left the employers with the same dilemma as before, and lessons from the strike could be drawn to support the views of both camps. For those who preferred a path of conciliation, the failure of the hard-line tactic could be taken as proof of its inefficacy. It was clearly not the case that a decisive act by the government would be capable of restoring order and bringing dangerous union leaders under control—on the contrary, one of the effects of the intervention had been to leave the strike leaderless and almost out of control. One of the reasons for the final concessions in May had been the fear that a further stoppage would strengthen the hand of the more militant elements in the three unions of the southern belt and make future dealings with them even more complicated. For all these reasons, it could be argued that a more conciliatory line would be advisable.

However, the proponents of more repressive measures could also draw support from the events of the strike. When ideas about union reform and the introduction of the right to strike were first widely discussed in 1977, many industrialists claimed that a union movement with greater freedom would be acceptable, but it is likely that they had expected the unions to be much weaker and less militant than the Metalworkers of São Bernardo turned out to be in 1979. The March strike showed that the workers were not easy to defeat and that the union would continue to adopt a more political and militant stance in the face of State and management intransigence on the fundamental questions of the structure and rights of trade unions. Therefore, in the short term at least, many employers would have had their misgivings about the further strengthening of trade unionism in Brazil. Whatever the long-term possibilities of reform, they could make a case for bringing more order and control into industrial relations. The failure to inflict a decisive defeat on the unions only meant that the employers and the State would have to try harder the next time.[8]

THE WORKERS AND THE UNIONS

If the lessons for management were pointing in two different directions, for the unions the message seemed to be clear: they would obtain no concessions from either management or the State without a struggle, and the preparation for 1980 would have to be better than for 1979. The policy of the hard-liners among the employers was most evident to the union leaders, and the positions of the more liberal managements were considered as mere talk or plain lies. In particular, the claim of the auto companies to be more progressive than the smaller firms was viewed with cynicism. The unions felt that the employers and the State had tried to destroy them. ''Jack Steel's'' column in the union newspaper included the following in a letter to the Minister of Labor:

[8] The conflicts over strategy among employers will be examined further in the last section of this chapter and in chapter eight.

Certainly, few of the people around you (and in that group I include the bosses as well) expected us to return. After all, you really came in heavily on top of us, and you really wanted to destroy us. Because of this we went through some terrible times, and many workers felt batons on their bodies and the effects of the tear-gas bombs. For all the things that you did to us, we should be very angry. (Free translation of a letter in *Tribuna Metalúrgica*, June 1979)

The Metalworkers of Santo André also viewed the strike as an attempt to destroy the union, as this account of it in their newspaper indicates:

At dawn on March 23, the three unions are occupied by the military. The Minister fulfills the promise given to the bosses, decreeing an intervention. . . . With this act, they truly declared war against us. . . . At this point it is possible to imagine that the bosses would be starting to laugh. After all, with this cleanup operation the movement should have been definitively liquidated. And the bosses would have achieved their political objective (to crush the unionism of ABC, which first appeared in May of last year, grew rapidly, and became an example for all other workers). (*O Metalúrgico*, May 1979)

The unions saw the strike's events, particularly the State intervention, as an attempt to destroy them, which it clearly had been for some of the employers, and their mistrust of both the employers and the State had been heightened by the experience.

The unions had survived because of the resistance of workers both during and after the strike, but the difficulties of this resistance pointed toward the need for three basic reforms in the trade union structure. Firstly, the limited penetration of the unions into the plants made it difficult to mount a long-term strike. Although the union directors had done a good job, their activities were restricted to a few plants, and during the strike many smaller firms carried on working. In the second week of the strike the Metalworkers of São Bernardo were increasingly forced to concentrate on the few large factories in the auto industry and leave the rest alone. Experience indicated that when the union attempted to develop its organization and activities without using directors, the activists were fired because they had no protection against dismissal. Therefore, the question of getting union delegates into the plants was once more brought to the fore. Only with delegates would the union be able to organize in the smaller plants. At the same time, the lack of an organized intermediate layer of militants in the plants meant that running the strike had not been easy. During the strike, the creation of a Wage Committee of between thirty and forty activists partly solved the problem, but its relation with the union directors had been uncertain. According to one of the participants, the Wage Committee had had neither the authority to take over the running of the strike once the union's leaders were neutralized by the intervention nor the continuity to play an active role in union affairs once the strike was over. The solution to all these problems lay in a scheme drawn up by the union for a network of delegates. Workers in the plants would elect delegates to plant committees. These committees would, in turn, elect representatives to liaise with the union's directors, thus providing a link between the plant committees and the official union structure.

The second basic reform related to union finances. By law, unions were not allowed to use the funds they received from the Trade Union Contribution to support strikers, but as the strike went on it became apparent that the workers could be forced back to work by a lack of money. The provision of food was one temporary measure adopted during the strike, but in the longer term the union saw a need for a strike fund. The implication of such a fund would be that the general funding of the union should be altered and taken out of the hands of the State. After the strike there was a lot of discussion about a strike fund and how one could be set up.

The third item related to the role of the State. As can be seen from quotes selected above, the unions were in no doubt about the State: they saw it as on the employers' side. Far from acting as a neutral arbiter of conflicts between capital and labor, the State seemed to have supported the hard-line group among the employers. The legislation relating to the powers of the Ministry of Labor encouraged the employers to provoke confrontations and then ask the State to resolve the disputes by force. The power of the Ministry of Labor could be suspended temporarily, as in May 1978, but it remained a threat to the unions and an encouragement to the more reactionary elements among the employers. The experience of the strike underlined the need for a modification (or elimination) of the Ministry of Labor's power over the unions. The pressure for better wages and working conditions had come up against the constraints of the labor system designed to contain and control it.

Given the apparent hostility of the State to the unions, further pursuit of fundamental changes in the law and practice on union questions required a shift to a more openly political struggle. Democratization was clearly on the agenda, and the unions were not prepared to wait for it. It was noted in chapter five that in its early period the union in São Bernardo had adopted an "anti-political" stance, concentrating on issues of direct relevance to its members. After the struggles in 1978 and 1979, the issues of direct relevance to its members were political ones, and in the latter part of 1979 the union pushed more strongly for political reforms and pushed forward proposals for the formation of a Workers Party that would represent working-class interests. The union supported general political campaigns on issues not solely relating to workers, such as amnesty for political prisoners, a Constituent Assembly, and the repeal of repressive legislation. This kind of activity was a long way from "apolitical business unionism," and it reflected three basic developments. Firstly, the union was much freer to express political opinions in 1979 than it had been a few years before, and this undoubtedly made a difference. Secondly, the union's leaders had developed their own political viewpoints in the course of the struggles in which they had been involved. Thirdly, the union had come up against political barriers in the course of its long struggle for union reform and freedom of action. Even the most "businesslike" of demands can have political implications and consequences.

Auto Workers Take On the State

The events of March and April accelerated the rise to prominence of the Metalworkers of São Bernardo and the group of "authentic"[9] union leaders allied to it. The immensity of the tasks and the generality of both the support for the union during the strike and the demands it was raising naturally led to a consideration of a wider grouping of trade unionists as the vehicle for further progress. In 1978, after the May stoppages, Lula and some other "authentic" union leaders took a program to the Congress of the National Confederation of Industrial Workers, an organization dominated by long-serving union bureaucrats sympathetic to the government. After being outvoted in the Congress, the progressive group issued a statement of their principles, entitled the "Letter of the Authentic Leaders" (published in the *Tribuna Metalúrgica*, September 1978). Around this document were grouped the leaders of the Metalworkers of São Bernardo, Santos, and João Monlevade (in Minas Gerais), the Tanker Drivers of Campinas, the Bank Workers of Porto Alegre, the Gas and Electricity Workers of Rio de Janeiro, and a number of others. They were united in their opposition to the dominant current in the official union structure and in their support for a broad program which included democratization (and a series of specific movements toward it—a Constituent Assembly, amnesty for political prisoners, direct elections), a more just economic strategy, freedom for unions and workers, and a reform of labor legislation. After the March strike, this group of union leaders became more active. As in the case of union directors in the plants and the *reposição salarial*, action was added to words. Realizing that the overall development of the labor movement would be crucially affected by specific strikes, the group of "authentic" leaders gradually became involved in strikes occurring outside of their own unions. When the strike of Building Workers in Belo Horizonte threatened to get out of hand as a result of union incompetence and bad policing, the "authentic" leaders went to the workers and restored some

---

[9] This was the name accepted by these unionists, and it expressed their claim truly to represent the interests of the working class.

discipline to the strike. In the words of Lula: "If our dream is
that workers should go on strike to release themselves from constraints and improve their standard of living, then we cannot allow
them to become victims of small groups. On these trips—as in
the case of Belo Horizonte—our concern is to avoid radicalization
and guarantee that things remain peaceful so that there is no
tightening up in the political sphere" (interview in *Isto É*, 19/9/
1979). But if in Belo Horizonte this meant calming down an
explosive situation that had led to a large-scale riot, in Porto
Alegre it meant giving active support to the Bankworkers Union
when it was involved in a disciplined war of attrition with the
employers and the State. The progressive group was referred to
as the "informal CUT,"[10] and it acquired a national prestige,
much to the annoyance of the government. Lula himself became
a national union figure, often preferred by workers to their own
leaders, and he could draw massive crowds when he traveled.

The March strike was important for all employers and workers
because of the national significance of the Metalworkers of São
Bernardo and its policies. Just as in 1978, the union was exploring
new ground and setting an example to other groups of workers.
One of the reasons for the bitterness of the strike was its symbolic
importance, and in more practical terms the elimination of Lula
would have been a severe blow for the "authentic" group of
unionists. Such general importance is far removed from the notion
that the Metalworkers of São Bernardo were an actual or potential
labor aristocracy, whose politics would be of interest only to
workers in the dynamic industries. Their basic demands had not
changed. They were still in favor of the right to strike, direct
negotiations with the employers (implying the end of the *dissídio
coletivo* and the role of the Labor Courts), and the eventual elimination of the Trade Union Contribution as the means of financing
the unions. These policies were the same as those put forward in
1972, and they were similar to the policies of the "renewal"
currents in the union movement in the early sixties (see Souza

[10] CUT stands for Central Único dos Trabalhadores, a single unifying Labor
Confederation, controlled by the unions directly.

Martins, 1979:84-88).[11] But whereas in the early sixties the renewal current was marginal to the union movement as a whole and represented a challenge to the pro-Populist currents within it, in 1979 the demands for reform were demands for an end to State oppression. Resistance to the State, within the unions and in society at large, was identified with the practical resistance of the São Bernardo metalworkers to the constraints of the State-controlled labor system. The decline of the Populist currents within the labor movement, the increasing importance of the dynamic sectors within the working class, and the dramatic change in the use of the labor system after 1964 gave the same demands a very different content within the struggles of the working class. A further examination of this content and the possible effects of such demands in a democratic period will be undertaken in chapter nine.

In 1979, the effect of the struggle of the Metalworkers of São Bernardo was clear: the March strike was followed by an upsurge of working-class activity. According to the *Jornal do Brasil*, there were eighty-three major strikes in the five months following the presidential succession in March (JB, 19/8/1979), and in some areas the strike movement took the form of mass local strikes, with different groups of workers going on strike at the same time. The nature of these strikes is more important than the numbers. As Morris has pointed out, strikes in underdeveloped countries are often little more than "isolated, spontaneous expressions of immediate grievances. They do not arise out of any pre-existing formal or semiformal organization, nor do they necessarily establish the conditions for the development of permanent institutions for collective action" (1969:215). Some of the strikes in 1978 and 1979 clearly had this character, but many did not, and they showed a degree of determination and discipline that indicated the presence of stable organization. Such organization was

[11] The one major demand of the "renewal" current not accepted by the Metalworkers of São Bernardo was trade union pluralism, but even this had been advocated by Lula as late as March 1978 (*Pasquim*, 24/3/1978). Trade union unity (only one union for each category of workers) was adopted decisively at the union's Third Congress in October 1978.

not confined to the workers in the dynamic industries. For example, in the case of the Union of Workers in the Leather and Plastic Goods Industries of São Paulo, an agreement was reached with the larger firms in the category for rises of between 59 percent and 61 percent for most workers, and the gains obtained by stoppages in 1978 were not to be discounted. These increases, about 15 percent higher than the employers' original offer, had been secured by the threat of strike action, even though the Labor Court had declared in favor of the employers' initial offer. In spite of the opposition of the Labor Court, the Regional Labor Office, and the Employers Federation, the union managed to generalize the settlement to all the firms in the category by means of strike action in the smaller firms.[12] The Metalworkers of Recife, in the Northeast, showed similar organization. After prolonged negotiations the union decided to call a strike in spite of an improved final offer from the employers. But when it became apparent that the strike movement would be weakened by this final increase, the union negotiators returned to the bargaining table and accepted it, along with a guarantee of stability of employment for the negotiating team. The impressive feature of this episode was the ability of the union's leaders to mobilize the members and then reach a negotiated settlement. The leaders were fully in control. An auto industry executive who participated in the final stages of the negotiations commented: "They could mobilize the workers. I felt this. There's no doubt about it, there are new leaders, not only in the metalworkers but in the whole of Brazil. New leaders are emerging who are overrunning the *pelegos*" (interviewed in AF1). Thus the new current was capable of attracting support and encouraging others to emulate it even in the more distant industrial areas. Even in the Clothing Workers Union in Porto Alegre, whose members were mainly women employed in small firms, union delegates were introduced into the plant as part of an agreement over shift changes. The working conditions in the industry were bad, but the introduction of delegates with stability of employment

[12] This account is taken from the union's newspaper, *Notícias Sindicais*, August 1979.

quickly led to improvements, because they were able to secure better enforcement of the law.[13]

These cases show that the revitalization of the trade union movement was not confined to workers in the dynamic industries in the major industrial areas. The demands raised by the Metalworkers of São Bernardo had a general appeal to workers in many industries and areas, and the political importance of its struggle extended to the whole of the working class. For both the future of the unions and also the future of democratization, the Metalworkers of São Bernardo and the sections of the labor movement grouped around it were of fundamental importance.

Entering the Eighties

In 1978 and 1979 the militant unions had been able to act with much greater freedom than earlier in the decade. In particular, legal and institutional restraints had been partly suspended. However, the corporate labor system had not been altered, and the unions and workers had every reason to believe that the government was hoping to implement democratization while keeping the labor system intact. The government's strategy seemed at times to be almost a conscious rerun of 1945-1946, with care being taken to give the pro-government forces a political majority. In spite of Lula's optimism following the first strikes in 1978, when he said, "I think that these strikes have already decreed the bankruptcy of the existing trade union structure and also of the current strike law" (interview, *Cara a Cara*, 1978:57), the government was more concerned with reviving and revitalizing the system than calling in the receivers. In 1972 the winning slate in the elections for the Metalworkers of São Bernardo had put forward a program which supported the introduction of direct negotiations with employers, union delegates in the plants, plant committees, and full autonomy for workers' associations (see chapter five). None of these demands had been conceded by 1979. Although

---

[13] This information comes from an interview with the President of the union, carried out by Werner Würtele.

some changes were envisioned in the government's draft proposals for the reform of the CLT—made public in 1979—they did not go far enough for the unions. The modified CLT would preserve much of the existing legislation, including restrictions on the right to strike, the wages policy, and the Trade Union Contribution. The proposed legislation did allow the possibility of direct negotiations and union delegates, but the existing CLT allowed them as well. The unions felt that the very existence of corporate institutions encouraged the employers to exploit the legalism and State orientation of the CLT to the full. For this reason, they demanded much more thoroughgoing reforms.

The attitude of the government and some employers appeared to be that labor unrest could be curtailed by a series of minor reforms that would demobilize the working class and isolate the radical elements in the unions from the mass of workers. This was seen most clearly in the introduction of a new wages policy late in 1979. The policy offered a new system of tying wages to the rate of inflation, six-monthly wage adjustments, bigger rises for the lower-paid, and sectoral (not national) negotiations on productivity increases. The intention of the government was to head off discontent among the lower-paid in order to isolate the union leaderships. One of the designers of the new policy made the following prediction about its likely effects: "I think that there should be a cooling down of the pressure. The unions will pressurize but the workers in general will not be very inclined to stop work, because they will not gain very much from it. Above all, the workers on the lowest pay scales will not support strikes, because their wages will rise more. . . . The (new) wages policy has put an end to the need for negotiations" (interviewed in AF1 in September 1979). This view was quite widespread in government and industry: minor changes in the wages policy would put an end to union mobilizations and obviate the need for major reforms.

In the plants, too, many employers saw little reason to make major changes. Following the 1979 strike, the tactics used in 1978—the control of militants and the resolution of minor grievances—were continued. Some firms began to modify their wage structures (speeding up promotion), while others attempted to co-opt or neutralize activists by offering training, promotion, and transfers. Two comments from militants in Santo André, interviewed in August 1979, illustrate the pressures on them:

> In . . . [a large multinational company] they don't sack people. They give rises and promotions so that you are cut off from the workers. A lot of people have gone along with this—they are almost forced to.

> In . . . [another multinational] they called me to the office and said, "What would you like? A salaried job?" They do everything to try and buy off the most active workers.

At the end of 1979 there was little sign of significant concessions from management. On the contrary, many firms believed that 1980 would provide the opportunity for a definitive defeat of the union.

The government, too, had its reasons for wanting to inflict a defeat on the Metalworkers of São Bernardo. Although its plans for controlled democratization were being implemented with some success, the government viewed the increasing influence of the São Bernardo union with concern. The regime at that time still needed both control over the unions and a circumscribed political arena. The former was directly threatened by the Metalworkers of São Bernardo and all that it stood for in the Brazilian labor movement, and the Workers Party formed by the "authentic" union leaders was the only serious challenge to the regime's plans to allow a gradual democratization while keeping power for the ruling group. The struggle for basic trade union freedom had led the Metalworkers of São Bernardo to the center of working-class mobilization. As important, the strategy of the leaders of the "new unionism" and the Workers Party was to press ahead for reforms. They were unhappy with the slow pace of change and would not wait for democracy, or adopt the line that any reform would be better than no reform at all.

The situation in São Bernardo was complicated by broader

issues.[14] The development of industrial relations in the large firms was influenced not only by labor-management relations in the plants but also by the general policies on industrial relations being developed by employers and the State, and the political struggle between the Workers Party and the government. In the runup to the 1980 negotiations, political considerations appeared to count for more than industrial relations. The union was anxious to translate its hard-won influence into something more than limited and temporary monetary gains that could easily be wiped out by inflation. To do this, it needed to challenge the labor system head-on. Opposed to the union stood the employers and the State. Frustrated by their failure to defeat the union in 1979, and bolstered by the predictions of the demobilizing impact of the new wages policy, the employers were ready to fight again. They could make common cause with the State, which was determined to halt the forward march of the Workers Party and the "new unionism." In the latter part of 1979 a tougher line against militant unions had been demonstrated in the Porto Alegre Bankworkers strike. After the employers had refused to make any concessions during negotiations, a well-supported and highly organized strike began. The government responded by taking over the union and imprisoning its President, Olívio Dutra, one of the leading "authentic" unionists. Although Dutra was released when the strike eventually ceased, the union remained under the Ministry of Labor's control. This was both a clear warning to the Metalworkers of São Bernardo and an indication to the employers that they could look to the State for support.

However, the 1979 strike had shown that force would not resolve industrial-relations problems if the workers could not be subdued. The encephalitic tendencies of corporatist trade unionism had made decapitation an effective remedy, but in São Bernardo the union's body—the organization and strength of its members in the plants—was developing rapidly. Far from losing its mass support after the 1979 strike, the union was expanding its

[14] In this chapter attention will be focused on events in São Bernardo in 1980-1981. A more general analysis will be undertaken in chapters eight and nine.

links with plant militants. After three months of meetings with workers in all the major factories the union was able to form a 480-strong Committee of Mobilization and Wages with representatives elected from all over the district. It was expressly designed to be able to take over the running of a strike after the Ministry of Labor intervened in the union and imprisoned its executive. In 1979 the State had been able to end the strike by the use of force, but it could not produce a permanent victory. The concessions made in May 1979 were a clear sign that the State could not resolve all the employers' problems. But the lesson was not learnt. In 1980 and 1981 the same conflicts and problems were played out in a more prolonged and destructive manner.

The union produced a long list of demands for the 1980 negotiations, including a 15 percent wage rise (over and above a wage adjustment to compensate for inflation), a forty-hour week without reduction in pay, stability of labor for all workers for one year, union delegates, and priority for dismissed workers when rehiring took place. The most important demands were for the wage rise and stability of employment. Although the union managed to secure an offer of a 7 percent increase in real wages—an acceptable compromise in view of the employers' initial 4 percent offer—negotiations broke down over the issue of stability of employment. The employers argued that it was totally unacceptable and unrealistic, whereas the union thought that without a guarantee of stability, wage rises were useless—workers would not be employed long enough to benefit from them. In 1980, as in 1979, many employers did not believe that the union could sustain a strike, particularly as the issue at stake was not wages. Once again they were wrong. The strike started without the use of pickets and it continued even after the union was taken over and its leaders imprisoned in the third week. It became a national political event, with support coming from other unions, rallies and fund-raising concerts, and, above all, the Catholic Church, whose leaders supported it publicly.[15]

[15] The Church's community organizations in working-class districts were possibly the main basis for continuing the strike once the police curtailed activities

But the government was determined to hold out. In spite of street battles between strikers and the security forces following the arrest of Lula on April 19, and in spite of a demonstration of 120,000 people in support of the strike on May 1, no concessions were made. Even though some firms suffered great losses during the strike,[16] the government merely promised financial support to firms in difficulty. FIESP was not allowed to negotiate a settlement: the State took full control of the dispute. Finally, after forty-one days the strikers accepted defeat. It seemed that the employers had won the outright victory denied them in 1979. At the end of the strike there was no concession on pay and no return of the deposed union leaders. In some major plants, the employers took advantage of the intervention by the Ministry of Labor to get rid of the union directors who hitherto had had immunity from dismissal. The union's ex-leaders also faced the threat of prosecution under the National Security Law for their activities during the strike; and many people predicted that eventually Lula would be transformed from a prestigious trade union leader to an ineffective politician within the ranks of the Workers Party.

In spite of this clear political victory, the big employers in São Bernardo still faced the problem of how to relate to their employees. The American auto companies generally thought that some form of negotiation with the union would be necessary, and Ford's Industrial Relations management, in particular, did not believe that the deposed union leaders would lose their influence in the region.[17] The strength of the union was so great in Ford's São Bernardo plant that management was very wary of any attempt to break it. The ability to mobilize at plant level independently

---

in and near the plants. Expressions of support for the strike and the strikers from the Church hierarchy provoked President Figueiredo to suggest to reporters that Cardinal Arns of São Paulo was "inciting the strike" (a criminal offense) (*Isto É*, 30/4/1980).

[16] The auto plants were virtually paralyzed throughout the strike, losing thousands of vehicles in production.

[17] Ford was the most important of the American companies. General Motors does not have a plant in São Bernardo, and Chrysler, much smaller, was in the process of being absorbed by Volkswagen. However, the Industrial Relations management in all three firms had similar perspectives.

of the other metalworkers in the area—seen in May 1978 and also in the stoppage in May 1979 over stopping wages for the days of the strike—was a significant factor. In view of this, and given management's general aim of establishing normal relations with the workers' representatives, the union directors in the plant were not dismissed, and management attempted to continue negotiating with them. Some sections of the Ford management, at least, were anxious to repair the damage of what they saw as a pointless and damaging political strike.[18] Far from judging the strike to have been a success from the employers' point of view, they regarded the takeover of the union as creating two serious problems: how to conduct negotiations without legitimate workers' representatives and how to give back the union to the only leaders recognized by the workers, the deposed executive. The strike and its aftermath had merely made the job of creating a viable industrial-relations policy that much more difficult. One executive in an American auto company graphically assessed the workers' reaction to the situation with the comment, "The workers carry on accumulating hatred because of the violence and deaths." The hard-line policy of the State would strengthen the workers' opposition in São Bernardo, not weaken it.

The European firms assessed the situation rather differently. Led by Volkswagen, they saw the defeat of the union as a chance to develop a new system of industrial relations. In general, the European firms had been more paternalistic with their employees, and following the rise in worker militancy this paternalism had been transformed into an antiunion sentiment. The union was seen as a threat to the relation between workers and employer. Following the 1980 strike, these firms tightened up discipline in the plants and also used the police to stop the deposed union leaders meeting workers at the factory gates. In the months after the strike many activists were dismissed.

This attack on the union was only the first step. Aware that the union would return to represent the workers' interests if an alter-

[18] The Americans thought that one major reason for the strike was the inability of the employers to negotiate, although it should be pointed out that some advisers on the union side were critical of the union's performance as well.

native was not provided, Volkswagen announced a new plan for employee representation in September 1980. At the main plant in São Bernardo there were to be seventeen workers' representatives.[19] These representatives would meet three times a year to transmit information and suggestions to management and would also *inform* management about problems relating to work in the area they represented. In spite of the enthusiastic welcome given to the plan by the Minister of Labor, who announced it as an advance for the workers, its most noticeable features were the strict limitation on the functions of the representatives and the extraordinary measures adopted by the company to prevent the union gaining control of the scheme. The functions of the representatives were narrowly circumscribed. They could offer suggestions and provide information for the firm, but they could not represent workers in grievance procedures, take on any responsibility for matters outside of their own immediate area, or represent workers to third parties outside of the plants.[20] In addition, the resolution stated that any representative "taking advantage of the position granted to him (her) for ends different from those foreseen in this resolution will lose his (her) mandate" (item 3.10). The decision on loss of mandate would be taken by a committee of seven—three persons nominated by the company, three representatives (or their deputies) from the electoral area of the representative being judged, and the Director of Industrial Relations, acting as Chairman and having a tie-breaking vote (item 16.1). These devices alone would have made it difficult for the union to gain control of the scheme, but the plan further restricted the union's participation by dividing representation into union and nonunion categories. The seventeen representatives were split into

[19] All the details of the plan are taken from the full text of the resolution as published in FSP, 11/9/1980.

[20] In view of the suggestions made in chapter four concerning the parallels between labor control in the prewar U.S. auto industry and in Brazil in the seventies, it is interesting to note the similarity between the Volkswagen plan and the representation schemes in the U.S.A. in the twenties, as discussed by Edwards (1979:105-109). In fact, the Volkswagen plan was more limited than the plan put into operation by General Electric in the U.S.A.

three groups: three white-collar staff, seven unionized hourly-paid workers, and seven nonunionized hourly-paid workers. Given the low level of unionization among white-collar workers, this practically ensured that the unionized representatives would be a minority. The further restriction that only workers with at least five years' employment in the firm would be eligible for election barred the access of young, militant workers to the scheme. Finally, as a last safeguard, the company reserved the right to change the plan at any time without consultation or notice.

The plan had a clearly antiunion character. It was designed to marginalize the union within the plant by providing an alternative form of representation. This was made clear by the Director of Industrial Relations, Admon Ganem: "We want representatives of the workers, and not of the union, because the problems of the firm should be resolved within the firm itself. The union should take care of the general questions of the category" (quoted in *Movimento*, 24/11/1980). The Volkswagen answer to the union's longstanding demand for union delegates in the plant was, then, to substitute a purely firm-based system of controlled and limited representation.

The deposed leadership of the Metalworkers of São Bernardo was resolutely opposed to the scheme and decided to call for a boycott of it, rather than attempt to use it for the union's ends. Lula said that metalworkers participating in the scheme would be "traitors" (*Em Tempo*, 25/9/1980), and the union organized a campaign in favor of a write-in vote for the union's mascot, João Ferrador. Following intense campaigning by both sides, the final result was inconclusive. Of 27,203 votes cast at the Volkswagen plant in São Bernardo, 6,978 were for nonexistent candidates (including João Ferrador), 9,867 were either blank or wrongly filled in, and 10,358 were correctly cast (OESP, 25/11/1980). Lack of information on the reasons for the 9,867 incorrectly cast votes left enough room for both sides to claim a moderate victory.

The ability of the deposed union leaders to mount a campaign against the Volkswagen plan was the first major sign that the Ministry of Labor's takeover of the union had not solved the "labor question" in the area. The problem of what to do with the union became more pressing as the 1981 negotiations approached. The CLT specifies (Articles 553 and 554) that after the Ministry of Labor removes an executive from office it should appoint an intervenor and call fresh elections within ninety days. In practice, the Ministry normally replaces its intervenor by an appointed executive, delaying elections for as long as is thought desirable. But in São Bernardo a representative of the workers was needed to conduct the 1981 negotiations. The President of FIESP made it clear that there would be little point in negotiating with the intervenor, and yet little could be gained by nominating an unrepresentative executive to run the union. The Ministry searched for, but could not find, a group of workers which would both have authority and be independent of, or opposed to, the deposed leadership. Finally, after a series of delays, the new executive was announced in February. Much to the surprise of those not already party to the decision, the workers appointed to run the union were favorable to the deposed leadership. The Ministry had been forced to recognize that only Lula and his group commanded support in São Bernardo. Two of the five workers appointed to the executive had been on the executive before (in 1965-1969 and 1965-1975), and the new union President summed up his attitude to the old leadership with the comment: "The union is open to the category, and since Lula is a metalworker I accept his leadership" (*Em Tempo*, 19/2/1981). Although the deposed leadership still wanted fresh elections, the appointed executive was much more sympathetic to their cause than they could have expected. The selection of such a committee was ample evidence of the continuing strength of the old leaders and a major climbdown by the Ministry of Labor and the government.

In spite of this retreat by the Ministry of Labor, the union was not prepared for a major confrontation during the 1981 negotiations. The union put forward much the same demands as in the previous year, but also presented six demands to the government. These were for a unified national minimum wage, stability of employment, unemployment pay, more control of the social funds administered by the State, greater union liberty and autonomy, and a freeze on rents.[21] After much discussion, and with evident reluctance, the union accepted the employers' proposals, which conceded little. This acceptance could have been taken as a sign of weakness, and since the government's new economic policy had provoked a sharp downturn for the auto industry it might have appeared that economic recession was achieving what repression could not. But the quiet passing of the annual negotiations did not herald a period of calm.

The onset of recession in the auto industry increased militancy among workers rather than decreasing it, because it threw into sharp relief the problem of instability of employment. This issue had been the breaking point in the 1980 negotiations, and in 1981 it became a central problem as a credit squeeze cut into auto sales; employment in the auto industry fell by 14,500 in the first six months of 1981 (OESP, 18/7/1981). The first sign of trouble in São Bernardo came in April, when Volkswagen put forward a proposal to reduce both the working hours and pay of production workers by approximately 20 percent. Although the Representative Committee produced a petition of 22,000 signatures in favor of this proposal, the proposed change in working patterns required the consent of the union, since it was, in effect, a renegotiation of the annual contract. A ballot of hourly-paid workers in the plant organized by the union produced a vote of 16,048 against the proposal, 7,687 in favor, and 7,065 nonvoters. The union refused to accept the company's proposal, given the workers' vote against it, and the company responded by threatening to go ahead with 5,000 redundancies. This produced an outcry from a number of quarters. The union threatened strike action, the President of ANFAVEA and Director of the Company, Mário Garnero, offered his resignation in protest, and the President of the Republic made it clear that the government would not offer any financial support. The government suggested that since the company had made profits in the past, it should make some sacrifices in the short term (see FSP, 29/4/1981). After a meeting with President Figueiredo

[21] This information is taken from the union's handout to workers on the 1981 claim.

on May 6, the head of Volkswagen, Wolfgang Sauer, announced the suspension of the redundancies (FSP, 7/5/1981).

The next major confrontation over dismissals in São Bernardo came when Ford dismissed 400 workers on Friday, July 3. On the following Monday both the day and night shifts decided to stop work and demand the readmission of the 400 workers, a guarantee of stability of employment for all workers, and payment for the time lost during the stoppage itself. The strike took the form of entering the factory but not working, as in May 1978, and to some extent management cooperated by not forcing the strikers out into the street and by offering a place to meet inside the factory. On the fourth day of the strike a committee of fourteen was elected, and from this point on the management conducted parallel negotiations with, on the one hand, the union at the Regional Labor Office and, on the other, the factory committee directly. After five and a half days on strike the workers finally accepted a compromise. The 400 dismissed workers were given priority for readmission, all the workers in the plant were guaranteed four months' stability, and the firm formally recognized the factory committee. The days lost would be discounted from wages, but only from September and in four installments, and the firm would not take away the eight-hour "paid Sunday" or reduce holiday pay. The final meeting which accepted the compromise was controlled by Lula, as were the previous meetings. Both parties to the dispute appeared to be satisfied.[22]

Fifteen months after their imprisonment, the old leaders appeared to be back in control. Without any legal status, they were representing workers, and their marginalization was merely provoking situations where management was forced to negotiate through unofficial as well as official channels, as had happened at Ford. This problem was partly resolved when new elections were held for the union executive in August. Although the deposed leaders were not allowed to stand, the slate they supported defeated an opposition slate (formed by a group opposed to the Workers Party)

[22] The development of the stoppage and the agreement which brought it to an end were widely reported in the São Paulo newspapers in the second week of July.

by a margin of more than six votes to one. Far from being destroyed, the old leadership was gaining strength, as were the Workers Party and groups in other unions opposed to right-wing incumbent leaderships. In São Bernardo, at least, this was not because of any reluctance by the government to take a firm line with militant union leaders but because of the contradictions faced by the large employers. Unappetizing as it was for some employers to have to deal with Lula and his group, trying not to deal with them was even more difficult. In particular, in the most organized plants, such as Ford, the decline of the system of control that had worked so well in the early and mid-seventies meant that some accommodation had to be reached with the new union current. Although the government had imposed a defeat on the metalworkers' leadership in São Bernardo in 1980 for political reasons, the victory could not be sustained in the plants.

The complexity of factors—local and national, union and political—which affect the situation in São Bernardo makes it impossible to specify what will happen in the remainder of the nineteen-eighties. The development of national politics will influence events at São Bernardo, just as the failure of the government to repress the "new unionism" at its strongest point will have repercussions on its union and political strategies. At the same time, industrial relations in the large plants cannot develop in total isolation from the rest of manufacturing industry. Although the future cannot be predicted, it is possible to discuss certain issues which will be crucially important for the further development of trade unionism in Brazil. In line with the analysis undertaken so far, attention will be paid to aspects of capital-labor relations and relations between sections of the working class. Therefore, chapter eight examines the attitudes of employers to union reform and the strategies that managements might adopt in a democratic period, and chapter nine discusses the implications of the struggles of workers in São Bernardo for the working class as a whole.

8

Employer Strategies and Industrial Relations

IN THE EARLY SEVENTIES the bourgeoisie were content to see the existing system of industrial relations continue without change, just as they were content to support the military regime. However, with the impact of the world recession and the crisis in Brazil's own pattern of accumulation, the consensus among the different sections of capital began to break down. Concern was expressed about long-term economic strategy and political stability, and it became clearer that the model that had provided rapid growth during the "economic miracle" needed some revision. The model's short-term problems, coupled with doubts about the form of decision-making and the content of decisions on economic policy, provided the impetus for opposition to the State by sections of the bourgeoisie. Criticism of the government was further stimulated by the military's own doubts and divisions about economic policy and political reform.

Employers' Attitudes to Changes in Industrial-Relations Practices

The concern of Brazilian industrialists in 1976 and 1977 centered on three main areas of economic policy. Firstly, there was considerable worry about the expansion of the State sector. In a period of increasing economic difficulty, private capital wanted to curb the expansion of, and competition from, the more dynamic State companies such as Petrobrás and Vale do Rio Doce. Secondly, there was conflict over the role played by foreign capital. In spite of the considerable degree of integration between Brazilian firms and multinational companies (see Evans, 1979), local industrialists were worried about the incursion of foreign capital into sectors of the economy perceived as the domain of local industry (such as auto components). Thirdly, at a time of increasing inflation, price controls, and credit squeeze, there were complaints about the role of the financial sector and the banks. Industrialists argued that the financial system profited from adjustments made to financial values to compensate for inflation (at the expense of industry), and they were well aware that high interest rates and tight money policies increased the financial sector's profits at the expense of borrowers such as industrial firms. The power of the financial institutions and their close links with the State were a source of suspicion and envy for industrialists.

At stake in the dispute over economic policy between the government and local industrialists were the direction of future economic growth and the distribution of the costs of adjusting the Brazilian economy to the realities of the post-miracle period. The first overt expression of discontent with the regime's handling of economic policy came from businessmen linked to the heavy industrial sector in São Paulo, which had developed rapidly through State incentives in the sixties and seventies. Isolated from the centers of economic decision-making, and fearful of the influence of banks, State corporations, and foreign capital, a group of Paulista industrialists finally set out proposals for a resolution of the country's difficulties in a document issued in June 1978, following lengthy debate in the previous year. The document proposed an emphasis on the development of basic industry, the strengthening of national firms, the cleansing of the financial system, and the disciplining of foreign firms (Prieto, 1979:14).[1] In addition, it proposed a "just wages policy," "trade union freedom," and a democratic regime.

---

[1] These demands reflect the underlying issue of economic development at the time, which was the need to develop a capital-goods sector. This would require a restructuring of all economic relations, just as the implantation of the consumer-durables industries necessitated much broader changes in the economy (see chapter two). For a discussion of the crisis of the Brazilian economy at this time and the role of the capital-goods sector, see the excellent analysis by Oliveira (1977:107-111).

There were a number of reasons why businessmen representing locally owned manufacturing industry should link their demands for increased political participation to demands for the freer discussion of more general political reforms. Firstly, among the group of industrialists who raised the question of economic policy and policy-making there were some genuine liberals who had an ideological commitment to democracy. Secondly, industrialists could rightly feel that the domination of the technocrats in the military regime could only be effectively challenged if the political system upon which their power rested was also challenged, because there were entrenched groups in government who would not willingly relinquish their control. Therefore, a move to democracy would be a way of shifting power toward the Brazilian industrialist group. At the same time, union reform could be seen as either a precondition or a likely result of such a democratization. Thirdly, the call for democracy, combined with reassuring statements about the acceptability of union reform, could have been a strategy to gain the support of sections of the labor movement for the policies being advocated by the national industrialists. Finally, in this crisis requiring new economic policies, some businessmen certainly felt that the government was losing the legitimacy conferred upon it by the success of the economic miracle. Hence a new initiative was needed to revitalize the political system.

However, there was no *necessary* connection between criticisms of the government's economic policy and support for democratization and union reform. It was perfectly possible for local industrialists to demand a better deal for themselves while at the same time calling for the kind of control over labor that would keep down wages and increase productivity. Even among those industrialists who favored some degree of democratization, there was ample scope for disagreement about the extent and speed of both political reform and reforms of the laws and institutions controlling industrial relations and trade unions. In the 1978 document the content of democracy and trade union freedom were left vague, and although some industrialists were prepared to confront the difficulties involved in reform, many others became concerned by the mobilization of the working class in 1978 and 1979. Although a leading liberal industrialist such as José Mindlin was still prepared in August 1979 to view strikes as an inevitable result of "years of repressed demands" (OESP, 10/8/1979), other influential figures in employers' organizations were ready to qualify any commitment they might have to union reform with reservations about the need for profits, wage restraint, and controls on union organization in the workplace.[2] The practical effects of these attitudes were seen, of course, in the intransigent positions taken by employers during annual negotiations.

The gulf between the demands of the unions for reform and the caution of leading industrialists was also seen on the broader questions of democratization. The Metalworkers of São Bernardo grew increasingly impatient with the pace of democratization in 1979, and in June the union's newspaper called for a full amnesty for political prisoners, a Constituent Assembly, and the formation of a Workers Party. Union leaders were worried that democratization did not seem to include plans for either union reform or genuine political participation for the working class. This limitation of the content of democratization was acceptable to businessmen, however. The government's plans for a slow, controlled return to democracy specified the forms of election, the formation of political parties, electoral boundaries and weighting, and the timetable for change. The decision on each of these matters was determined solely by the government's desire to ensure that the ruling group could maintain control after free elections.[3] While trade union leaders were unhappy about the slowness and limitations of democratization, the employers were, on the whole, either satisfied or concerned that it was going too far and too fast.

[2] These positions will be discussed later in this section.

[3] A striking feature of Brazilian military governments since 1964 has been their combination of electoral politics and shameless electoral manipulation. Whenever the rules of the electoral game appeared to endanger the government's control, they were changed. This started with the abolition of parties in 1965, and it carried on throughout the seventies with restrictions on the use of television after the opposition's success in 1974, shifts from direct to indirect elections for State Governors, the introduction of Senators appointed by the President, and the extinction of the two-party system in 1979.

Employer Strategies

The opposition of sections of local capital to union reform was not based solely on perceptions of the difficulties encountered in the transition to a new pattern of capital-labor relations. There was also a deep-seated opposition to reform because of its direct impact on companies. This is clearly seen if one examines the attitudes of industrialists on the two issues which were most salient in the 1979 negotiations with the Metalworkers of São Bernardo—wages and union representation in the workplace. An examination of published statements, combined with interviews with a small number of industrialists in Greater São Paulo a few months after the dispute, graphically illustrate the gulf between the unions and the employers at this time.[4]

For the unions, 1978-1979 was a time to regain some of the losses sustained during the period of wage control, instituted after 1964. Workers and unions had clear expectations that employers could and should pay higher wages. Employers, however, believed that higher wages were neither desirable nor necessary. Cláudio Bardella, a leading São Paulo entrepreneur, said that "Brazilian trade unionism has yet to become aware of the fact that there is a greater priority that comes before wage demands, which is the creation of employment" (JT, 13/8/1979). Similarly, the President of the Union of Auto Component Employers, Luis Eulálio Bueno Vidigal Filho, declared that the *reposição salarial* was a nonissue because workers had already received compensation for lost wages. A similar position was expressed by the managing director of a large components-company who said that "the campaign for the *reposição salarial* was not truthful. It was only relevant for workers who earned the minimum wage. Most workers gain more than that, so the compensation has already taken place." Even if employers admitted that real wages might have fallen, this could be regarded as only a minor problem for the working class: "The real wage fell slightly, but there was full employment. We have had years and years of improvement in the cost of living, combined with order. It has been a wonderful

[4] Eight owners or managing directors of firms were interviewed. Three came from the "liberal" group of employers, active in 1979. The other five were chosen to represent different sectors and sizes of firm.

212

thing. . . . In Brazil there has been ample freedom. There are degrees of liberty and license'' (owner of a small textile firm). As a result of these attitudes, businessmen refused to recognize the demands of the unions as genuine expressions of the anxieties and problems of the working class, thus making it easy to justify State action against union leaders such as Lula. For these employers, even the generally accepted opinion that wages were too low and workers too poor in Brazil was tempered by the argument that the creation of new jobs was more important than raising wages[5] and that profitability and the control of inflation were the keys to prosperity.

On the question of wages, employers and unions could at least negotiate about percentages. On the issue of union representation in the workplace, they were divided by a huge gulf. It was seen in chapters three and four that employment practices in the auto industry were based on a largely unfettered management power that dispensed with negotiation procedures outside of the formalities of the *dissídio coletivo*. Industrial relations were completely subordinate to questions of finance and production, and the mentality of command, not negotiation, permeated all management levels. In the smaller companies, the direct authority of the owners or senior management was freely exercised, often in a paternalistic fashion. The demands of the authentic unions challenged these forms of control. In opposition to the unfettered power of management, the unions proposed negotiation and the limitation of management freedom. Rejecting the presupposition of harmony between capital and labor, the unions stressed that conflict and contestation were a normal feature of industrial life.[6] Rejecting the primacy of the relation between the employer and ''his'' workers, the unions suggested that they had the right to

[5] This argument, when put forward by employers, assumes that higher wages lead to lower productivity, decreased investment, and fewer new jobs. The unions, on the other hand, are more likely to stress that higher wages increase consumption and create new jobs, as does government spending on social programs.

[6] In spite of the employment practices outlined earlier, the presupposition of harmony was still a part of management thinking, even in the auto industry (see Silva, 1979).

represent all workers and to do this even within the workplace. Refusing to accept the State as the guardian of the interests of both capital and labor, the unions proposed that the State was solely on the side of the employers and should be excluded from the normal arena of relations between capital and labor. In this sense, the union's demands struck at the heart of a whole mentality, as well as at the organizational forms that reflected and reinforced it. To accept these demands, managers would have had to abandon three basic beliefs that had guided their activities. The first of these was that workers did not have the knowledge or the right to make demands on their employers. The latter, therefore, should be left to determine wages, working conditions, and the day-to-day running of the enterprise in accordance with their own best judgment. The second was that employers would naturally do as much as possible for the workers in their care and that their benevolence was limited only by the constraint of the profitability needed to finance growth. The final principle was that there were fair and knowable levels of wages and effort, which constituted the "just" situation, and that in cases of dispute the State was the best arbiter for determining those levels.

These attitudes left no room for legitimate conflict between capital and labor, nor did they place any faith in bargaining or the play of contending forces as a means of arriving at acceptable compromises between the two sides. Businessmen did not acknowledge conflict between workers and employers, even at the height of the operation of what the Cardinal-Archbishop of São Paulo, Dom Evaristo Arns, called Brazil's "unbridled capitalism"[7] (GDN, 25/6/1980). Control over workers was justified by a mixture of paternalism and authoritarianism. The paternalistic outlook reduced the relation between capital and labor to a largely personal and specific relation between the worker and the paternal figure— foreman, manager, or owner. The individualizing of relations meant that no legitimacy was allowed for either collective action or outside representation of the workers. In a paternalistic struc-

[7] The Brazilian term *selvagem*, could be translated as "wild," "savage," or "fierce."

ture, a worker with a problem should approach his superior and request a solution. The assumption that there was neither conflict between capital and labor nor any fundamental inequality between worker and employer meant in practice the subordination of the worker to the authorities above her or him.

The undeniable power of the employer was justified by references to the backwardness of the workers (their inability to take responsibility) and by the attribution of resistance to outside agents (see Silva, 1979:17-18). The emphasis was on a just employment policy that would be in the interests of all, even though the needs of the firm would of necessity take priority over the wants of workers. Hence a leading industrialist, the President of the Association of Electrical Manufacturers, could be unsympathetic to union demands for plant delegates because Brazilian workers were not prepared for them and because they disturbed the smooth running of the plants: "The factory committees adopted in a very few highly industrialized countries are an instrument that leads to co-gestion. They are not suitable for countries in the process of development because in the few cases where they have been adopted they have created disturbances in work and have had to be stopped. For this reason, we are not favorable to their creation here" (Manoel da Costa Santos, *Jornal da República*, 17/9/1979). In the strongly corporatist version of this outlook, the stress on the factory as a community allowed those who opposed management policy to be viewed as "enemies of the group, the firm, who have to be dismissed." The person making this comment saw himself in the role of guardian of the workers: "Union delegates? Anyone who is against them today is called a reactionary. But what are they for? If they are meant to enforce the law, then I want to be the delegate. I have the most ability and the most knowledge of what is going on. I want the law to be obeyed" (owner of a small components-plant). The union's only permissible function was, therefore, better assumed by management, whose benevolence was not put into question by the inadequacies of employment conditions. The owner of this components factory viewed it as a "community," in spite of a turnover rate of over 70 percent per annum. Even in the auto industry, management often emphasized the importance of a "just" policy.[8]

The more directly authoritarian attitude emphasized the right of management to determine what was best for capital and labor. The right to strike, for example, was superfluous and harmful because it could only reduce production and force wage rates above the "correct" level, while the role of factory delegates was restricted to enforcing the law and cooperating with management:

> Q. Could a factory delegate take up issues like the representation of workers facing disciplinary action?

> A. Well, discipline is usually carried out through the supervisory staff, and industry is hierarchical, rather military in fact. Therefore, to appeal against a disciplinary warning is something that a delegate might do, but he should not interfere in the relation between the worker and the supervisor. Otherwise the foreman would lose authority and discipline would collapse. Discipline and hierarchy have to be carefully looked after. (manager of a large components-firm)

> The union delegate should demand the fulfillment of the law and defend workers. But he should not interfere with the firm. There should be no disrespect of the administrative order of the firm. (owner of a small textile-firm)

Similarly, the owner of a paper-products firm could not countenance the delegate's operating outside of a situation where there were clearly defined norms. The delegate was seen as a kind of union industrial-relations officer, working with the company's management:

> If the delegate was a man who understood the situation, he should demand that the workers produce a normal amount, but not more. If the firm demands more than that, the delegate should say that the worker cannot do it. But demagogues are

---

[8] Silva's work (1979) examines the ideology of Industrial Relations personnel in a large auto plant, contrasting it with actual conditions and the attitudes of workers.

pernicious. They are only on the side of the workers and only want to protect them.

In contrast, the President of the Metalworkers of São Bernardo, when interviewed in 1978, described the delegate as the figure to oppose the many functionaries in the plants whose jobs were to impose increasing workloads on the workers.[9]

Expressions of management authority were often combined with an emphasis on the mediating role of the State. The State was viewed by managers as a substitute for the union, limiting the otherwise unfettered power of capital, and as the arbiter of the relation between capital and labor. The State guaranteed fair play and also ensured that capital-labor relations operated in the general interest of society. Thus, for example, the State was expected to protect consumers against excessive wage increases that might be conceded by firms in a monopoly position and to ensure that any wage settlements fell within the limits demanded by overall economic policy. This left no place for the development of free collective bargaining, since working conditions, too, were to be controlled by the State. Few employers accepted that such matters might be the subject of bargaining: they assumed that any matter not the subject of legislation was entirely within the prerogative of management. This is why union delegates were expected only to enforce the law. Although the unions saw the State as totally on the side of the employers, the latter still expressed a belief in its neutrality.

It is not possible to say to what extent these beliefs were completely and truthfully held, but employers advanced them as reasons for supporting the existing labor system. There could be little doubt such justifications for the system would be voiced in opposition to the pressures resulting from democratization and increased working-class power. Democratization would be likely to involve a transfer of wealth from capital to labor, and this would adversely affect the marginal firms in the economy. Capital as a whole would be able to cope with some redistribution of income, but this would be achieved only through the rationalization of

[9] Once again this interview was made available by Werner Würtele.

217

production and the centralization and concentration of capital. The economic crisis of the mid-seventies had placed smaller and weaker firms at the risk of elimination by increased competitive pressure, and conflict between industrial and banking capital had increased. At issue was economic policy in the areas of price controls, interest rates, inflation adjustment, and subsidies for industry. In 1979, some sections of the bourgeoisie already favored a return to the "golden age" of the miracle.

Reform of the Labor System and Democratization

In spite of their reservations concerning union reform, employers will have to respond to a considerable challenge from the labor movement. Even if democratization does not proceed further, the employers will face an increasing difficulty in controlling labor at the point of production, as was indicated in chapter seven. In other words, in spite of the evident reluctance of employers to consider major reforms in the labor system, they cannot avoid a struggle. The analysis carried out so far does not allow predictions to be made about the outcome, but it does provide a basis for specifying the kinds of issues that will arise.

At the beginning of the analysis of the working class in Brazil and the situation of auto workers, it was argued that the two major features shaping the working class were the changing structure of industry and the political transformations in the period after 1964. In chapter two a first empirical specification of these changes as they affected the working class in general was mapped out. The transformations in the composition of the class and in its relations with the bourgeoisie and the State were described. Following the analysis of auto workers in chapters three through seven a more precise specification of these two aspects of the transformation of the class can be made.

The "industrial structure" and the "development of modern industry" can be seen to be references to the development of the modern, capitalist organization of production. The "modern" factory is not merely modern because of the technology that it uses but also because of its management practices. In the case of the auto industry, the uniqueness of its role in the development of industrial relations and trade unionism was attributable to both use-value aspects (the size of the plants, the concentration of workers, and the nature of the work performed) and exchange-value aspects (the pressure for productivity and cost control) of production. In the auto industry, this resulted in a specific pattern of organization of work and control of labor which broke down paternalism and encouraged collective workers' resistance.[10]

The "political situation" was originally defined in terms of the coming to power of the new regime in 1964 and its impact on the unions and labor legislation. In fact, what is being referred to is the development of the institutional forms and practices of capital-labor relations in a given historical period, including the accumulated experiences of both capital and labor in their use. Clearly, the State has a crucial role in the definition of such institutions, but it has been shown that employers, unions, and workers, too, have a say in how such institutions work in practice.

It has been argued that the development of a definite pattern of industrial relations in the auto industry, combined with the specific manner in which the CLT was utilized by the State and the employers after 1964, produced a strong movement in favor of an independent unionism oriented toward the rank and file and the resolution of grievances over wages and working conditions through negotiation with the employers. At the same time, it has

---

[10] The analysis of labor markets presented here is closer to the "radical" viewpoint, particularly the version argued by Edwards (1979), than to the orthodox school criticized in chapter three. Edwards himself suggests that in countries such as Brazil and South Korea the forms of control adopted by management will be similar to those found in mass-production industries in the U.S.A. in the pre-union period (1979:181). However, there are two main differences between the position adopted in this work and that of Edwards. Firstly, use-value considerations are taken to be important constraints on the forms of control adopted by management. In production labor is not only controlled but also has to produce specific items, and this affects class composition, workers' resistance, etc. In Edwards's analysis, control strategies are taken to be primary and the techniques and organization of work are arranged to create or sustain them (1979:179). Secondly, the analysis in chapters three and four clearly shows that elements of what Edwards considers to be three largely distinct control systems—the simple, the technical, and the bureaucratic—can be combined in one plant or industry.

219

been shown how this movement became politicized through the struggle for better working conditions and greater union autonomy in the latter part of the nineteen-seventies. This analysis avoids the problems of reductionism and voluntarism discussed in the Introduction by showing how the general effects of capital accumulation in Brazil—in particular the growth of modern capitalist forms of labor control and pressure for productivity—produced pressure for change of a specific type in a very specific historical-political situation.

In the analysis of the labor movement and democratization in Brazil, the problems of reductionism and voluntarism can be avoided by applying the same kind of approach. Democratization is not merely a transition from authoritarianism to democracy, with the latter being the political form which will allow full expression to the tendencies within the labor movement suppressed by the former. On the one hand, the period of "transition" is itself a time of prolonged struggle in which forms and experiences of struggle develop rapidly, leaving an important legacy for the following democratic period. Democracy in Brazil in 1982, for example, will be affected by the struggles in 1979 and 1980 that led to the formation and growth of the Workers Party. On the other hand, there is no one type of democracy to which Brazil will necessarily evolve. Democracy can take various forms, and within the range of political systems that could be called democratic there is also a considerable variation in labor-movement structures and labor-management relations. In the auto industry alone, there is a very wide variety of industrial-relations systems within the democratic countries of the developed world (see Turner et al., 1967:300-325).

From 1978 to 1981, the specific institutional forms controlling labor-management relations were an important determinant of the patterns taken by workers' struggles. Following the analysis in chapters six and seven one can point to, for example, the effects of the grouping together of unskilled and skilled workers in the same union, the complications for the State of having regular union elections in which only unionized members of the category could present themselves as candidates, and the cyclical rhythm of conflicts created by the obligation of annual negotiations between unions and employers. The framework of labor-management relations is far more complicated than that which can be encompassed in the simple dichotomies of controlled versus free unions, or corporate versus noncorporate labor systems. If democratization proceeds in Brazil, it is the variation in institutional forms that will be the object of most conflict.

After a long period of authoritarian rule and the close control of unions and workers, the most obvious effect of democratization on the labor movement will be the relaxation of State control, just as *distensão* (relaxation) was the first step along the path of controlled democratization in the political sphere. From here it is all too easy to assume that further democratization will lead to a rapid increase in working-class power and influence. The experience of Spain in the latter part of the seventies suggests a more complex picture. The cycles of liberalization and clampdown experienced by the Spanish working class in the sixties and seventies were themselves uneven (see Claudin, 1975:99-121), but after the death of Franco events became even more unpredictable. Although initially there were rapid changes in the structure and freedom of action of the unions which went well beyond the reforms proposed by the government (see Morcillo et al., 1978:11-38), once a democratic form of government was implanted the working class seemed to lose ground. Its parties were not successful in the elections, and in the plants the role of the Plant Committees was curtailed. In effect, they were subordinated to the trade unions, which were more concerned with national policy and the protection of democracy than workers' struggles in the plant. Democracy did not leave the Spanish employers bereft of strategies for control.

In Brazil it is possible to foresee certain ways in which managements and employers' organizations will respond to democratization. Leaving aside the minor responses to increasing workers' resistance of the sort discussed in chapters six and seven (improvements in working conditions and better grievance-resolution procedures), the two basic issues to be faced will be, firstly, the definition of the general framework of industrial relations, and, secondly, the establishment of specific patterns of relations between unions and employers. On the first issue, it is essential to note that the redefinition of the State's role in capital-labor relations does not mean that the State will have no role at all. Even in countries where the law and the State are not actively involved in day-to-day industrial relations, the frameworks within which workers, unions, and employers carry on their activities are often laid down in law. In Brazil, the rights and duties of the different parties and the procedures they follow will all be open to negotiation. Among the matters likely to be discussed will be the right to strike (including the designation of areas where strikes are forbidden, union immunities, the right of workers not to be dismissed for going on strike, and procedures for deciding to take strike action), the rights of pickets, the enforceability of contracts, periods of notice, the application of minimum-wage legislation, the formation of bargaining groups, the minimum conditions of labor contracts, protection for union delegates in the plants, and the stability of employment.

In the short term these debates on the framework of labor-management relations will take place in the context of discussions about the aspects of existing legislation to be retained in the democratic period. The CLT guaranteed the right for a recognized union to be the sole representative of workers in the category and to have sole bargaining rights. It was argued in chapter five that in spite of its problems, the system of one union for each group of workers did confer some advantages. Some authentic union leaders expressed their desire to keep the one-union system but to remove the controls of the Ministry of Labor. The employers may seek to do the opposite. In 1979, a labor lawyer linked to the Employers Federation in São Paulo, Dr. Otávio Bueno Magana, argued that a liberalization of the controls over unions should also entail the loss of automatic bargaining rights.[11] This issue will be linked to the question of the Trade Union Contribution. Although many union leaders are against it, the timing and circumstances of its termination will be important, and a sudden

---

[11] This statement was made at the First Congress on Trade Unionism in Brazil, organized by the Associação Paulista de Administração de Pessoal.

withdrawal of this form of finance would leave some unions in a difficult position.

The union structure will also be the object of debate. In the seventies membership and power were concentrated in the metal-working unions, and the employers will almost certainly attempt to diminish their roles. Consideration was given in 1979 to the possibility of either splitting the metalworkers into a number of sections—auto, mechanical, etc.—or perhaps dividing skilled and unskilled workers in the plants. In addition, the employers might well encourage the divisions that exist between the unions by allowing the formation of rival union federations and confederations. Union leaders were conscious of the problems that this would bring, and the employers, too, must have given it some consideration.

After the basic framework of capital-labor relations is established, the employers will have to decide how to relate to the unions. Two basic strategies were distinguished in chapter six. The first of these was to try to marginalize the union as much as possible, reducing its influence and role; the second, to develop a working relation with it and control it by co-option. The first strategy is still possible in a democratic period. In chapters three and four it was argued that the labor system operating in Brazil in the seventies resembled the system found in the United States before the Second World War, in a democratic regime. In Brazil, where there are more workers than jobs, it would be possible to bribe activists, screen entrants, and intimidate workers by persecuting the militants. In Fiat in Italy, for example, a determined attack was mounted in the fifties on militants and their organization. The tactics included the use of a company union, a special bonus for workers who did not strike, sackings of political activists, the isolation of militants in special departments, favoritism from the foremen, and the harassment of opposition elements at a time of union elections (Partridge, 1980:420-425). Such tactics are particularly effective when the unions that might represent workers in the plants are either divided or uncertain about the positions they should be taking. For this reason, the general framework considered above will be an important factor in the selection of this kind of strategy.

The opposite strategy is to accept the union as the legitimate workers' representative and use it to management ends. Although the largest employers may have the means to adopt a strategy of eliminating the union (as described above), they are also the most susceptible to workers' resistance. In the auto industry even the employment practices described in chapters three and four were not sufficient to prevent that industry becoming the center of workers' organization. The high-wage strategy was an indication that productivity is very important in the auto industry, and in large-scale integrated production processes, inadequate control of the labor force is a serious problem. Therefore, large firms may find that a policy of resistance to the influence of the union is either ineffective or too expensive. As an alternative, they may try to use the union as a moderating and regulating force in the plants. For example, if the unions experience a phase of opposition from the auto firms along the lines described in the first strategy, they might be prepared to negotiate a recognition agreement that imposed certain limitations: for example, a union shop and full bargaining rights in return for limits on strike action during the life of a contract, centralized bargaining to reduce plant power, limited powers for the union delegates in the plants, and complex, formal negotiation and disciplinary procedures. In this kind of agreement, the union obtains a secure position and has some power to limit management "excesses," but it is tied into a set of formal procedures that inevitably give management the upper hand because it generally retains the initiative for the determination of working conditions.[12] This employers' strategy is found in the North American auto industry, and it might be the case that a new Brazilian model would be derived from this source, just as the system used in the seventies resembled the pre-union system in Detroit.

The choices facing both employers and unions will be very

[12] The shortcomings of this system from the workers' point of view are the same as for the use of the law to regulate working practices (as discussed in chapter one).

complicated.[13] Certain institutions and practices have a broad range of effects, some desirable and some undesirable, which cannot be disaggregated. This is why the debates over the reform of the Trade Union Contribution and the single-union system become so heated. More important, the content and operation of any formal structure can itself vary considerably over time, as the experience of unionism in the Argentine auto industry clearly demonstrates. In the nineteen-fifties, workers in the newly developing auto industry were kept out of the powerful metalworking union because the government did not want this union to be strengthened by the affiliation of large numbers of new workers from a potentially important industry. Instead, the workers were allocated to the tiny and inexpressive motor mechanics' union, SMATA. In the course of the sixties, workers in Córdoba used the independence given by their membership in a small union to build up a militant plant activity that would have been impossible within the metalworkers' union (see Evans et al., 1979). Although SMATA may have been a good option for the employers in 1960, it was not so good in 1970.

In this discussion of the labor system and industrial-relations practices in a democratic period, emphasis has been placed on the variability of possible reforms and the importance of the struggle between employers and labor in determining the outcome. Does this mean, then, that the ineluctable historical specificity of society and class struggle in Brazil forces any analysis away from reductionism and toward merely a description of events as they unfold? The analysis of the seventies undertaken in this book has attempted to demonstrate that this is not so. In particular, the events of May 1978 were unpredictable but not inexplicable. So, too, the eighties are not predictable, but events in the decade will move over a terrain that defines certain limits. A major limit is the need of capital to maintain control of labor at the point of production. This requires the adoption of one of the two strategies

[13] There will not be, of course, just one option chosen by the employers and the unions. There will be differences within the ranks of the employers and also, potentially, differences between union leaders, rank-and-file militants, and the mass of workers.

specified here—the marginalization of the union or the establishment of some formal relation to it. Neither goal can be attained without further conditions being created. The analysis of events in 1980 and 1981 showed that labor-management relations in the auto industry were not merely to be determined by national political considerations. Management in the eighties will have to come to terms with the working class that capital has created and shaped through its expansion and through its own policies toward labor.

9

Auto Workers and the Brazilian Working Class

LIBERALIZATION AND THE MOVEMENT toward democratization pose problems for the employers. They also pose problems for the working class. The class is unified by dictatorship: economic and political demands are fused together because economic issues are politicized by the ever-present intervention of the State. At the same time, the limited freedom of expression allowed to the class tends to suppress differences within it. Once democratization, or even the beginnings of a movement toward it, occurs, then divisions emerge. Rival leaderships and differences in tactics and strategies quickly come into the open when greater freedom of expression and greater room for political maneuver is obtained. In Brazil, the major split in the labor movement in 1979 and 1980 was between the "authentic unionists" and those union leaders and political currents grouped around the Unidade Sindical and the Communist Party. At the political level the same division developed over the formation of the Workers Party. The immediate dispute concerned the extent to which the pace of democratization should be forced and the manner in which working-class unity should be obtained. The Metalworkers of São Bernardo, for example, were criticized by Hércules Correia, a Communist leader, for their "lack of political realism" and for failing to appreciate the power of the employers at the time of the 1980 strike (see *Em Tempo*, 20/11/1980). In contrast, the Communist Party has been criticized for demobilizing the working class by subordinating its economic struggles to the political end of securing continued democratization by a display of moderation.[1]

---

[1] The demobilization of the working class through the subordination of economic struggles to political ends (such as the consolidation of democratic forms by displays of "moderation") was, according to Weffort (1973), an aspect of the

227

Auto Workers and the Working Class

Behind these debates about political tactics in the short term lie important differences in beliefs about the correlation of political forces, the nature of the working class, and its capabilities. Positions on questions such as the formation of political parties, union strategies in relation to the State, demands for union reform, and the bases for unity within the labor movement depend on often unquestioned beliefs about the composition of the working class. In spite of the development of the new union current and the advances made from 1978 to 1981, basically the same issues as were outlined in chapter one remain in contention. All parties to the dispute agree that the "new unionism" in São Bernardo has something new about it, but they disagree about how it is new and what its relevance for other sections of the working class might be. This final chapter attempts to provide an evaluation of the likely impact of union reform.

The Debate on Union Reform

Are workers in modern industry demanding the kinds of reforms that are in the interests of the working class in general? Is the "new unionism" in São Bernardo a general advance for the Brazilian working class or the expression of a split within it?[2] It might appear that the answer to these questions is a foregone conclusion. After all, it was argued in chapter three that the notion of a structural differentiation of industry was at the root of a position which identified workers in modern sectors as a privileged group with superior wages and working conditions. The assumptions of this position with regard to the situation of auto workers were shown to be incorrect. And if the analysis in chapters three and four were not enough to dispel doubts about the role of auto

---

Communist Party's strategy in the democratization period following the demise of the Estado Novo. Partridge puts forward a similar critique of the Italian Communist Party's position in the same period (1980:418-419).

[2] This discussion will be limited to the organized working class: in other words, to the relation between the different currents within the union movement. It is not attempting to go into the relation of industrial workers to agricultural workers or to those not engaged in waged employment.

workers, then the analysis of chapters six and seven might be considered sufficient. There it was argued that auto workers, instead of apolitically pursuing their own self-interest, were forced into an increasingly political confrontation with the State. If the arguments in these chapters are accepted, then the notion of auto workers as a privileged elite pursuing policies of self-interest at the expense of other workers would appear to be unfounded. The support for the union's President, Lula, and the upsurge in working-class activity that accompanied the strikes in 1978 and 1979 indicated the general resonance that auto workers encountered within the working class. Far from being integrated into the political sphere of the dominant classes, or accepting the existing system because of holding a privileged position within it, the Metalworkers of São Bernardo and the "authentic" current within the union movement provided the most serious opposition to the mlitary regime.

However, the experience of the seventies and the struggle against the military regime do not prove that auto workers will not, or could not, act as a privileged group (or labor aristocracy)[3] at some point in the future. In her analysis of the workers in the dynamic sectors in Argentina, for example, Ramos (1973) is able to reconcile her argument that they were a potential labor aristocracy with the objective fact of their militant role in the late sixties. Ramos argues that the undoubted vanguard role of auto workers and other relatively highly paid workers in the Cordobazo uprising in 1969[4] was entirely due to specific conjunctural factors. She suggests that the conditions of work in the dynamic industries generally favored the emergence of a "labor aristocracy" of re-

---

[3] The term "labor aristocracy" is used here to denote a section of the working class which has a privileged position and adopts policies which are not in the interests of the working class as a whole. This is the sense of the term as used by Hobsbawm in relation to the British working class in the late nineteenth century (1974:154-158) and Arrighi and Saul (1973) in their analyses of labor in sub-Saharan Africa.

[4] On the activities of auto workers in this period in Argentina, see Jelin, 1975:105-109. For an excellent analysis of another group of highly paid but militant and politically active workers, see the excellent study by Roldan (1978) of the power-generation workers' union, Luz y Fuerza.

formist trade unions[5] and that only a crisis in Argentine capitalism stopped this from happening. The crisis led to an intensification of exploitation in the auto industry and the rapid development of militancy among auto workers (1973:170-172 and 182). It is implied that had the crisis not occurred, then workers in the dynamic industries would have supported anti-Peronist, reformist currents in the labor movement. For Ramos, then, an evaluation of workers as an actual or potential labor aristocracy depends not upon their behavior at a given point in time but rather on the answers to three fundamental questions:

1. Are they placed in a situation that would lead them to pose distinctive demands?
2. Would the pursuit of these demands and the formation of institutional frameworks adequate to them (types of union, bargaining procedures, etc.) prejudice other sections of the working class, or the working class as a whole?
3. Is there an alternative strategy available for all or part of the working class which would be preferable?[6]

Although Ramos's argument is generally couched in terms of a suppressed tendency for a labor aristocracy to emerge, and is, therefore, inclined to reductionism, her refusal to extrapolate the past behavior of auto workers to their future behavior is entirely correct. It follows from the argument advanced in the previous chapter that the auto workers' assumption of a vanguard role in Brazil in the late seventies does not indicate that they will continue to play that role in changed circumstances.

The analysis presented so far has not denied that the working class is differentiated: it is obvious that wages and working con-

---

[5] Ramos uses the term "labor aristocracy" to refer to the leadership of workers in the dynamic sectors, but in this context she clearly implies that the situation of the workers in these sectors will determine the success or failure of such leaderships.

[6] In Ramos's case the alternative strategy is support for revolutionary Peronist unionism. In contrast, the analysis of Arrighi and Saul does not specify any definite political line or movement to which the labor aristocracy of modern-sector workers should adhere other than an ill-defined anti-imperialism.

ditions vary considerably within and between industrial sectors. Rather, I have tried to show that (i) the differentiation is not along the lines predicted by theories of the structural heterogeneity of industry and labor-market segmentation, and (ii) in the seventies at least, the factors which distinguished auto workers from other sections of the working class enabled them to adopt a vanguard role. This vanguard role consisted of their taking full advantage of *distensão* and liberalization to struggle against the constraints imposed by the CLT and the Ministry of Labor, thus expanding the space available to all unions. The effects of their struggle to achieve union autonomy and union reform in opposition to the military regime were beneficial to the working class in general, even if they were also self-interested. However, this does not mean that the kinds of reforms sought by the Metalworkers of São Bernardo would themselves be necessarily beneficial to the class. Almeida makes a clear statement that they would not, and on the basis of this statement she assumes that the Metalworkers of São Bernado cannot play the vanguard role:

> Could the workers in the modern sector transform themselves into a vanguard capable of speaking in the name of all those in the plants, as Humphrey would wish? Raising the banner of decentralized negotiations, will they manage to unify around it those who have no bargaining power in relation to the bosses? Demanding wage increases according to productivity, will they succeed in arousing the interest of those whose major concern is a rise in the minimum wage? Will the maintenance of the employment link appeal to workers in firms permanently threatened by bankruptcy? Demanding the establishment of free play between the forces of capital and labor, will they find an echo among those whose rights are only respected thanks to the mediating intervention of the State? (1978:491)

Written before the struggles in 1978, this statement fails to identify the radical, political, and universalizing tendencies within the practices of the Metalworkers of São Bernardo. It is a poor predictor of the period 1978-1981. But this does not disqualify it as an evaluation of the divisions that might occur if the metalworkers' project for union reform is successful in the eighties.

Almeida's hypothesis is that the situation of workers in large firms is so distinct from that of the mass of workers that the forms of wage determination and bargaining, the legal framework, and the political activity favored by the former are prejudicial to the latter. The points made by her and by another writer on this issue, Annez Troyano, can be clarified into four basic propositions, which will be discussed in the next section. The first of these is that workers in the dynamic industries favor free collective bargaining because of the high productivity in these sectors. The effect of free bargaining would be to increase wage differentiation because productivity in the traditional sectors is much lower. In these circumstances, centralized wage determination would be preferable for traditional-sector workers. The second proposition is that the question of working conditions takes different forms in modern and traditional industries. Troyano argues that the CLT is adequate for the traditional sectors of the economy but inadequate to control the conditions of work in the newer dynamic industries. Therefore, the workers in the dynamic sectors will prefer to abandon the CLT and regulate working conditions by direct means (1978:86-87 and 179-180). Similarly, Almeida sees the typical demands of workers in the dynamic industries as relating to the internal functioning of the enterprise (hierarchy, promotion, job classifications, recruitment, the working day, overtime, shifts, dirty and unsafe working conditions), as opposed to the basic issues of work and the reduction in the precariousness of employment that she claims are the major concerns of workers in the traditional sectors (1978:479-480). The former issues can be resolved by direct negotiation, whereas the latter require the intervention of the State.

The third proposition states that workers in the traditional industries, even if they share some of the interests of the dynamic-sector workers, do not have the strength to pursue them by direct negotiation. As the quote above argues, these workers are without bargaining power and need the protection of the State to guarantee wages and working conditions. Finally, the fourth proposition asserts that the inclination to establish direct relations between capital and labor leads to a nonpolitical outlook. For Almeida, the orientation of unions such as the Metalworkers of São Bernardo can at best lead to a critical awareness of the situation of workers and to a strongly independent trade union action that implies conflict with the employers. At worst, it can lead to an acceptance of the logic of the monopoly capitalist system and a trade union system integrated into it. In both cases, however, union activity is essentially nonpolitical. Almeida argues that because unions in the traditional sectors have to take up demands through the State, they are led to put questions of development, the State, and politics more centrally into their bargaining thematic (1978:479). This line of argument is echoed by Troyano, who regards the political orientation of the unions in the Populist period as better than the essentially economistic outlook of unions in the dynamic sectors (1978:87-88).

These four related points make certain specific claims about the nature of employment in the modern and traditional sectors, the demands being raised by unions and workers in the modern sectors (and in particular by the Metalworkers of São Bernardo), and the effectiveness of the Populist style of trade union organization in protecting the interests of workers in the traditional industries. I shall show that each point in turn can be contradicted by the evidence from Brazil.

The Dynamics of Interunion Relations

WAGE BARGAINING

The Metalworkers of São Bernardo called for the replacement of the *dissídio coletivo* by a collective labor contract, which would have reduced the role of the State in wage bargaining and put greater emphasis on negotiations between employers and unions. It is not clear how this would damage the interests of workers in the traditional sectors. Although common sense might appear to suggest that workers in the strong unions would secure large wage claims and leave the workers in the weaker unions behind, the evidence is more complicated. Wage levels and the evolution of wages over time closely follow patterns of productivity, irrespective of the system of wage determination being used. Therefore, wage differentials are not significantly affected by the system in force. It was seen in table 2-4 that the evolution of wages in different industries and sizes of firms varied greatly in the period after 1964, even though wage settlements were highly centralized and uniform. Similarly, Almeida herself has noted that wage differentiation in Brazil was greater within sectors than between them (1978:478-479), which implies that wage differentials are greater within groups of workers represented by the same union than between workers in strong and weak unions. For these reasons it can be argued that a move to a form of wage bargaining that lays less emphasis on the centralized determination of wage settlements (but does not necessarily abandon the minimum wage) is not likely to harm low-paid workers.[7] In fact, the release from the constraints of centralized bargaining could enable the unions in the dynamic sectors (or subsectors) to make trend-setting wage settlements that would raise the level of pay for all workers. Given the insertion of workers in the dynamic industries into general labor markets, and allowing for cooperation between unions, the workers in the traditional sectors might well find that their real wages rose more through free bargaining than through a system of State regulation. The interests of workers in small firms could be guaranteed by either a State-determined minimum wage or negotiations at a union or interunion level that established generally applicable minimum levels. The Metalworkers of São Benardo have not expressed opposition to either of these methods of giving minimum guarantees to low-paid workers, although such guarantees may be

[7] Although Sanchez and Arnaudo argue that free bargaining led to an increase in wage differentiation in Argentina between 1959 and 1963 (1973:191-193), Marshall (1975:386-387) and Gerchunoff and Llach (1975:31) show that wage differentiation was as strong or stronger in periods of centralized wage determination. The evidence from Argentina also confirms the Brazilian experience that there is a big difference between wage settlements and wage increases (Chirico, 1976, part 3:25-27).

ineffective. On the question of wage differentiation, therefore, Almeida's argument is incorrect.

WORKING CONDITIONS

Two distinct claims are advanced about working conditions in the dynamic industries. On the one hand, Troyano asserts that the drive for productivity is greater in the dynamic sectors (1978:86-87), while on the other Almeida sees the structures and practices of modern industry as being significantly different from those of the traditional sectors. The result would be the same in both cases: a shift away from seeking the protection of the law and toward an increase reliance on the direct negotiation of issues relating to working conditions.

The CLT provided for a general regulation of the conditions of work, but it left management with a free hand to organize production within the basic limits of hygiene and safety. The freedom given to management by the law was reinforced by the absence of any official trade union representation in the plants and the reliance on the Labor Courts for the resolution of conflicts arising in the workplace. The Metalworkers of São Bernardo sought to offset this by emphasizing plant organizing, but this alone does not imply that they have problems and ways of resolving them different from those of workers in the traditional sectors. It was argued in chapters three and four that the complex system of promotion and classification in the auto industry did not correspond to the opportunities for advancement available to workers. This system did not divert workers' concern away from the basic problems that they faced in their daily work: wage levels, intensity of work, security of employment, hygiene and safety, overtime (length of the working day), and discipline. Because Almeida assumes that wages and working conditions are relatively good in the auto industry she assumes that workers' attention can be displaced to other matters, but this is not borne out by an examination of the situation. The auto workers' problems were similar to those of other workers, and they tried to resolve them in much the same way. Even in the early part of the century, workers' problems were those of wages (piece rates), hygiene, protection from accidents, overtime, and the length of the working day;[8] and the solution was seen as a combination of legislation and workers' organization. In 1906 the delegates of the First Workers Congress were aware that the passing of laws could guarantee neither the eight-hour day nor workers' safety (Pinheiro and Hall, 1979:54 and 57-58), and in the seventies, too, a mass of legislation proved inadequate to protect workers. The response of the Metalworkers of São Bernardo was not to abandon the law but to attempt to strengthen and enforce it. In the field of health and safety, the union proposed improving the law by means of supplementary negotiation and the use of union delegates in the plants to regulate working conditions. Far from abandoning the law, the union sought to improve its provisions in the fields of stability of employment, accident compensation, and the minimum terms of individual contracts.

The outlook of the Metalworkers of São Bernardo is different from that of the unions in the Populist period, which did not seriously attempt to enforce the law at plant level. They either relied on the State to enforce the law or followed Miglioli's line of argument and assumed that conditions at plant level were not important (see chapter one). The new trade unionism breaks with the Populist model, but it does not thereby prejudice workers in the traditional industries. The degree of overlap in the area of workers' problems and the solutions to them is greater than the degree of difference. On the question of productivity, for example, the large, modern firm has a greater ability to reorganize work and enforce a greater intensity of labor because of the higher development of capital's control, but this does not mean that workers in the modern sectors have no problems or demands in common with workers in the traditional industries. In the modern sectors, the length of the working day was a serious problem, as was seen in chapter three, while in the more traditional industries the rapid modernization that took place from the fifties onward

---

[8] These problems were reported by the Rio de Janeiro Weavers Association in 1913 (Pinheiro and Hall, 1979:132-138). If "modern" industry developed in the nineteen-fifties, the problems expressed in 1913 could not have been those of the modern sector.

led to such transformations that it is nonsense to adhere to the stereotype of the small, low-productivity, low-wage, backward firm as dominant in such sectors as textiles, food, and clothing. For this reason alone, workers in modern and traditional industries might have demands in common, but there is one further aspect that needs to be taken into account. The workers in the large, modern firm are not isolated from the general situation of the working class, as Almeida supposed, but rather exposed to it by high wage and turnover policies. Therefore, workers in the dynamic industries would be obliged, and were obliged, to seek general changes in the law, trade union practice, and economic policy that would give them better conditions in which to pursue their struggle against the domination of capital. In addition, the development of the authentic current of union leaders in 1979 showed clearly that the unions representing workers in the more dynamic industries realized that they could not succeed without obtaining the support of other workers. For this reason, the policies of the new union current were designed to avoid the isolation from the rest of the working class that Almeida predicted. The common ground shared by different sections of the working class gave some chance of success to the "authentic" unionists.

If the proposals of the authentic current were put into practice, the workers in the traditional sectors would benefit in two ways. Firstly, the establishment of better legislation on working conditions and improvements in the protection given to workers would enable workers in the less organized and small-scale sectors to develop their own organization. Secondly, the example set in the dynamic industries would encourage workers elsewhere. In the case of the clothing workers in Porto Alegre, cited in chapter seven, the metalworkers' demand for union delegates in the plants was taken up by a relatively weak union and obtained with great effect.[9] The dynamic of relations between traditional and modern sectors is not understood by either Almeida or Troyano.

[9] Brant has noted that many of the "gains" of the Estado Novo period were, in fact, the generalization by law of conquests made by the stronger sections of the working class (1980:33).

237

THE POWER TO NEGOTIATE

The third step in the argument was that workers in the traditional industries would not have the power to defend their interests through direct negotiations. According to Almeida, the introduction of collective labor contracts would allow the strong unions to gain big advantages while leaving the weak at the mercy of the employers. In the light of the arguments on the previous two steps, this point also falls, because the dynamic of relations between the weaker and stronger unions is different from that assumed by Almeida. Almeida is unable to distinguish between a rejection of the role of law and the State as it was seen in the Populist period and a complete rejection of the role of law in capital-labor relations. Just how important the law would be in a non-Populist system was seen in chapter eight, and the many common features of workers in the dynamic and traditional sectors provide a basis for a common interest in legal protection, as was outlined above. It was seen in chapters six and seven that there was widespread support for the proposals for union reform advocated initially by the Metalworkers of São Bernardo. Similarly, the development of the "informal CUT" in 1979 (see chapter seven) was a practical statement of the need for the interunion solidarity and support that the corporate labor system negates.[10]

Some unions are weaker than others, and in any union structure some workers are more difficult to organize because of their dispersion, age, or nonpermanence in work. Such workers were not protected by either the corporate union structure or the Populist unions. The subordination of the unions to the State discouraged them from actively defending the interests of their members, and the smaller unions were largely bureaucratic and top-heavy, with little or no active membership. In many cases they were under the influence of the employers and hostile to rank-and-file militants.[11] The workers in the less organized sectors would probably

[10] I am grateful to Vinícius Brant for first emphasizing to me the many ways in which the corporate union structure actively discourages interunion cooperation.

[11] This is one of the reasons why some "authentic unionists" are not prepared to defend either the Trade Union Contribution or the single-union system. They feel that these devices merely encourage unrepresentative and inactive unions. To

gain more from the freedom of the stronger unions to make fresh advances than from the fettering of the most organized sectors of the working class.

THE UNIONS AND POLITICS

The final step in the argument, the supposedly apolitical position of unions in the dynamic sectors, is also devoid of foundation. Pizzorno has noted that unions are able to pursue purely economic strategies only when they are either strong enough to ignore the State completely or content with the general framework in which they operate (1973:77). If it is assumed that auto workers are a stable, privileged elite whose basic conditions of work are highly desirable, then the hypothesis of a nonpolitical outlook is plausible. However, it was shown that the basic demands of the auto workers and the union for better wages and working conditions came into direct conflict with the system of control exercised by the employers and the State. This made a nonpolitical outlook impossible, and it was seen in chapter seven that the union's struggle became increasingly focused on political issues in 1978 and 1979. Unless the economic situation changes beyond all recognition in the nineteen-eighties,[12] the dynamic-sector unions will continue to have an interest in political issues and the problems of national development. The "authentic" unionists and the Workers Party have discussed such questions as the role of the multinationals, agrarian reform, and policies for lowering the prices of basic commodities. The difference between this form of politics and the strategy of the Populist unions is that the "authentic" unionists did not attempt to derive their political power from their relation with the State. They rejected "political bargaining" as a device for improving the situation of the working class and concentrated on building up an independent base. The emphasis on

the charge that union pluralism divides the working class, they reply that unity can only be forged in practice and struggle, not by formal organization.

[12] In the auto industry the pressure for increased productivity is likely to become stronger in the eighties as Brazilian production is integrated into the Latin American and world vehicle-production strategies of the multinational firms (see, for example, the analysis of the pressure on Scania, FT 23/5/1980).

plant issues and the immediate interests of workers (which Almeida completely misinterprets) stemmed from the understanding that the working class could not be mobilized and drawn into the union's activities on the basis of general political demands.[13] It is worth noting that even in the case of the Metalworkers of Osasco in 1967-1968, the union's leaders were able to engage in an intensely political struggle against the State, but only after a long period of struggle over issues in the plants (Ibrahim, 1978).

The political struggle will not stop with democracy, because the specific trade union structures that will be developed in the democratic period will also be an object of political debate, as will be the economic and social policies of any future democratically elected government. At the same time, it is hard to imagine that a union which may well have to struggle for a long time to achieve full democratization—if the analysis in chapter eight is correct—will abandon the political struggle as soon as the space for a full participation in democratic political life is opened up. More generally, the distinctions between unions oriented to the State and unions concerned with economic issues does not appear to have any substance: unions with the strongest economic bases often play a significant political role. It may be the case that unions with strong rank-and-file bases and private employers may be less inclined to take up certain types of political struggles— particularly those in support of national-populist regimes—but this is a very different claim.

The Analysis of the Working Class

The discussion of the unity of the working class and the effects of the new current within the trade unions has centered on two basic issues: the characterization of the dynamic sectors and assumptions about the best means of protecting the interests of workers in the traditional industries. On both aspects the analysis based on the notion of the structural heterogeneity of industry has

[13] Roldan's study of the intensely political and militant union Luz y Fuerza, in Córdoba, shows that at the height of its activity the majority of the members assessed its effectiveness according to its success on the question of wages.

proved to be inadequate and misleading. Theories about the development of the working class which begin with the notion of the structural differentiation of industry fail because they are technologically determinist. The development of industry itself is reduced to the implantation of new productive techniques, and these techniques are assumed to determine certain forms of labor market and labor use. In this sense, the situation of workers in the dynamic industries—their problems, demands, and forms of organization—is held to be determined by the nature of modern technology. The uneven implantation of such technology leads, it is assumed, to an inevitable and increasing differentiation within the working class itself. On the one hand, there are the workers in the traditional sectors, whose forms of activities and organization (Populist unions, orientation to the State) correspond to the type of industry developed in the earlier period of industrialization. On the other, the Metalworkers of São Bernardo is the most developed form of that unionism which corresponds to the situation of workers in the dynamic industries. In both cases, the patterns of union activity and strategy are assumed to be functional for a specific type of industry. It is this assumption of functionality that allows Almeida to be so mistaken about workers in the traditional sectors and yet so sure about what is in their interests.[14]

In this book, the analysis of the auto industry started from two basic premises. The first was that the development of industry is part of a process of accumulation of capital. This process involves not merely shifts in technology but also changes in the relation between different capitals, a restructuring of the relation between capital and labor, and changes in the role of the State. Hence a shift from one phase of capital accumulation to another sets in train a series of changes that affect the working class as a whole. Some of these changes were outlined in chapter two, where it

---

[14] Almeida does attempt to justify the pattern of trade unionism found in the Populist period, but it is symptomatic of her approach that she holds a discussion of the effects of Populist unionism before 1964 to be adequate for an analysis of the options available to workers in the traditional sectors in the nineteen-seventies. She sees the traditional sectors as largely unaffected by the transformation in the Brazilian economy.

was shown that after 1964 the situation of the working class was transformed by the new labor legislation and the activities of the Ministry of Labor. The second premise was that production processes in capitalism are both labor processes and valorization processes.[15] The modern factory is not merely the site of modern techniques but rather the site of modern capitalist production, which involves both the production under capitalist control of specific socially useful products and the production of commodities that can be sold at a profit. The work of those employed by capital has to be directed and controlled by its agents (managers, supervisors) in such a way that production is profitable. The control of capital at the point of production depends on both the organization of the labor process and more general labor-market, social, and political conditions. It was shown in chapter four that in the Brazilian auto industry management developed a system of labor use and control in the seventies that combined high wages, complicated wage structures, and the rotation of labor. By emphasizing the need for control and profit, as opposed to the technical requirements of production, it was possible to show how that system worked and where its points of weakness lay. By showing the grievances generated by that system, along with its shortcomings, it was possible to explain the increasing importance and specific characteristics of the demands for reform voiced by workers in the auto industry. The location of the system within a given political framework explained the nature of the opposition expressed by auto workers and, in particular, accounted for its political content. The explanation of the labor-control system used in the auto industry situated the events of 1978 and 1979 in their proper context and also provided the basis for a discussion of possible future patterns of industrial relations in the auto industry.

This analysis has two major implications for research on the working class. The first is that the factory is an important site for research. In the context of the view that tends to reduce industrial development to the acquisition of technology and technology to

---

[15] A valorization process is one in which money-capital is invested in such a way as to produce a larger quantity of money-capital at the end of the cycle of investment than at the beginning.

machines, the factory is rather uninteresting and no more important for social development than other organizations. Because work is reduced in this perspective to a technologically determined process, the factory lacks social content, and the struggles of workers in the factories are reduced to the most abstract level—the fight for wages or the struggle against the alienation of modern production. If, on the other hand, technology is seen as both embodying social relations and as operating within socially determined systems of communication and control, then the labor process in the workplace becomes a much more significant indicator of social relations generally. At the same time, if the labor process is also a valorization process, then the situation in the workplace is related to the general question of capital accumulation. Given these two relations, the situation in the workplace acquires a much more definite relation to society at large and can be seen as the point at which a series of economic, political, and social contradictions are located. Instead of merely defining abstract problems—such as the alienation of modern man—the factory is the point of expression of extremely specific contradictions and can form the basis of concrete struggles against them. This was why careful attention was given in chapters two, three, and four to the determination of the situation in the plants, and why this attention provided the basis for the analysis in the following chapters. This is not to argue that the workplace is the only site of contradictions or the only area for the study of the working class, but it does mean, firstly, that the workplace deserves much more than the neglect it has generally received in Latin America,[16] and, secondly, that it should be studied from a point of view that emphasizes production as both a labor process and a valorization process (on this see Brighton Labour Process Group, 1977, and Braverman, 1975, among others).

The second implication is that the study of the working class cannot be abstracted from history, the accumulation of capital, and class struggle. It was noted in the Introduction that the adop-

---

[16] The bulk of research on the working class in Latin America has concentrated on unions, the labor movement, and specific strikes rather than the workplace.

tion of a labor-process approach to auto workers would not, of itself, resolve the problem of reductionism. Indeed, the militancy of auto workers in many countries of the world, which often takes the form of opposition to the State and to the established union structure, has led some writers to apply the concept of the "mass worker" to workers in the industry. The "mass worker," it is argued, is the young, unskilled production-line worker who rejects the patterns of struggle established by skilled workers (the defense of professional interests through formal union channels) and, instead, favors direct, sometimes violent struggle at the point of production.[17] The "mass worker" thesis can be as reductionist as any theory of the structural heterogeneity of industry when patterns of struggle and resistance are related solely to capital-labor relations at the point of production. Although it has been argued that an analysis of the labor process provides a valuable approach to the issue of workers' struggles in the auto industry, it is also clear that such struggles have taken on markedly different forms in different situations. In the U.S.A. in the thirties the auto workers spawned the struggles for union recognition, and in the sixties Detroit gave rise to the League of Revolutionary Black Workers (see Geschwender, 1977). In Argentina, auto workers were involved in revolutionary unionism and urban insurrection in the sixties, and in Mexico they have fostered some of the stronger independent unions. In each of these cases, both the forms of struggle adopted by the auto workers and the consequences have been quite distinct. The specificity of each case can only be understood by examining not only the composition of the working class but also the development of workers' struggles against capital in a specific historical-political context.

Having said this, it is equally true that the analysis of the working class must be grounded in an examination of the relation between labor and capital at the point of production. Without such a grounding, analyses of strikes, labor-movement organizations, and the political development of the class will continue to oscillate

[17] The "mass worker" thesis was first developed in Italy, and its main exponents have been Italian. However, at least one attempt has been made to apply the concept to auto workers in Latin America (see Quiroz, 1981).

between reductionism and mere description. Both errors derive from a failure to examine the material existence of the working class, and they are often combined in analyses which pass from descriptive and voluntaristic accounts of the development of events and organizations to the mechanistic attribution of such developments to underlying structural characteristics of the class. At a time when strikes in Brazil have become more frequent and political activity within the working class more overt, the hitherto neglected analysis of capital-labor relations at the point of production becomes indispensable for an understanding of political and social change.

Bibliography

Acero, Liliana. 1981. "Control y Resistencia de los Trabajadores en la Cotidianeidad Textil de Brasil." Paper presented at Conference on Crisis, New Technology and the Labor Process, UNAM, Mexico City, July 20-31.

Almeida, Angela Mendes, and Michael Lowy. 1976. "Union Structure and Labor Organization in the Recent History of Brazil." *Latin American Perspectives* (Winter), 8:98-119.

Almeida, María Hermínia Tavares de. 1975. "O Sindicato no Brasil: Novos Problemas: Velhas Estruturas." *Debate e Crítica* (July), 6:49-74.

———. 1977. "A Autonomia Sindical." *Movimento*, 18/7/1977.

———. 1978. "Desarrollo Capitalista y Acción Sindical." *Revista Mexicana de Sociología* (April-June), 40(2):467-492.

Amsden, John. 1972. *Collective Bargaining and Class Conflict in Spain.* London: Weidenfeld and Nicholson.

Andrade, Regis de Castro. 1979. "The Evolution of the Working Class Movement in Brazil from 1930: An Outline." Paper presented at Workshop on the Working Class in Latin America, London, March 9-10.

Arrighi, Giovanni, and John Saul. 1973. "Nationalism and Revolution in Sub-Saharan Africa," in *Essays on the Political Economy of Africa.* New York: Monthly Review.

Bacha, Edmar L. 1975. "Hierarquia e Remuneração Gerencial," in *A Controvérsia sobre a Distribuição da Renda no Brasil*, Ricardo Tolipan and Arthur Tinelli, eds. Rio: Zahar.

———. 1976. "Issues and Evidence in Recent Brazilian Economic Growth." Discussion Paper No. 12, Harvard Institute for International Development.

Beynon, Huw. 1973. *Working for Ford.* Harmondsworth: Penguin.

Brant, Vinícius C. 1980. "Sindicatos de Trabalhadores," in *São Paulo: O Povo em Movimento*, Paulo Singer and Vinícius Brant, eds. Petrópolis: Vozes.

Braverman, Harry. 1975. *Labor and Monopoly Capital.* New York: Monthly Review.

Bright, James R. 1966. "The Relationship of Increasing Automation to Skill Requirements," in *The Employment Impact of Technical Change,*

Bibliography

vol. 2, National Commission on Technology and Economic Progress. Washington D.C.: U.S. Government Printing Office.

Brighton Labour Process Group. 1977. "The Capitalist Labour Process." *Capital and Class* (Spring), 1:3-26.

Cadernos do Presente. 1978. *Greves Operárias (1968-1978)*, Cadernos do Presente, No. 2. São Paulo: Aparte.

Capistrano, David. 1980. Untitled résumé of a talk given at a Conference on the Brazilian Working Class, Archívio Stórico del Movimento Operaio Brasiliano, Milan, March 26-30.

Cara a Cara. 1978. "São Bernardo: Uma Experiência de Sindicalismo 'Autêntico.' " *Cara a Cara* (July-December), 1(2):54-66.

Cardoso, Fernando H. 1980. "Os Impasses do Regime Autoritário: O Caso Brasileiro." *Estudos CEBRAP*, 26:169-194.

Central Policy Review Staff. 1975. *The Future of the British Car Industry*. London: H.M.S.O.

Cesarino, A. F., Jr. 1970. *Direito Social Brasileiro*, 6th ed. São Paulo: Saraiva.

Chinoy, Ely. 1955. *Automobile Workers and the American Dream*. New York: Random House.

Chirico, Maria Magdalena. 1976. "La Inserción de la Clase Obrera en la Estructura Económica de la Argentina, 1955-1972." Mimeo. Buenos Aires: CEUR.

Claudin, Fernando. 1975. "El Movimiento Obrero Español," in *Movimiento Obrero y Acción Política*, Lucio Magri et al., eds. Mexico City: Era.

Confederação Nacional da Indústria. N.d. *Análise e Perspectivas da Indústria Automobilística*. São Paulo: C.N.I.

Crozier, Michel T. 1967. *The Bureaucratic Phenomenon*. Chicago: University of Chicago Press.

DIEESE. 1975. *Dez Anos da Política Salarial*, Estudos Sócio-Econômicos, no. 3. São Paulo: DIEESE.

——. 1977. "Distribuição Salarial em São Paulo Segundo Gúias da Contribuição Sindical." Mimeo. São Paulo: DIEESE.

Doeringer, Peter B., and Michael J. Piore. 1971. *Internal Labor Markets and Manpower Analysis*. Lexington, Mass.: D. C. Heath.

Edwards, Richard. 1979. *Contested Terrain*. New York: Basic Books.

Erickson, Kenneth P. 1977. *The Brazilian Corporative State and Working Class Politics*. Berkeley: University of California Press.

Erikkson, John R. 1966. "Wage Structures in Economic Development

Bibliography

in Selected Latin American Countries: A Comparative Analysis.'' Ph.D. dissertation, University of California, Berkeley.

Evans, Judith, Paul Hoeffel and Daniel James. 1979. ''Labor in the Argentine Motor Industry.'' Paper presented at a Workshop on the Auto Industry in Latin America, Boston, May.

Evans, Peter. 1979. *Dependent Development: the Alliance of Multinational, State, and Local Capital in Brazil.* Princeton, N.J.: Princeton University Press.

Fajnzylber, Fernando. 1971. *Sistema Industrial e Exportação de Manufaturados.* Rio: IPEA/INPES.

Ferrante, Vera Lúcia Botta. 1978. ''História Operária e Legislação Trabalhista: O F.G.T.S. e a Perda da Estabilidade.'' *Escrito Ensaio*, 2(4):43-50.

Fischlow, Albert. 1974. ''Algumas Reflexões sobre a Política Econômica Brasileira Após-1964.'' *Estudos CEBRAP* (January-March), 7:5-65.

Ford, Henry. 1926. *Today and Tomorrow.* London: Heinemann.

Foxley, Alejandro, and Oscar Muñoz. 1977. ''Políticas de Empleo en Economías Heterogéneas.'' *Revista Paraguaya de Sociología* (January-April), 14(38):81-100.

Frederico, Celso. 1978. *Consciência Operária no Brasil.* São Paulo: Ática.

————. 1979. *A Vanguardia Operária.* São Paulo: Símbolo.

Gerchunoff, Pablo, and Juan J. Llach. 1975. ''Capitalismo Industrial, Desarrollo Asociado y Distribución del Ingreso entre los Gobiernos Peronistas: 1950-1972.'' *Desarrollo Económico* (April-June), 57:3-51.

Geschwender, James A. 1977. *Class, Race and Worker Insurgency.* Cambridge: At the University Press.

Gouldner, Alvin. 1954. *Wildcat Strike.* New Jersey: Antioch.

Gramsci, Antonio. 1971. *The Prison Notebooks.* London: Lawrence and Wishart.

História Imediata. 1978. *A Greve na Voz dos Trabalhadores*, História Imediata no. 2. São Paulo: Alfa-Omega.

Hobsbawm, Eric J. 1974. ''The Labor Aristocracy in Nineteenth Century Britain,'' in *Workers in the Industrial Revolution*, P. N. Stearns and D. J. Walkowitz, eds. Edison, N.J.: Transaction.

Hoffmann, Helga. 1976. ''Wage Indexation and Anti-Inflationary Incomes Policy in Brazil.'' *Bulletin of the Society for Latin American Studies*, 24:81-100.

Humphrey, John. 1977. ''The Development of Industry and the Bases

Bibliography

for Trade Unionism: A Case Study of Car Workers in São Paulo, Brazil.'' D.Phil. dissertation, Sussex University.

IBGE. N.d. *Censo Industrial, São Paulo, 1960*. Rio: IBGE.

——. 1974a. *Censo Industrial, Brasil, 1970*. Rio: IBGE.

——. 1974b. *Censo Industrial, São Paulo, 1970*. Rio: IBGE.

——. 1976. *Pesquisa Industrial, Centro-Sul, 1974*. Rio: IBGE.

——. 1978. *Anuário Estatístico do Brasil, 1978*. Rio: IBGE.

Ibrahim, José. 1978. ''A História do Movimento de Osasco,'' in *Greves Operárias 1968-1978*, Cadernos do Presente, no. 2. São Paulo: Aparte.

Jelin, Elizabeth. 1975. ''Espontaneidad y Organización en el Movimiento Obrero.'' *Revista Latinoamericana de Sociología*, 2:77-118.

Latin American Perspectives. 1979. ''Interview with Luis Inácio da Silva (Lula), President of the Sindicato dos Metalúrgicos de São Bernardo do Campo.'' *Latin American Perspectives* (Fall), 23:90-100.

Lobos, Julio Alejandro. 1976. ''Technology and Organization Structure: A Comparative Case-Study of Automotive and Processing Firms in Brazil.'' Ph.D. dissertation, Cornell University.

Lopes, Juarez R. Brandão. 1964. *Sociedade Industrial no Brasil*. São Paulo: DIFEL.

McPherson, William H. 1940. *Labor Relations in the Automobile Industry*. Washington, D.C.: Brookings Institute.

Magana, Otávio B. 1966. ''Revisão da Estabilidade.'' *Revista Legislação do Trabalho*, 30.

Maragliano, Rubens. 1966. ''Elaboração das Leis do Trabalho e o Problema de Estabilidade no Emprego.'' *Revista Legislação do Trabalho*, 30.

Maranhão, Ricardo. 1975. ''Operários, Partido e Organização de Base.'' Mimeo. São Paulo.

Marshall, Adriana. 1975. ''Mercado de Trabajo y Crecimiento de los Salarios en la Argentina.'' *Desarrollo Económico* (October-December), 59:373-397.

Martins, Luciano. 1976. *Pouvoir et Développement Économique: Formation et Évolution des Structures Politiques au Brésil*. Paris: Anthropos.

Mata, Milton da, and Edmar L. Bacha. 1973. ''Emprego e Salários na Indústria de Transformação, 1949/69.'' *Pesquisa e Planejamento Econômico* (June), 3(2):303-340.

Mericle, Kenneth S. 1974. ''Conflict Regulation in the Brazilian Indus-

Bibliography

trial Relations System.'' Ph.D. dissertation, University of Wisconsin.

Miglioli, J. 1963. *Como São Feitas as Greves no Brasil?* Rio: Civilização Brasileira.

Miller, Richard U. 1971. ''The Relevance of Surplus Labor Theory to the Urban Labor Markets of Latin American.'' *International Institute for Labour Studies Bulletin*, 8:220-245.

Moisés, José Álvaro. 1979. ''Current Issues in the Labor Movement in Brazil.'' *Latin American Perspectives* (Fall), 23:51-70.

Morcillo, Fernando Almendros, et al. 1978. *El Sindicalismo de Clase en España (1939-1977)*. Barcelona: Peninsula.

Morris, Morris D. 1969. ''Labor Relations: Developing Countries,'' in *Comparative Perspectives on Industrial Society*, William A. Faunce and William II. Form, eds. Boston: Little Brown

Munck, Ronaldo. 1979. ''State Intervention in Brazil: Issues and Debates.'' *Latin American Perspectives* (Fall), 23:16-31.

Nun, José. 1978. ''Despidos en la Industria Automotriz Argentina: Estudio de un Caso de Superpoblación Flotante.'' *Revista Mexicana de Sociología* (January-March), 40(1):55-106.

Oliveira, Francisco de. 1977. *A Economia da Dependência Imperfeita*. Rio: Graal.

Oliveira, Francisco de, and María Angélica Travolo. 1979. *El Complejo Automotor en Brasil*. Mexico City: ILET/Nueva Imagem.

Partridge, Hilary. 1980. ''Italy's FIAT in Turin in the 1950s,'' in *Capital and Labour*, Theo Nichols, ed. London: Fontana.

Pinheiro, Paulo Sérgio, and Michael Hall. 1979. *A Classe Operária no Brasil: Documentos 1889-1930*, vol. 1. São Paulo: Alfa-Omega.

Pinto, Aníbal. 1965. ''La Concentración de Progreso Técnico y de sus Frutos en el Desarrollo Latinoamericano.'' *El Trimestre Económico* (January-March), 125.

Pizzorno, Alessandro. 1973. ''Los Sindicatos y la Acción Política,'' in *Economía y Política en la Acción Sindical*, Cadernos de Pasado y Presente, no. 44. Cordoba: Pasado y Presente.

Prebisch, Raul. 1969. ''The System and Social Structure of Latin America,'' in *Latin American Radicalism*, I. L. Horowitz et al., eds. New York: Vintage.

Prieto, Helios. 1979. ''La Emergencia de la Oposición Sindical en Brasil.'' *Debate* (March-April), 3(8):9-17.

Quartim, João. 1971. *Dictatorship and Armed Struggle in Brazil*. London: New Left Books.

251

Bibliography

Quijano, Anibal. 1974. "The Marginal Pole of the Economy and the Marginalized Labor Force." *Economy and Society* (November), 3(4):393-428.

Quiroz, Othón. 1981. "Tecnología, Reestructuración Capitalista y Composición de Clase en la Industria Automotriz Mexicana." Paper presented at Conference on Crisis, New Technology and the Labor Process, UNAM, Mexico City, July 20-31.

Ramos, Mónica Peralta. 1973. *Etapas de Acumulación y Alianzas de Clases en la Argentina (1930-1970)*. Buenos Aires: Siglo Veintiuno.

Ray, G. F. 1969. "The Diffusion of New Technology." *National Institute Economic Review* (May), 48:40-83.

Rodrigues, Leôncio Martins. 1970. *Industrialização e Atitudes Operárias*. São Paulo: Brasiliense.

Roldan, Martha. 1978. *Sindicatos y Protesto Social en la Argentina*. Amsterdam: CEDLA.

Sanchez, Carlos E., and Aldo A. Arnaudo. 1973. "The Economic Power of Argentine Manufacturing Labor Unions," in *The International Labor Movement in Transition*, Adolfo Sturmthal and James Scoville, eds. Illinois: University of Illinois Press.

Sellier, François. 1971. "Les Transformations de la Négociation Collective et de l'Organisation Syndicale en Italie." *Sociologie du Travail* (April-June), 13(2):141-158.

Silva, Moacyr Pinto da. 1979. "Relações de Trabalho na Moderna Empresa Brasileira." Paper presented at Second Seminar on Labor Relations and Social Movements, CEDEC, São Paulo, May.

Souza, Amaury de, and Bolivar Lamounier. 1980. "Escaping the Black Hole: Government-Labor Relations in Brazil in the Eighties." Mimeo. Rio.

Souza, Paulo R. 1978. "Wage Disparities in the Urban Labor Market." *CEPAL Review* (1st semester), 5:199-224.

Souza Martins, Heloisa Helena Teixeira de. 1979. *O Estado e a Bureaucratização do Sindicato no Brasil*. São Paulo: Hucitec.

Telles, Jover. 1962. *O Movimento Sindical no Brasil*. Rio: Vitória.

Torre, Juan Carlos. 1974. "El Proceso Político Interno de los Sindicatos en Argentina." Documentos de Trabajo no. 89, Instituto Torcuato di Tella, Centro de Investigaciones Sociales, Buenos Aires.

Troyano, Annez Andraus. 1978. *Estado e Sindicalismo*. São Paulo: Símbolo.

Turner, H. A., Garfield Clack and Geoffrey Roberts. 1967. *Labour Relations in the Motor Industry*. London: George Allen and Unwin.

Bibliography

Vianna, Luiz Werneck. 1978a. "Estudos sobre Sindicalismo e Movimento Operário: Resenha de Algumas Tendências." *Dados*, 17:9-24.

———. 1978b. *Liberalismo e Sindicato no Brasil*. Rio: Paz e Terra.

———. 1978c. "Questões Atuais sobre o Sindicalismo." *Escrita Ensaio*, 2(4):19-23.

Weffort, Francisco C. 1972. *Participações e Conflito Industrial: Contagem e Osasco 1968*, Cadernos CEBRAP, no. 5. São Paulo: CEBRAP.

———. 1973. "Origens do Sindicalismo Populista no Brasil (a Conjuntura do Após-Guerra)." *Estudos CEBRAP* (April-May-June), 4:65-105.

———. 1974. "Partidos, Sindicatos e Democracia: Algumas Questões para a História do Periodo 1945-1964." Mimeo. São Paulo.

Widdick, B. J. 1976. "Work in Auto Plants, Then and Now," in *Auto Work and Its Discontents*, B. J. Widdick, ed. Baltimore: Johns Hopkins University Press.

Index

Aliança Nacional Libertadora, 13
Almeida, 28, 61-63, 133-134, 231-233, 238
arbitration. *See dissídio coletivo*
authentic unionism: challenge to employers, 213-214; idea of Ministry of Labor, 39, 130
authentic unionists, 191, 227, 239
auto firms, nomenclature used in text, 57. *See also* names of individual firms
auto industry: in Argentina, 110, 225, 229-230; concentration in São Bernardo, 3n, 50, 128-129, 139; definition of, 4n; history of, 48-49, 54; impact on industrial relations, 219; importance for working class, 3-4, 181, 231, 239; labor costs in, 109-110, 113; labor markets in, 63-72, 108-110; management strategy options in, 167-169, 200-201; output, 49-50; production process in, 55-56; recession in, 205; recruitment of workers to, 63-67; size of plants in, 50-52, 137, 139; skills in, 63-67; turnover in, 87-89, 98-100; union in, 3n, 140-145, 175; in U.S.A., 106; wages in, 52-53, 70-71, 73-74, 110; wages compared with other sectors, 52-53, 68-70, 77-78. *See also dissídio coletivo*; stoppages; strikes

Bacha, 42-43
bankworkers, Porto Alegre, 192, 198
Braverman, 106
bus drivers, 125
business unionism, 133-134, 169-170

Campos, Roberto, 37-38
Cardoso, 150
Catholic Church, 160, 199
Chrysler, 162
clothing workers, Porto Alegre, 194-195
CLT, 13, 15, 115, 141; relevance for dynamic sectors, 235-236. *See also* labor system
Cobrasma, 116
Communist Party, 18, 227
Contagem, 25
Costa Santos, 215

definitions: of auto industry, 4n; of dynamic sectors, 32-33; of firms cited anonymously in text, 55, 57; of workers sampled in auto plants, 56
democratization: and employers, 209, 217; impact on labor, 210, 220; and Metalworkers of São Bernardo, 190; and the military, 150; postwar, 17; in Spain, 221
DIEESE, 132, 153-154
discipline, 100-104
dissídio coletivo, 15; for Metalworkers of São Bernardo, 156-157, 157-158, 177-178, 198, 199, 204-205; in seventies, 115-116
Doeringer and Piore, 59
dynamic sectors, 23, 32-33, 33-34. *See also* modern and traditional sectors

earnings, 42-43. *See also* wages
economic growth, 31-33, 150
employers: and economic policy,

Index

Index

Index

strikes, 166-167, 193-194, 197; in auto industry, 161-165, 180-181, 186-187, 191, 199-200; right to strike, 18, 24, 38, 148-149
structural heterogeneity. *See* modern and traditional sectors

toolroom workers. *See* skilled workers
Trade Union Contribution, 14, 189; elimination of, 192, 222-223, 225
Trade Union Opposition, 126
trade unions. *See* unions
traditional sectors, 35
Troyano, 232, 233
turnover, 87-100; impact on workers' struggles, 103-104; relation to wages, 112-114. *See also* stability of labor

union delegates, 22, 189; employers' resistance to, 215-217; in 1979 negotiations, 189. *See also* union directors
union directors: in auto plants, 140-145, 173-174; in CLT, 141; and management, 141-143. *See also* union delegates
union elections, 129n; in São Bernardo, 138, 206-207
unionization in auto industry, 140, 143-144, 175

union reform. *See* labor system
unions: jurisdiction of, 130n; in labor system, 14, 15; in Populist period, 238. *See also* labor system, and names of individual unions

Vidigal, 212
Volkswagen: conflict in, 54, 126, 164-165, 180, 181; dismissals, 174, 205; employee representation plan, 202-203

wages: in auto industry, 68-69, 73-74; and collective bargaining, 234; evaluation by auto workers, 76-78; high-wage strategy, 58, 107-109, 112-114; impact of wages policy on, 42-44; in metalworking industries and textiles, 43-44, 68-70. *See also dissídio coletivo*
wages policy, 40-43; reform of, 196. *See also dissídio coletivo*
wage structure in auto industry, 70-71, 110; in Argentina and Brazil, 110; workers' discontent with, 79
Weffort, 20, 25, 28, 227
Workers Party, 190, 239; and Metalworkers of São Bernardo, 197
working conditions, 21-22, 194-195, 235-237; in auto industry, 80-104
workplace as focus of study, 5, 243

258

Library of Congress Cataloging in Publication Data

Humphrey, John.
  Capitalist control and workers' struggle in the
Brazilian auto industry.

  Bibliography: p.
  Includes index.
  1. Automobile industry workers—Brazil.
2. Trade-unions—Automobile industry workers—
Brazil.   3. Strikes and lockouts—Automobile
industry Brazil.   4. Automobile industry and
trade—Brazil.   I. Title.
HD8039.A82B736   331.88'1292'0981   82-47599
ISBN 0-691-09400-4   AACR2